VISUAL QUICKSTART GUIDE

SEARCH ENGINES

FOR THE WORLD WIDE WEB

Alfred and Emily Glossbrenner

 Peachpit Press

Visual QuickStart Guide
Search Engines for the World Wide Web
Alfred and Emily Glossbrenner

Peachpit Press
1249 Eighth Street
Berkeley, CA 94710
510/548-4393
510/548-5991 (fax)

Find us on the World Wide Web at: http://www.peachpit.com

Peachpit Press is a division of Addison Wesley Longman

Copyright © 1998 by Alfred and Emily Glossbrenner

Editor: Jeremy Judson
Copy editor: Chrisa Hotchkiss
Production: David Van Ness
Inhouse production: Kate Reber
Cover design: The Visual Group

Notice of rights
All rights reserved. No part of this book may be reproduced or transmitted in any form or by any means, electronic, mechanical, photocopying, recording, or otherwise, without prior written permission of the publisher. For more information on getting permission for reprints and excerpts, contact Trish Booth at Peachpit Press.

Notice of liability
The information in this book is distributed on an "As is" basis, without warranty. While every precaution has been taken in the preparation of this book, neither the author nor Peachpit Press shall have any liability to any person or entity with respect to any loss or damage caused or alleged to be caused directly or indirectly by the instructions contained in this book or by the computer software and hardware products described herein.

ISBN: 0-201-69642-8

0 9 8 7 6 5 4 3 2

Printed and bound in the United States of America

♻ Printed on recycled paper

About the Authors

Alfred Glossbrenner is the author of some 40 books on personal computers, online services, the Internet, and other topics. Hailed as "The Great Communicator" by *The New York Times*, he has been a freelance writer, editor, and book packager since graduating from Princeton in 1972. He wrote his first book on online searching, *How to Look It Up Online*, for St. Martin's Press in 1987 and it went on to become a best-seller. The most popular of his non-computer books are *The Art of Hitting .300* (Hawthorn, 1980) and *The Winning Hitter* (Hearst, 1984), both written with the late, great Charley Lau. The thread that unites these books with his computer titles is an uncanny knack for explaining complex subjects in a way that anyone can understand.

Emily Glossbrenner has over two decades' experience with computers and online services, including nine years with the IBM Corporation as a marketing representative and marketing manager for Fortune 500 accounts. She is the co-author of *Computer Sourcebook* (Random House, 1997), *The Little Web Book* (Peachpit Press, 1996), *Making More Money on the Internet* and *Internet 101* (McGraw-Hill, 1996), and many other titles. In addition, she has contributed to numerous books and articles about the Internet, personal computers, and online services.

The Glossbrenners live in a 1790s farmhouse on the Delaware River in Bucks County, Pennsylvania. You can reach them online at **gloss@gloss.com**.

Recent Glossbrenner Books

The Information Broker's Handbook, Third Edition
by Sue Rugge and Alfred Glossbrenner, 1997.

Computer Sourcebook
by Alfred and Emily Glossbrenner, 1997.

The Little Web Book
by Alfred and Emily Glossbrenner, 1996.

Making More Money on the Internet
by Alfred and Emily Glossbrenner, 1996.

Internet 101: A College Student's Guide, Third Edition
by Alfred and Emily Glossbrenner, 1996.

The Little Online Book
by Alfred Glossbrenner, 1995.

The Complete Modem Handbook
by Alfred and Emily Glossbrenner, 1995.

Online Resources for Business
by Alfred Glossbrenner and John Rosenberg, 1995.

Finding a Job on the Internet
by Alfred and Emily Glossbrenner, 1995.

TABLE OF CONTENTS

Introduction   **ix**

PART 1: GETTING COMFORTABLE WITH SEARCH BASICS

Chapter 1: Search Engines and How They Work   **3**
Enter Search Engines 4
How Search Engines Work 6

Chapter 2: Unique Keywords   **9**
The Challenge of Full-Text Searching 9
Choosing the Right Keywords. 11

Chapter 3: Basic Search Tools   **15**
Searching in Plain English. 16
Searching for Multiple Words and Phrases 16
AND searches 17
OR searches. 18
NOT searches 19
NEAR (or Proximity) searches 20
Creating More Complex Queries. 21
Using Wildcards 21
Dealing with Stopwords 22

Chapter 4: Tips and Techniques   **23**
The Seven Habits of Highly Effective
    Web Searchers 24
Customizing Your Web Browser 28
Keyboard Shortcuts and Other Time Savers 30

PART 2: USING THE LEADING SEARCH ENGINES

Chapter 5: AltaVista   **35**
Using AltaVista's Simple Search. 37
Creating Simple Search Queries 39
Improving Web search results
    with field search 42
Searching Usenet newsgroups
    for information in specific fields 44
Using AltaVista's Advanced Search. 46

Searching the Web and Newsgroups
with Advanced Search 47
Refining Simple or Advanced Searches
with LiveTopics 50
Using the LiveTopics Java interface 52
Using the LiveTopics JavaScript and
Text interfaces 54

Chapter 6: Excite   57
Using Excite's main search page 59
Searching the Web with Excite 61
Creating Excite Queries. 63
Zeroing in on the best Web sites 66
Searching by topic for the best Web sites 68
Searching Usenet newsgroups 70
Searching for current news with Excite. 72
Using Excite to find travel information 74

Chapter 7: HotBot   77
Using HotBot's basic search form 79
Refining your HotBot searches 82
Advanced searching with HotBot 84
Exploring the Web by topic. 88

Chapter 8: Infoseek   91
Using Infoseek's main search page 93
Basic Web searching with Infoseek 96
Creating more effective queries 98
Field searching with Infoseek 100
Searching Usenet newsgroups 103
Searching for current news with Infoseek. 105
Searching other Infoseek databases 107
Power searching with Ultraseek 110

Chapter 9: Lycos   113
Using the main Lycos search page 115
Searching for the best Web sites 119
Searching for images and sounds 121
Custom searching with Lycos Pro 123
Using other Lycos search tools 127

Chapter 10: Yahoo!   129
Using Yahoo!'s main search page. 131
Searching with Yahoo!. 133
Customizing your Yahoo! searches 135
Using Yahoo!'s Web directory 138
Exploring the Web by topic. 140

TABLE OF CONTENTS

PART 3:	USING SPECIALIZED SEARCH ENGINES	

Chapter 11: Searching Newsgroups with Deja News   **145**
Using Deja News to search newsgroups 147

Chapter 12: Searching Mailing Lists with Liszt   **151**
Using the Liszt directory 153

Chapter 13: Searching Subject Guides with the Argus Clearinghouse   **157**
Finding subject guides 159

Chapter 14: Searching for People with Four11   **163**
Finding e-mail addresses with Four11 165
Finding home addresses and telephone
     numbers with Four11 167

Chapter 15: Searching for Businessses with Zip2 Yellow Pages   **171**
Finding businesses with Zip2 173

Chapter 16: Searching for Everything from Authors to ZIP Codes   **177**
Amazon.com Books 178
CDNow 178
C|Net's Shareware.com 179
Consumer World 179
DineNet Menus Online 180
Edmund's Automobile Buyer's Guides 180
Electric Library 181
Epicurious Food 181
FedEx Package Tracking 182
FindLaw Internet Legal Resources 182
HealthAtoZ 183
Internet Movie Database 183
MapQuest 184
Microsoft Technical Support 184
The New York Times Book Reviews 185
Online Career Center 185
Parent Soup 186
Peterson's Education & Career Center 186
Project Gutenberg 187
Tax Information: 1040.com 188
Thomas Legislative Information 188
UPS Package Tracking 189

The Wall Street Journal Interactive Edition 189
ZDNet Software Library and Reviews 189
ZIP Code Lookups 190

Appendix A: Search Engine Quick Reference   191
AltaVista 192
Argus Clearinghouse 195
Deja News 195
Excite 197
Four11 198
HotBot 199
InfoSeek 201
Liszt 202
Lycos 203
Yahoo! 206
Zip2 Yellow Pages 207

**Appendix B: Internet Domains
and Country Codes   209**
Common Internet Domains 209
Country Codes (Alphabetical by Country) 210
Country Codes (Alphabetical by Code) 212

Appendix C: Usenet Newsgroup Hierarchies   215

Appendix D: The Web Searcher's Toolkit   217
Essential Tools for Windows Users 218
Glossbrenner's Choice Order Form 221

Index   223

INTRODUCTION

The amount of information available on the Internet and the World Wide Web is vast and growing at a staggering rate. But how does anyone find anything? That's the $64,000 question. If you're like us, the fascination of "browsing the Web" wore off a long time ago. We want to sign on, get the information we need, sign off, and go about our business and our lives.

Fortunately, the tools now exist for doing just that. Dozens of them, in fact. They're called *search engines* and some now rank among the most popular sites on the Internet.

But now we have a new problem and a whole new set of questions. With so many search engines out there (one popular Internet directory currently lists 145 and the number keeps growing), how do we find out what the really good ones are? Does it make any difference which one we choose? Will a search for **Tamagotchis** or **virtual pets** produce the same results whether we use AltaVista or Yahoo!?

This book will answer all of these questions and more. And like all the books in the *Visual QuickStart* series, it's designed to do so with a minimum of technical jargon and extraneous information. You'll find lots of step-by-step instructions and specific examples for using search engines in general, and the very best ones in particular.

How to Get the Most out of This Book

In writing the book, we've made just a few basic assumptions about you:

- You know the fundamentals of working with a computer, such as how to use a mouse and how to choose menu commands.

- You have access to the Internet—either through an Internet Service Provider (ISP) or a major online service like America Online or CompuServe—and you know how to sign onto the Net.

- You have some experience using a Web browser program like Netscape Navigator, Netscape Communicator, or Microsoft Internet Explorer to visit Web sites, and now you're ready to learn how to do more than just "surf the Net."

If you're not quite ready on one or more of these fronts, you may want to hold off on this book for the time being. Instead, check your favorite bookstore or your local library for *The Little Web Book: A Gentle Introduction to the World Wide Web and the Internet* (also published by Peachpit Press). We wrote *Little Web* for people who are venturing onto the Internet for the very first time. Once you've read it and spent some time exploring Web sites on your own, the information presented in this book will make a lot more sense.

How the Book is Organized

Here's how *Search Engines for the World Wide Web* is organized:

Part 1, **Getting Comfortable with Search Basics**, introduces you to the concept of search engines and how they work. You'll also learn about *keywords*—how to choose the right ones and the various methods of combining them for more effective searches. We round things out with some specific tips and techniques for using any search engine.

Part 2, **Using the Leading Search Engines**, gets down to specifics with chapters on six of the most popular Web search engines. By the time you're finished, you'll know about their strengths and weaknesses and how to use the major features. Perhaps best of all, each chapter includes at least one Quick Reference guide that summarizes the key commands and search rules for each search engine.

Part 3, **Using Specialized Search Engines**, presents some alternatives to the all-purpose "Swiss Army Knife" approach of the search engines covered in Part 2. Just as cooks and carpenters need special tools from time to time, so too do Web searchers. We'll introduce you to some of the best of these special tools and help you understand when to use them for faster, more efficient searches.

Appendix A, **Search Engine Quick Reference**, is a collection of all the Quick Reference guides from throughout the book, organized alphabetically by search engine. Our thought is that when you're online and need a quick reminder of, say, the AltaVista or Lycos search commands, you'll find it more convenient to turn to this appendix instead of going back to the individual search engine chapter.

Appendix B, **Internet Domains and Country Codes**, will help you take advantage of power-searching techniques like zeroing in on a specific *type* of organization (based on the *Internet domain* designation in its Web address), or locating sites that originate in a particular country.

Appendix C, **Usenet Newsgroup Hierarchies**, explains how newsgroups are named and gives you the information you need to limit your queries to specific newsgroups, a feature offered by some search engines.

Appendix D, **Web Searcher's Toolkit**, tells you about the Windows and DOS programs we've found to be especially useful for getting the most out of the Internet. All of the programs are public domain or shareware, and they are available on the Net. But as a convenience to our readers, we've put them on 3.5-inch high-density disks and offer them by mail, separately or as a complete toolkit. (See the order form in the back of the book to get these disks.)

HOW THE BOOK IS ORGANIZED

PART 1

GETTING COMFORTABLE WITH SEARCH BASICS

Chapter 1: Search Engines and
How They Work   3

Chapter 2: Unique Keywords   9

Chapter 3: Basic Search Tools   15

Chapter 4: Tips and Tricks   23

Getting Comfortable with Search Basics

If you're new to online searching, we suggest that you read the four chapters in this part of the book from start to finish. With this information under your belt, you'll get a lot more out of the specific search engine chapters in Parts 2 and 3.

Chapter 1, **Search Engines and How They Work**, brings you up to speed on what search engines are all about and how they accomplish the mammoth task of collecting information from Web sites around the world.

Chapter 2, **Unique Keywords**, lays out specific steps for choosing the best search terms for your Web searches. Coming up with the right keywords is the essence of effective searching, and this chapter will show you how to do just that.

Chapter 3, **Basic Search Tools**, builds on the keyword concept by showing you how to enter and combine search terms. Each search engine has its own way of doing things, but the basic concepts are similar from one search engine to the next. Once you know the basics, you'll be well equipped to deal with almost any search engine.

Chapter 4, **Tips and Techniques**, presents some of our favorite Web-searching techniques, shortcuts, and time-savers.

SEARCH ENGINES AND HOW THEY WORK

The Perils of Internet Searching

Clifford Stoll is an experienced Internet searcher. In fact, some years ago he used his considerable search skills to track down the infamous "Hanover Hacker" on the Net—a trail that led to a KGB-backed spy ring. The tale is recounted in his best-selling book, *The Cuckoo's Egg*. His most recent book is *Silicon Snake Oil—Second Thoughts on the Information Highway*.

Here's what this longtime Internaut had to say in *Newsweek* (February 27, 1995) about the frustration of doing research on the Internet:

What the Internet hucksters won't tell you is that the Internet is an ocean of unedited data, without any pretense of completeness. Lacking editors, reviewers, or critics, the Internet has become a wasteland of unfiltered data. You don't know what to ignore and what's worth reading.

Logged on to the World Wide Web, I hunt for the date of the Battle of Trafalgar. Hundreds of files show up, and it takes 15 minutes to unravel them—one's a biography written by an eighth grader, the second is a computer game that doesn't work, and the third is an image of a London monument. None answers my question, and my search is periodically interrupted by messages like "Too many connections, try again later."

Listening to the evening news and reading the daily paper, you could easily get the impression that the Internet and the World Wide Web hold the answers to virtually any question you could possibly ask. Sign on, tap a few keys, and all the world's knowledge is there for the taking. It couldn't be simpler.

But ask anyone who has actually tried to use the Internet to answer a specific question or track down a particular fact or figure and you're likely to hear a far different story: "I can't find *anything* on the Net." Or "There was so much information, most of it useless, that I gave up."

Even longtime, experienced searchers like author Clifford Stoll (see the sidebar, "The Perils of Internet Searching"), have expressed great frustration in doing research on the Internet. So what hope is there for less experienced searchers?

Enter Search Engines

The good news is that things have improved dramatically since 1995 when Clifford Stoll's lament about the problems of finding useful information on the Internet first appeared—at least in terms of the tools available for dealing with what he referred to as the Internet's "wasteland of unfiltered data."

Today we can choose from among dozens of *search engines*—tools that let you explore databases containing the text from tens of millions of Web pages. When the search engine software finds pages that match your search request (often referred to as *hits*), it presents them to you with brief descriptions and clickable links to take you there.

Some search engines, like AltaVista (**Figure 1.1**), concentrate exclusively on providing a powerful search capability. Most, however, also offer a multi-level *topic directory* that you can browse for information on a given subject. Topic directories are usually prepared by search engine employees who spend their days visiting, selecting, and classifying Web sites based on content. Excite (**Figure 1.2**) is a good example of a search engine that offers both sophisticated searching as well as an excellent topic directory.

Of all the general-purpose search engines available today, several are especially impressive. We'll have much more to say about them in Part 2 of this book, but if you'd like to visit them now, here's where to find them:

AltaVista	www.altavista.digital.com
Excite	www.excite.com
HotBot	www.hotbot.com
Infoseek	www.infoseek.com
Lycos	www.lycos.com
Yahoo!	www.yahoo.com

Figure 1.1 AltaVista emphasizes *searching*—rather than browsing the Web by topic. It's one of the few search engines without a topic directory on its home page.

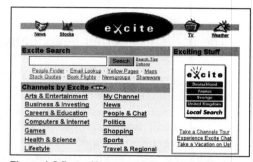

Figure 1.2 Excite, like most other major search engines, gives you two ways to look for information. You can type a query in the search form or click on one of the topics (Excite calls them *Channels*) to explore a broad subject area.

ENTER SEARCH ENGINES

✔ Tips

- The official address, or URL (Uniform Resource Locator), for any Web site always begins with http://. However, with Web browsers like Netscape Navigator, Netscape Communicator, and Internet Explorer, it's no longer necessary to include this portion of the address.

- With Netscape Navigator and Communicator, you can even omit the www and com portion of the address. Try it with any of the addresses in our search engines list: altavista.digital, excite, hotbot, etc.

- Netscape devotes a special page to search engines and other Internet search tools. To get there, go to the Netscape home page at home.netscape.com, scroll down to the bottom of the page, and click on Net Search.

- Yahoo!, one of the best search engines and Internet directories going, is also an excellent one-stop source of search engine information. From the Yahoo! home page at www.yahoo.com, click on Computers and Internet, then Internet, then World Wide Web, and finally Searching the Web. Prepare to be overwhelmed!

- Don't feel you have to spend too much time at either of these sites—unless you're truly interested in making an exhaustive study of Internet search tools. We tell you about them simply to make the point that there are a lot of tools out there. If you want to concentrate on the best ones, stick with the information presented in this book.

ENTER SEARCH ENGINES

How Search Engines Work

Search engines are designed to make it as easy as possible for you to find what you want on the Internet. But with tens of millions of Web pages stored on computers all over the world—and more being added all the time—how can search engines possibly collect them all? And what do they do with the information once they get it?

Most search engines deploy robot programs called *spiders* or *crawlers*. Some of them even have names and personalities, like "Scooter," the AltaVista spider shown and described in **Figure 1.3**. Scooter and other such programs are designed to track down Web pages, follow the links they contain, and add any new information they encounter to a master database or *index*.

You don't really need to know the specifics. The key point to understand is that each search engine has its own way of doing things. Some have programmed their spiders or crawlers to search for only the *titles* of Web pages and the first few lines of text. Others snare every single word, ignoring only the graphics, video, sound, and other multimedia files.

Search engines also differ in the methods they use for calculating *relevancy*—usually reported as a percentage indicating how well a particular Web page matches your search request. (See **Figure 1.4** for an example.)

The formulas for calculating relevancy are constantly changing as search engines attempt to stay one step ahead of Web developers who engage in a practice called *spamdexing*—doctoring a Web page to fool search engines into putting it high on the list of search results. One of the most common spamdexing tricks is to load a Web page with words—like *free* or *money* or *sex*—that may or may not have anything to do with the site.

Where does the index come from? How do you decide what information gets indexed?
The AltaVista index is created by our Web spider, called Scooter (isn't he cute?), that roams the Web collecting Web pages-approximately six million per day. Scooter then takes the pages back to AltaVista and gives them to our N12 indexing software, which then indexes each word from every page. The index saves each instance of each word, including instances of different capitalization, as well as the URL of the page on which it appears and some information about its location in that document. Also, the index software indexes words with non-Latin characters using English-equivalent letters. These details are what allow you to search for individual words, phrases in which word order is essential, and words or phrases with specific capitalization or accents.

Figure 1.3 Scooter is the spider responsible for building the Web page database for AltaVista.

CL: Windsor Chairs--Types of Windsor Chairs
Windsor Chairs Types of Windsor Chairs Despite the subtle differences that evolved in various regions of the country, specific styles of Windsor chairs were widespread over the course ...
100% http://homearts.com/cl/collect/10windb4.htm   (Size 2.2K)

CL: Windsor Chairs--British Influence
Windsor Chairs British Influence PHOTOGRAPHY WINTERTHUR MUSEUM One English influence American cabinetmakers retained for their Windsor chairs was a painted finish. Since many ...
95% http://homearts.com/cl/collect/10windb3.htm   (Size 2.4K)

Frontera-Greg Long Windsor Chairs
Handmade colonial windsor chairs. Our windsors are built using traditional tools and techniques to create beautiful heirlooms of museum quality. Free catalog.
93% http://www.frontera.com/pages/long.htm   (Size 2.9K)

Frontera -History of Windsors
Early history of windsor chair design, manufacture and use. Link to Frontera Trading Company, Texas' mail order retailer of fine colonial and pioneer furniture. Free catalog.
90% http://www.neosoft.com/~frontera/pages/winhist.htm   (Size 4.1K)

CL: Windsor Chairs--Comb-back
Windsor Chairs Comb-back The earliest Philadelphia Windsor chairs are called comb-backs, because their tall, straight spindles resemble the teeth of a comb. Comb-back Windsors are ...
87% http://homearts.com/cl/collect/10windb5.htm   (Size 1.4K)

Figure 1.4 Search results are usually presented in order based on *relevancy*, reported as a percentage. Here, the first site listed has a rating of 100 percent. The fifth item down the list has a rating of 87 percent.

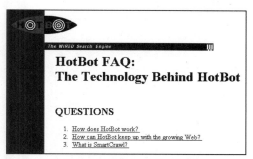

Figure 1.5 HotBot shares some of its search engine secrets on the HotBot FAQ (Frequently Asked Questions) page.

Lycos has responded to this tactic by changing its relevancy formula to give a *lower* ranking to pages with a lot of repeated words.

The beauty of spiders and crawlers is that they operate around the clock. But some take longer than others to make their rounds, and even the best of them take days or even weeks to cover the entire Web. That's one of the reasons you may find a certain Web site with one search engine but not another. If you check back in a couple of days, chances are it will be there.

✔ Tips

■ Many search engines provide basic information about how their spiders operate—what they search for, how many sites they visit in a day, how often the master database is updated, and so forth. But you might have to dig a bit to find it. AltaVista's spider (**Figure 1.3**) is described in an "About AltaVista" page. HotBot presents similar information about its spider in a FAQ (Frequently Asked Questions) page called "The Technology Behind HotBot" (**Figure 1.5**). Other search engines include it with the "Search Tips" or "Help" information accessible from their home pages.

■ Keep in mind that when you use a search engine to search the Web, what you are actually searching is a database of information that's been collected automatically by a spider or crawler program. If you choose instead to explore a subject using a search engine's topic directory, you're likely to get far fewer hits. But the sites you find will all have been selected and classified by human beings.

Unique Keywords

```
Records 1 through 1 of 103 returned.

Author:        Vonnegut, Kurt.
Title:         Cat's cradle.
Edition:       [1st ed.]
Published:     New York, Holt, Rinehart and Winston [1963]
Description:   233 p. 22 cm.
LC Call No.:   PZ4.V948 Cat
Subjects:      Humorous stories. gsafd
               Science fiction. gsafd
               Satire. gsafd
Control No.:   63010930 /L/r952
```

Figure 2.1 Search for author Kurt Vonnegut at your local library and you'll get information like this for each of his books.

The biggest challenge with any type of online searching is choosing the right search terms or *keywords*. This goes double for Web searching because, as you know from Chapter 1, what you are typically searching when you use tools like AltaVista or Excite is the full *text* of Web pages collected automatically by spider or crawler programs.

That sounds great in theory, but as any professional searcher will tell you, it's actually the most difficult type of searching in the online world.

The Challenge of Full-Text Searching

Traditional databases, like the electronic card catalog at your local library, let you do *field searches*. If you're interested in the writer Kurt Vonnegut, for example, you can search for **Vonnegut** in the database's Author field to produce a list of his books. Click on a title and all the relevant information about that book will be presented in familiar, card-catalog format (**Figure 2.1**).

If, on the other hand, you're looking for his biography or other information *about* him, you can search for his name in the Subject field. Or maybe what you really want is recent magazine articles that feature Kurt Vonnegut, in which case you'd use the Periodicals database instead of the one for the library's collection of books.

Web search engine databases, in contrast, make no distinction between the various types of information available about Kurt Vonnegut. Do a search on his name and you'll get a hodge-podge of Web sites, many of them personal home pages created by Vonnegut fans (**Figure 2.2**).

Field searching with Web search engines, if it's available at all, is limited to fields having to do with the Web page itself—its title, Web address or URL (Uniform Resource Locator), the date the page was created, and so forth— not the information *on* the page.

Searching these Web page fields can be quite useful, but it comes nowhere close to matching the precision and sophistication of traditional database field searching. Which brings us back to our original point: To be an effective Web searcher, you'll need to get quite good at coming up with the *right* keywords.

✔ Tip

- Of the major search engines covered in this book, AltaVista, HotBot, Infoseek, and Yahoo! all offer field searching of one sort or another. For details, see the individual search engine chapters in Part 2 or the Search Engine Quick Reference in Appendix A.

Welcome to the Monkey House **86%** (Size 12.2K)
Vonnegut Scholarship Critical Sources. Abadi-Nagy, Zoltan. "The Skilful **80%** (Size 4.6K)
Alt.books.kurt-vonnegut FAQ **77%** (Size 32.5K)
Kurt Vonnegut Web **76%** (Size 7.8K)
Alpha Ralpha Boulevard: Kurt Vonnegut **76%** (Size 1.4K)
Kurt Vonnegut Quote **75%** (Size 3.7K)
alt.books.kurt-vonnegut **75%** (Size 2.2K)
The High School Honors Project Kurt Vonnegut Page **74%** (Size 11.0K)
The George Page -- Kurt Vonnegut. **74%** (Size 2.6K)
PHOAKS: Resources for alt.books.kurt-vonnegut **74%** (Size 28.6K)
Kurt Vonnegut Essay Collection **73%** (Size 4.2K)
The Kurt Vonnegut Web: Formal Honors **73%** (Size 2.9K)
Alt.books.kurt-vonnegut FAQ **73%** (Size 34.9K)
A Post-modern Pierrot: Kurt Vonnegut arrives at the UW **73%** (Size 14.1K)
NIC - alt.books.kurt-vonnegut **72%** (Size 1.0K)
Welcome to the Monkey House: The Vonnegut Web **71%** (Size 7.7K)
Kurt Vonnegut **71%** (Size 3.6K)
Jaro's Web Pages Presents: Kurt Vonnegut Introduction to Vonnegut: Kurt **71%** (Size 2.4K)
H-Net Book Reviews: Bane on Mustazza,   Critical Response to Kurt Vonnegut **71%** (Size 4.2K)
Kurt Vonnegut: November 11, 1922 **70%** (Size 2.3K)

Sites 1 - 20 of 2,958   **Show Summaries**   next 20

Figure 2.2 Search the Web for Kurt Vonnegut and there's no telling what you'll come up with, as these results show.

Figure 2.3 Searching for a unique keyword like **Sumatran tiger** is more likely to produce a site like this near the top of your search results list than would a search for the far more common **tigers**.

Choosing the Right Keywords

Learning to come up with the most effective keywords for your Web searches will take time and practice. Don't be surprised or disappointed if you're not successful every time. After all, even the best online searchers find Web searching to be quite a challenge.

We don't pretend to have all the answers ourselves, but here are some points to keep in mind that can help you improve your Web searching success rate.

To get the best search results:

1. **Use the most unique keyword you can think of.**

   Take the time to think about the words that will almost certainly appear on the kind of Web page you have in mind. Then pick the most unique or unusual word from that list.

   If you're looking for information about efforts to save tiger populations in Asia, for example, don't use **tigers** as your search term. You'll be swamped with Web pages about the Detroit Tigers, the Princeton Tigers, and every other sports team that uses the word *tigers* in its name.

   Instead, try searching for a particular tiger species that you know to be on the endangered list—**Bengal tiger** or **Sumatran tiger** or **Siberian tiger**. (With some search engines, you'll need to enclose the words in double quotes to let them know you're doing a *phrase search*: "Bengal tiger".) Chances are, you'll find sites like the one in **Figure 2.3** near the top of the list.

2. **Make it a multi-step process.**

   Don't assume that you'll find what you
   want on the first try. Take your best shot.
   Then review the first couple of pages of
   results, paying particular attention to the
   sites that contain the kind of information
   you want. What unique words appear on
   those pages? Make a few notes and then
   do another search using those words.

3. **Narrow the field by searching
   just your previous results.**

   If your chosen keyword returns relatively
   good information but too much to review
   comfortably, try a second search of just
   those results—often referred to as *set searching*. Procedures for doing this vary from
   one search engine to the next. Infoseek
   makes it quite easy with a special "Search
   only these results" option (**Figure 2.4**).
   You can accomplish essentially the same
   thing with any search engine, however, by
   simply adding another keyword to your
   search request and submitting it again.

4. **Look for your keyword
   in the Web page title.**

   Often the best search strategy is to look
   first for your unique keyword in the *titles*
   of Web pages. (AltaVista and Infoseek both
   offer this type of field search.) If you're
   looking for information about marriage
   customs in the Middle Ages, for example,
   start with a search of Web pages that have
   the words *Middle Ages* in the title. Then do a
   second search of just those results, looking for *marriage customs*.

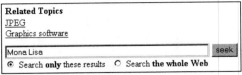

Figure 2.4 Set searching is easy with Infoseek. Once
you've located sites offering JPEG graphics files, for
example, you can look for images of the Mona Lisa by
doing a second search of just those results.

5. Find out if case counts.

It's important to know whether the search engine you're using pays attention to upper- and lowercase letters in your keywords. Will a search for Java, the Sun Microsystems program, also find sites that refer to the program as JAVA?

6. Check your spelling.

If you've used the best keyword you can think of and the search engine comes back with the message "No results found" or some such, check your spelling before you do anything else. Nine times out of ten, the reason a search engine comes up empty-handed is because of a spelling or typing error. At least that's been our experience.

✔ Tip

■ The Quick Reference guides in the search engine chapters of this book (and repeated in Appendix A) are a good place to look for specifics on set, field, and case-sensitive searching with different search engines.

BASIC SEARCH TOOLS

Search Tools at a Glance

Here are the basic search tools you'll read about in this chapter:

- Plain-English Searches
- AND Searches
- OR Searches
- NOT Searches
- NEAR (or Proximity) Searches
- Nested Searches
- Wildcards
- Stopwords

As we've said before, choosing the right keywords is the essence of effective searching. It's especially important for *Web* searching, because there's so much information out there—some of it worthwhile, much of it totally useless—and there's no single company or organization responsible for organizing and making sense of it.

But coming up with good, unique keywords is actually just half the battle. You also need to know how to enter and combine keywords, taking advantage of the basic search tools offered by the major search engines. Your success rate will improve dramatically once you learn what these tools are and when and how to use them.

Specific procedures vary from one search engine to the next, of course. In fact, some search engines have a different set of instructions depending on whether you're using their simple or advanced versions. But certain general concepts apply across the board. That's what we'll cover here.

Once you have this basic understanding of the tools that are available, you'll be better equipped to deal with just about any search engine you encounter on the Web. The chapters in Parts 2 and 3 will fill in the details for some of the best of them.

Searching in Plain English

For new Web searchers, one of the best tools going is *Plain-English* or *Natural-language* searching. Most of the leading search engines have developed techniques that are amazingly good at finding what you want, based on a simple question—especially if the question includes at least one unique keyword (**Figure 3.1**).

You'll get lots of hits, but the ones most likely to be of interest to you will appear at or near the top of the list (**Figure 3.2**).

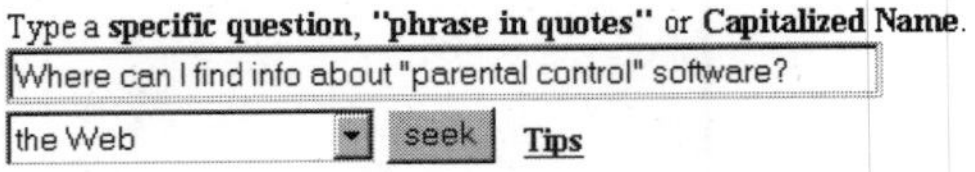

Searching for Multiple Words and Phrases

The most important thing to find out about any search engine is how to look for *multiple* words and phrases. Plain-English queries are great, and they can probably handle many of your search requirements. But sometimes you need more precision than you can get from a Plain-English search.

Here are the features to look for:

- How do you tell the search engine that you want to find Web sites that include references to Keyword A *and* Keyword B?

- How do you specify that it's not necessary for *both* keywords to appear in the results, as long as one or the other is present?

- How do you look for one keyword while specifically *excluding* another?

- How do you find two words or phrases in close *proximity* to one another?

The technical term for this type of searching is *Boolean* searching, and AND, OR, NOT, and NEAR are among the traditional *Boolean* operators. We'll use the more common names: AND, OR, NOT, and NEAR (or proximity) searches.

Type a **specific question**, **"phrase in quotes"** or **Capitalized Name**.

> Where can I find info about "parental control" software?

the Web ▾ | seek | **Tips**

Figure 3.1 Plain-English searches like this often produce excellent results. Many search engines encourage you to simply ask a question.

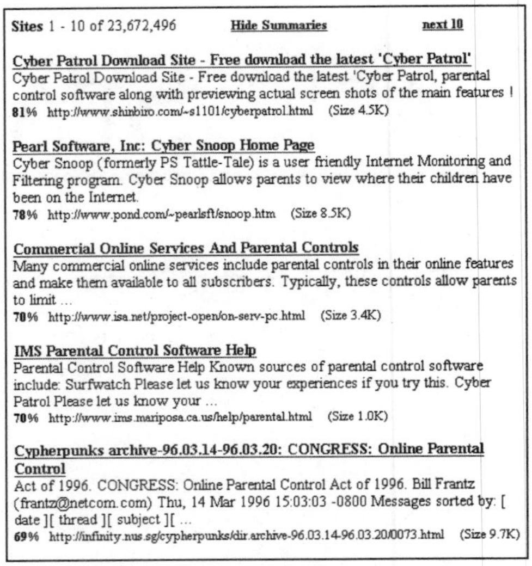

Sites 1 - 10 of 23,672,496   **Hide Summaries**   **next 10**

Cyber Patrol Download Site - Free download the latest 'Cyber Patrol'
Cyber Patrol Download Site - Free download the latest 'Cyber Patrol, parental control software along with previewing actual screen shots of the main features l
81% http://www.shinbiro.com/~s1101/cyberpatrol.html   (Size 4.5K)

Pearl Software, Inc: Cyber Snoop Home Page
Cyber Snoop (formerly PS Tattle-Tale) is a user friendly Internet Monitoring and Filtering program. Cyber Snoop allows parents to view where their children have been on the Internet.
78% http://www.pond.com/~pearlsft/snoop.htm   (Size 8.5K)

Commercial Online Services And Parental Controls
Many commercial online services include parental controls in their online features and make them available to all subscribers. Typically, these controls allow parents to limit ...
78% http://www.isa.net/project-open/on-serv-pc.html   (Size 3.4K)

IMS Parental Control Software Help
Parental Control Software Help Known sources of parental control software include: Surfwatch Please let us know your experiences if you try this. Cyber Patrol Please let us know your ...
78% http://www.ims.mariposa.ca.us/help/parental.html   (Size 1.0K)

Cypherpunks archive-96.03.14-96.03.20: CONGRESS: Online Parental Control
Act of 1996. CONGRESS: Online Parental Control Act of 1996. Bill Frantz (frantz@netcom.com) Thu, 14 Mar 1996 15:03:03 -0800 Messages sorted by: [date][thread][subject][...
69% http://infinity.nus.sg/cypherpunks/dir.archive-96.03.14-96.03.20/0073.html   (Size 9.7K)

Figure 3.2 The question posed in **Figure 3.1** identified millions of sites, but the first five (shown here) all look promising.

all the words ▾
all the words
any of the words
the exact phrase
words in the title
the person
links to this URL
the Boolean expression

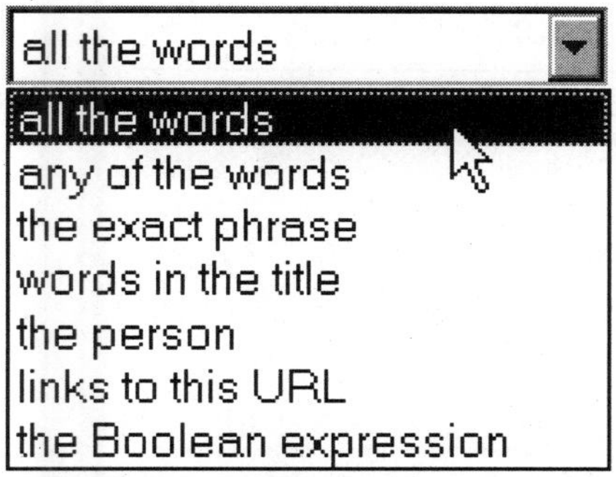

Figure 3.3 AND searches can sometimes be done by choosing "All the Words" from a menu like this one.

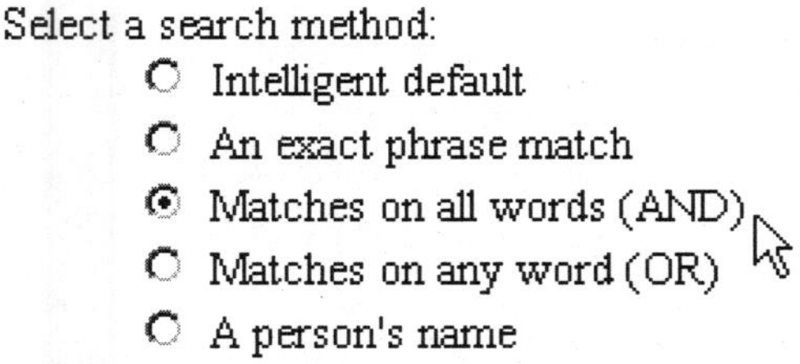

Select a search method:

○ Intelligent default

○ An exact phrase match

◉ Matches on all words (AND)

○ Matches on any word (OR)

○ A person's name

Figure 3.4 Some search engines let you specify an AND search by clicking on a radio button.

AND searches

Searching for two or more keywords—both of which must appear in the results—is an excellent strategy for doing precise searches and greatly reducing the number of search results you have to consider. Some search engines offer more than one method for doing AND searches, so you can choose the one you like best.

The most common way to tell a search engine that you want to do an AND search is to put a plus sign in front of each word or phrase that must appear in the results: **+Renaissance +sculpture**.

Other search engines require that you actually use the Boolean operator AND to combine words or phrases: **basket–weaving AND supplies**, for example, to look for references to both terms. Some search engines further require that you use full caps for AND, while others don't care. To avoid having to remember which is which, it's a good idea to get into the habit of using full caps all the time.

Some search engines make AND searching extremely easy by offering it as a menu option or radio button. You simply type two or more unique keywords or phrases and then choose "All the Words" from a drop-down menu (**Figure 3.3**) or click on the radio button with a similar label (**Figure 3.4**).

MULTIPLE WORDS & PHRASES: AND SEARCHES

OR Searches

OR searches cast a much broader net than AND searches and may result in a very large number of hits for you to consider. They make good sense, though, when there's more than one way that the person, object, or thing you're looking for might be referred to in a Web page or other document. If you're doing research on the Clinton presidency, for example, you'd want to look for references to *President Clinton* or *Bill Clinton* or *William Jefferson Clinton*.

Most search engines do an OR search by default. In other words, if you type several words or phrases, leaving a space between each one, the search engine assumes that you want to find references to *any one* of them: "President Clinton" "Bill Clinton" "William Jefferson Clinton".

Other search engines require that you actually type the word OR between the words or phrases: **Gingrich OR "Speaker of the House"**. Again, full caps may or may not be required for the word OR, but it's a good habit to get into.

Finally, some search engines offer OR searching as a menu option or radio button. You type your search words and phrases and then choose the option labeled "Any of the Words" or some such (as opposed to "All the Words"). See **Figures 3.5** and **3.6** for examples.

Common Methods for Doing OR Searches:

■ Search for UPS U.P.S.

■ Search for UPS OR U.P.S.

■ Search for UPS U.P.S and select "Any of the Words" option

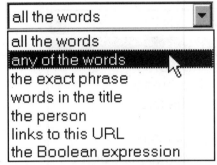

Figure 3.5 Choosing "Any of the Words" from a menu like this is the way you tell some search engines to do an OR search.

Select a search method:

○ Intelligent default

○ An exact phrase match

○ Matches on all words (AND)

⦿ Matches on any word (OR)

○ A person's name

Figure 3.6 Here's another approach to OR searching. You simply click on a radio button indicating that you want the search engine to look for any of the words you've typed in the search form.

NOT Searches

Here's the example you'll come across again and again to illustrate when to use a NOT search: You're looking for information on snakes and key in a search for **python**. Much to your dismay, your search results are dominated by Web pages created by devoted Monty Python fans. What to do?

The answer, of course, is to *exclude* Monty Python pages with a NOT search. Usually that means putting a minus sign in front of the word you want to avoid: **python –monty**. (Notice that there's no space between the minus sign and the word that's being excluded.)

Some search engines allow (or require) the use of the word NOT to exclude a word: **python NOT monty**.

AltaVista is one of the few search engines to require that you use AND NOT to exclude a word or phrase—but that applies only with its Advanced Search form: **python AND NOT monty**. For AltaVista's Simple Search form, NOT searches must be done with the minus sign: **python –monty**. (Be sure to put the minus sign directly in front of the word you want to exclude, without leaving a space.)

✔ Tips

■ NOT can be a very powerful operator. But it also makes it quite easy to unwittingly throw the baby out with the bath water. Suppose the definitive Web site on pythons—"The Master Python Page"—happens to have been created by someone named Monty Shields. The NOT search in our example could very well prevent you from ever finding it.

■ By all means, learn to use NOT searches. Just be aware of the potential for inadvertently excluding good material.

MULTIPLE WORDS & PHRASES: NOT SEARCHES

NEAR (or Proximity) Searches

Sometimes you're not just interested in finding multiple keywords that are *mentioned* in the same document. You want to be able to specify that they appear in *close proximity* to one another. That's what NEAR searching is for.

AltaVista and Lycos offer NEAR searching, but only as part of their advanced search capabilities (not on their basic search forms). The format is the same for both: **Clinton NEAR "foreign policy"**.

And just how near is NEAR? AltaVista defines it to mean within 10 words of each other. Lycos defines it as within 25 words but lets you change that with the addition of a forward slash and any number you choose: **Clinton NEAR/15 "foreign policy"** would expand the range to within 15 words.

See **Figures 3.7** and **3.8** for an example of NEAR searching with Lycos.

Search Engines Offering NEAR Searches

■ AltaVista (Advanced Search only)

Search for **Japan NEAR climate** to find the two terms within 10 words of each other.

■ Lycos (Lycos Pro with Java Power Panel only)

Search for **Japan NEAR climate** to find the two terms within 25 words of each other.

Use **NEAR/** followed by any number to specify some other distance: **Japan NEAR/5 climate**.

Figure 3.7 A NEAR search like this tells Lycos to find references to *Clinton* within 15 words of the phrase *foreign policy*.

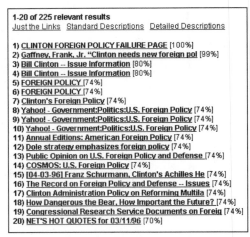

Figure 3.8 The first 20 sites found by the NEAR search in **Figure 3.7** look promising.

Creating More Complex Queries

Most search engines also allow you to create more complex queries by grouping AND, OR, NOT, and NEAR statements using parentheses: **Canton NEAR (Ohio OR OH)**. These are often called *nested searches* because they can get quite complex, with one search statement "nested" within another.

Our advice is to use parentheses in your searches sparingly, and only when you really need them. Complex nested searches are fine for the professionals. But for most search tasks, and especially for new online searchers, they're not worth the **mental AND (energy OR effort OR aggravation)**!

You'll be far better off concentrating on coming up with good, unique keywords and sticking to simple combinations like AND, OR, NOT (and possibly NEAR) searches.

Using Wildcards

Searching with *wildcards*—or *truncation* as it's sometimes called—means using an asterisk to indicate that you want to look for variations on a particular word, like **medic∗**, to find references to *medical, medicine, medicinal,* and *medication.*

It's usually a good idea to use a wildcard along with at least one other unique keyword: **anti–depressant NEAR medic∗**. Otherwise, your search may take painfully long and return too many hits to be truly useful.

Some search engines don't specifically offer wildcard searches, but they do a variation on it automatically. Excite, for example, routinely performs what it calls *concept-based searching*, looking for the words in your search request as well as words and concepts that are similar to it. Believe it or not, it works amazingly well.

CREATING COMPLEX QUERIES / USING WILDCARDS

Dealing with Stopwords

You may come across the term *stopwords* at search engine sites, often in the help information or search tips (**Figure 3.9**). Stopwords are words that search engines ignore because they're too common or because they're reserved for some special purpose.

The list varies from one search engine to the next, but it usually includes words like *the, to, with, from, for, of, that, who,* and all of the Boolean operators (AND, OR, NOT, NEAR, etc.).

Should you need to use a stopword as part of a search, you can usually ensure that it won't be ignored by setting it off in double quotes: Portland NEAR "OR". Search engines also typically pay attention to stopwords that are included as part of a phrase: "The Man Who Came to Dinner" or "to be or not to be".

✔ Tips

■ Most major search engines offer all of the basic tools described in this chapter. But keep in mind that the specifics vary from one to the next. In some cases, there's even a different set of rules depending on whether you're using the search engine's simple or advanced search form.

■ The chapters in Parts 2 and 3 of this book will introduce you to many of the specifics. Be sure to also check the online Search Tips and Help sections for any search engine you decide to use on a regular basis to learn about new features that may have been added.

Stopword Tips:

■ Every search engine ignores certain very common words (*stopwords*) like *the, to, with,* the Boolean operators, etc.

■ Stopwords in phrases won't be ignored by most search engines: "to be or not to be".

■ To look for words that might be confused with Boolean operators, put them in double quotes: Portland NEAR "OR".

❏ What are the Deja News stopwords?

1994	date	lines	s
1995	do	may	sender
1996	for	message-id	subject
a	from	newsgroups	t
an	gmt	nntp-posting-host	that
and	have	of	the
any	i	on	there
are	if	or	this
as	in	organization	to
be	is	path	uuneo
but	it	re	with
can	jan	references	you

Figure 3.9 The Deja News search engine includes its list of stopwords along with other Help information.

TIPS AND TECHNIQUES

So far we've covered search engines and how they work, the importance of choosing unique keywords, and the basic search tools offered by most search engines on the World Wide Web. We'll wrap up this part of the book with some specific tips and techniques that will help you get the most out of the time you spend online—no matter what search engine you decide to use on a regular basis.

We'll start with what we call "The Seven Habits of Highly Effective Web Searchers." Then we'll offer suggestions for customizing your Web browser so that you can access your favorite search tools automatically. We'll conclude with some advice on keyboard short-cuts and other time-savers.

The Seven Habits of Highly Effective Web Searchers

We're not professional searchers, but we've logged a lot of hours over the years searching the Internet and other online systems. We have a pretty good idea of what works and what doesn't. Here are our recommendations for effective Web searching, organized into seven steps, or "habits," that can make you a better searcher.

1. Develop the Internet habit.

When you have a question about anything—and we mean *anything*—your first step in nearly every case should be to check the Net. The answer may lie deep within a company-sponsored Web site, or in a newsgroup posting from two years ago, or among the millions of listings in a white or yellow pages directory, or somewhere else. But with the right search tool and search strategy, chances are you can find it.

2. Use the best tool for the job.

For day-to-day searching, you can't beat the all-purpose search engines listed nearby. Each has its strong points that you should take into consideration when choosing the one you'll use for a particular job.

But good as these search engines are, they're not the best tool for every job. You may sometimes need a *special-purpose* search engine—like Liszt (www.liszt.com) for finding Internet mailing lists or the Argus Clearinghouse (www.clearinghouse.net) for locating subject guides to the Net.

The Seven Habits at a Glance

1. Develop the Internet habit.
2. Use the best tool for the job.
3. Choose unique keywords.
4. Remember to check newsgroups.
5. Use multiple search engines.
6. Consider the source.
7. Know when to look elsewhere.

Leading Search Engines and What They Do Best

- **AltaVista** is fast, powerful, and comprehensive—great for finding obscure facts and phrases. It offers the best field-search capabilities.

- **Excite** has an excellent searchable database of site reviews. It's also particularly strong on locating current news articles and travel information.

- **HotBot** makes it exceptionally easy to search for multimedia files and to locate Web sites by geography.

- **Infoseek** handles Plain-English queries particularly well. Its topic directory is also quite good. And you can zero in on a search problem by doing a second search of just the results returned by your original query.

- **Lycos** offers some of the best Web site reviews and a good multimedia search feature.

- **Yahoo!** has the best, most detailed Web directory, making it an excellent choice for exploring a subject to find out what's available on the Net.

Figure 4.1 C|Net's Search.com site is a great place to look for special-purpose search engines. You can click on a topic or use the Find a Search feature.

Figure 4.2 A few words of a poem enclosed in double quotes is often all it takes to locate the complete work, as shown here.

Part 3 of this book will introduce you to 30 of our favorite special-purpose search engines, including these two. To locate others using a searchable directory, visit C|Net's Search.com site at **www.search.com** (**Figure 4.1**).

✔ Tip

One type of search engine we *don't* recommend is the so-called *meta-search engine* that lets you query several search engines simultaneously. It may sound good in theory. But you're sure to get a lot of duplicate hits, and you won't be able to take advantage of the advanced query features offered by each engine.

3. Choose unique keywords.

Before launching a search, take the time to think about what unique words or phrases are likely to appear on the pages you want to find. To locate sites devoted to impressionist painters, for example, try **Monet AND Renoir AND Degas**. That's sure to produce better results than a search for **impressionists** or **painters**.

What about the complete text of a famous quotation, literary work, or even a joke you heard at the office? Try a phrase search on some small portion that you remember: **"tiger tiger burning bright"** to locate the William Blake poem (**Figure 4.2**). Or **"man walks into a bar"** for that joke you'd like to add to your repertoire.

4. Remember to check newsgroups.

Usenet newsgroups (or *newsgroups* for short) are freewheeling "global conversations" on virtually every subject imaginable. They've been around far longer than the World Wide Web and are an excellent source of advice, personal opinions, and commentary. Think of them as expanding your circle of acquaintances. If you're looking for recipes, travel bargains, software fixes or workarounds—newsgroups may have the answer.

As you'll learn in Part 2, most search engines give you the option of searching newsgroups instead of the Web (**Figure 4.3**). But to take full advantage of newsgroups, be sure to try Deja News (**Figure 4.4**), a search engine specifically designed for newsgroups and covered in more detail in Chapter 11. You'll find Deja News on the Web at **www.dejanews.com**.

5. Use multiple search engines.

Every search engine has its own way of doing things, and none can truthfully claim to cover *everything*. So when thoroughness counts, you should plan on using several search engines.

6. Consider the source.

Just because it's on the Net doesn't mean the information is either accurate or true. Remember, anyone can "publish" anything on the Internet and the World Wide Web. So be skeptical at all times. If the information is on a Web site, try to determine the following: What person or organization created the information? What's the motivation behind it? When was the material last updated?

The same goes for newsgroup postings, where unscrupulous marketers sometimes plant positive comments about their own products and negative ones about their competitors'—making it appear as though the comments were made by actual users of the products.

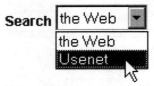

Figure 4.3 Usenet is short for Usenet newsgroups, which many search engines allow you to search instead of the Web.

Figure 4.4 Deja News is the ideal tool for searching newsgroups.

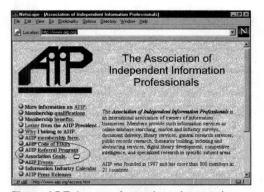

Figure 4.5 To hire a professional searcher, visit the AIIP Web site and look for information about their member Referral Program.

7. Know when to look elsewhere.

Don't assume that the Internet contains the sum total of human knowledge. The Net will always surprise you, both with the information that it does contain and with its lack of information on some specific topic.

Part of being a good online searcher is knowing when to stop. The information you want may or may not be available online. And if it is online, it may be buried so deep that it's not worth the time and trouble to locate it.

Your efforts may be better spent getting the information, fact, figure, or whatever you need using conventional printed reference works: almanacs, dictionaries, encyclopedias, and so forth. Start with the reference section at your local library, or ask the reference librarian for help.

✔ Tips

- If you don't mind paying for research services, you might try Answers.com (**www.answers.com**), an innovative online company that strives to provide 24-hour turnaround for its "Ask a Question, Get an Answer" service. Prices range from $2 to $20 depending on the level of difficulty. Custom quotes are provided for more complex searches.

- For really tough search assignments, your best bet may be to hire a professional searcher or *information broker*. The nonprofit Association of Independent Information Professionals (**Figure 4.5**) is a good place to start. Look for information about their Referral Program on the Web at **www.aiip.org**.

- To learn more about becoming a professional searcher, check your local library or bookstore for *The Information Broker's Handbook*, Third Edition by Sue Rugge and Alfred Glossbrenner (McGraw-Hill, 1997).

Customizing Your Web Browser

When we go online, it's usually to search for something. So we like to have our favorite search tools handy at all times. We've customized our Web browser software so that the search engine we use most often comes up automatically when we sign on. And we can get to it at any time by clicking on our browser's Home button (**Figure 4.6**) or the Home menu option (**Figure 4.7**). Our other favorite tools are easily available from the Bookmarks (or Favorites) list.

If you'd like to customize your Web browser for searching, here are the steps to follow.

To make your favorite search engine appear automatically:

- With Netscape Navigator 3.0, click on Options, then General Preferences, and then Appearance. In the Startup box, enter the complete Web address (including http://) of your favorite search engine. (See the nearby list for suggestions.) Also make sure that the Netscape Browser and Home Page Location boxes are selected.

- With Netscape Navigator 4.0 (a.k.a. Communicator), the process is even easier. Start by going to your favorite search engine site. Then click on Edit, then Preferences, and then Navigator. From the list of Navigator home-page choices, choose the option labeled "Home page" and then click on Use Current Page.

- With Microsoft's Internet Explorer, start by going to your favorite search engine. Then go to the View menu, click on Options, and then on the Navigation tab. Choose Start Page from the Page menu and finish by clicking on Use Current.

Figure 4.6 Once you've customized your Web browser with your preferred Home or Startup location, clicking on the Home button will take you there instantly.

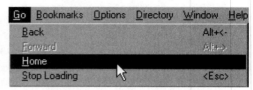

Figure 4.7 You can also get to your Home or Startup location using your browser's Home menu option.

Complete Web Addresses for Leading Search Engines

AltaVista	http://www.altavista.digital.com
Excite	http://www.excite.com
HotBot	http://www.hotbot.com
Infoseek	http://www.infoseek.com
Lycos	http://www.lycos.com
Yahoo!	http://www.yahoo.com

✔ Tips

■ Once you've set your browser's home page or startup location as described here, that's the site that will greet you whenever you sign on. It's also the one you'll be taken to when you click on the Home button or select the menu option that tells the browser you want to "Go Home."

■ Internet Explorer also gives you the option of customizing the Search button that appears in the toolbar. You might use it for quick access to your *second favorite* search site. Start by going to the site you want to be able to access with the Search button. Then go to the View menu, click on Options, and then on the Navigation tab. Choose Search Page from the Page menu and then click on Use Current.

To add other search engines to your Bookmarks or Favorites lists:

■ With Netscape Navigator (Versions 3.0 and 4.0), go to the search engine site and choose Add Bookmark from the Bookmarks menu.

■ With Microsoft's Internet Explorer, go to the search engine site and choose Add to Favorites from the Favorites menu.

CUSTOMIZING YOUR WEB BROWSER

Keyboard Shortcuts and Other Time Savers

Here are several tried and true techniques for making your online sessions easier and more productive.

Keyboard Shortcuts

Searching for menu commands can be a nuisance with any application, Web browsers included. We find that it's often faster and easier to perform common tasks with a couple of keystrokes. These keyboard shortcuts for Windows and Macintosh systems work with both Netscape Navigator and Microsoft's Internet Explorer.

Table 4.1

Keyboard Shortcuts		
TASK	WINDOWS SYSTEM	MACINTOSH SYSTEM
Go to the next Web page	Alt-Left Arrow	Command-Alt-Left Arrow
Go to the previous Web page	Alt-Right Arrow	Command-Alt-Right Arrow
Organize Bookmarks or Favorites	Ctrl-B	Command-B
Add current Web page to Bookmarks or Favorites	Ctrl-D	Command-D
Find text on a Web page	Ctrl-F	Command-F
Open History folder	Ctrl-H	Command-H
Open new Web page	Ctrl-L	Command-L
Open new Browser window	Ctrl-N	Command-N

Figure 4.8 With Netscape Navigator, you don't have to type **http://www.infoseek.com** in the Go To box to get to Infoseek. Just typing **infoseek** is enough.

Figure 4.9 Locating text on a Web page is a snap (or a click!) with Edit, Find.

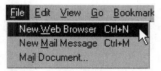

Figure 4.10 You can open a second Web browser window from the Netscape Navigator File menu shown here. Internet Explorer works much the same way.

Making Short Work of Web Addresses

We've mentioned this shortcut before but it bears repeating here: With the latest versions of Netscape Navigator and Microsoft's Internet Explorer, you don't have to type http:// in your browser's Go To or Address box to get to a Web site.

And with Netscape Navigator, you can even leave out www and com to get to your favorite search engine—or any site that begins and ends with those letters (**Figure 4.8**).

Searching Web pages with Edit, Find

Search engines often return pages that are loaded with text, and it's not immediately clear that the information you want is there. To avoid the time and trouble of scrolling and reading through page after page, let your Web browser do the work for you.

Just click on Edit and then Find (**Figure 4.9**). Or use the keyboard shortcut Ctrl-F (Command-F on the Mac). Then enter one of your keywords and hit Enter to search.

Opening a Second Web Browser

Sometimes the Web is painfully slow and a complicated search can seem to take forever to finish. When that happens, consider opening a second browser window so that you can go about your business and check back in a couple of minutes.

With Netscape Navigator, click on File and then New Web Browser (**Figure 4.10**). With Internet Explorer, the command sequence is File and then New Window.

Alternatively, you can use the keyboard shortcut Ctrl-N (Command-N on the Mac) with either browser.

KEYBOARD SHORTCUTS & OTHER TIME SAVERS

PART 2

USING THE LEADING SEARCH ENGINES

Chapter 5:	AltaVista	35
Chapter 6:	Excite	57
Chapter 7:	HotBot	77
Chapter 8:	Infoseek	91
Chapter 9:	Lycos	113
Chapter 10:	Yahoo!	129

Using the Leading Search Engines

Once you have a basic understanding of search engines and searching (either through direct experience or by reading Part 1), you'll be ready for the chapters in this part of the book on six of the very best search engines:

Chapter 5	**AltaVista**
Chapter 6	**Excite**
Chapter 7	**HotBot**
Chapter 8	**Infoseek**
Chapter 9	**Lycos**
Chapter 10	**Yahoo!**

As you can see, the search engines are presented in alphabetical order. Feel free to skip around, perhaps starting with a search engine you've used before or heard the most about.

And remember, it's not necessary to master all six of these search engines. Use the information presented here to learn about the strengths and weaknesses of each one. Work through the step-by-step examples, and try some sample searches of your own with the book opened to the appropriate Quick Reference guide.

Once you've identified the search engine you like best, consider making it the default starting location for your Web browser, as suggested in Chapter 4. Add the others to your browser's Bookmarks or Favorites list so that you can get to them quickly when you need to consult a second (or third) search engine.

ALTAVISTA

www.altavista.digital.com

What you can search

- World Wide Web
- Usenet newsgroups

Contact information

AltaVista Search
Digital Equipment Corporation
Maynard, MA
800/344-4825
508/493-5111
www.altavista.digital.com

AltaVista is generally considered to be one of the most powerful and comprehensive search engines available. You'll be amazed at how fast you can search both the Web and Usenet newsgroups using AltaVista's Simple or Advanced Search.

You'll probably use Simple Search most of the time, especially if you're good at coming up with a unique word or phrase that's likely to appear in your target document. You can even zero in on a particular part of a Web page or newsgroup posting using one of AltaVista's field-search terms.

For more complex queries—and for additional features like date searching and keyword weighting—AltaVista's Advanced Search is the way to go.

When you "search the Web" with AltaVista, what you're actually searching is a database created by the AltaVista spider—known as Scooter. Exploring the Web at a rate of 3 million pages a day, Scooter updates the AltaVista database every 24 hours. Thanks to these daily updates, you're not too likely to encounter pages that have moved or no longer exist, or to miss new pages that have just been added to the Web.

Of course, this power and comprehensiveness come at a price. Unlike other search engines, AltaVista starts you right out on its main

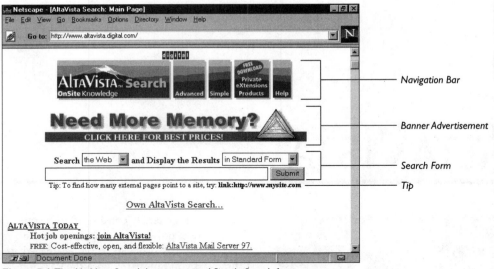

Figure 5.1 The AltaVista Search home page and Simple Search form.

search screen. It makes no attempt to rate sites or organize them into subject categories.

And unless you construct your AltaVista queries carefully, you're likely to be overwhelmed with far too many hits. You'll need to spend some time learning the rules of Simple and Advanced Searches to take full advantage of AltaVista. Once you do, you'll understand why this is the search engine of choice for most professional searchers.

✔ Tip

- Be sure to include the word *digital* in the AltaVista Web address. Otherwise, you'll find yourself at the site of another company, not the official AltaVista Web site.

- As you explore the Web, you may come across sites that offer search capabilities that are "powered by AltaVista." (Watch for a special logo as shown in the adjacent figure.) You can use the AltaVista search skills and strategies you learn about in this chapter whenever you encounter sites that are "powered by AltaVista."

Figure 5.2 Type a word or phrase in the Search text box. Putting words in quotes tells AltaVista to search for a phrase.

Word count: Battle of Trafalgar: about 100
Documents 1-10 of about 100 matching the query, best matches first.

Bass Radio Commercials
Bass Radio Commercials. [Follow Ups] [Post Followup] [Bass Ale Chat] Posted by Simon on May 24, 1996 at 13:48:35: I like the originality of the Bass.
http://www.bassale.com/chat/chats/70.html - size 3K - 12 Sep 96

A Moment In Time: List of Transcripts
This list of transcripts are those programs created and broadcast around the world on A Moment In Time. These and a list of resources used in preparing...
http://www.amomentintime.com/list.html - size 48K - 26 Feb 97

PORTSMOUTH WORLD CENTRE FOR MARITIME HERITAGE
Portsmouth World Centre for Maritime Heritage. HMS Victory. Mary Rose Artefacts. HMS Warrior. Portsmouth's Royal Dockyard - traditional home of the Royal.
http://www.resort-guide.co.uk/portsmouth/marhert.htm - size 5K - 17 May 96

Cranston Art Prints
Back to the Last Square Homepage. Back to the Catalog Index. Below you will find a listing of Cranston art and titles you may call us about at The Last...
http://www.lastsquare.com/cranston.html - size 65K - 1 Dec 95

J. Stanger: The Specter of the Press in Romantic Scenes of Writing
James Stanger jamesst@csnsys.com University of California-Riverside. The Specter of the Press in Romantic Scenes of Writing. Perhaps the most famous...
http://prometheus.cc.emory.edu/panels/4B/J.Stanger.html - size 34K - 4 Jul 96

Dave's Food and Drink Page
Top Cafes, Bars and Restaurants. (Sunday 3rd September 1995). My favourite wine at the LCBO at present is: Chateau la Faggotte (Haut-Medoc) which would...
http://ibm-0.mpa-garching.mpg.de/~sperfrest.html - size 10K - 27 Feb 97

Nelson Exhibition
Nelson Britain's greatest naval hero. February 1996 On the 190th anniversary of the Battle of Trafalgar and the day on which the 'Nelson Decade' was...
http://www.nmm.ac.uk/ww/pr/nelson.html - size 7K - 25 Feb 97

No Title
HERITAGE. No Nuns At The Well? Heritage Matters. Utopia Disaster. Trafalgar Remembered. No Nuns At The Nuns' Well? Freddie Gomez and his growing team of...
http://www.gibnet.gi/~gibmag/heritage.html - size 18K - 28 Feb 97

Heinemann (UK) - Technology Review May 1996
Nelson and his Navy Anglia Multimedia, KS3, £50+VAT; Format: Acorn, PC, Mac; From SCA, PO Box 18, Benfleet, Essex SS7 1AZ (01603) 615151. This visually...
http://www.heinemann.co.uk/heinemann/htoday/tech2000/nelson.html - size 3K - 31 Jul 96

All At Sea Art Corridor
The UK Electric Art Gallery. All At Sea. The Art World's Romantic Affair with the Sea. Cut the text and get straight through to the pictures. Pre 19th...
http://www.ukshops.co.uk:8000/gallery/sea.html - size 6K - 2 Apr 96

p. 1 2 3 4 5 6 7 8 9 10 11 12 13 14 15 16 17 [Next]

Figure 5.3 The first page of results from an AltaVista Web search. Best matches are listed first. For each one, you'll be given the document title, the first few lines of text, and the Web address. Click on the title or Web address to go directly to the site.

Using AltaVista's Simple Search

Most of your AltaVista searches will be done from the AltaVista Search home page (**Figure 5.1**). To get there, point your Web browser at **www.altavista.digital.com**.

Although AltaVista calls this page the Simple Search form, it's actually quite powerful. Once you learn to use the search terms and operators available to you with Simple Search, you'll probably find that you only rarely need to use the search engine's Advanced Search capabilities.

To search the Web:

1. Type a word or phrase in the Search text box (**Figure 5.2**).

2. Click Submit to start the search. Within seconds, AltaVista will display your results, 10 citations to a page, with the best matches listed first (**Figure 5.3**).

3. Scroll through the first couple of pages to see if you found the type of information you were looking for. If not, go back to the Search form, refine your query, and try again.

To search Usenet newsgroups:

1. To look for the same information in Usenet newsgroups, simply click on Usenet in the Search menu (**Figure 5.4**).

2. Click Submit to start the search.

3. AltaVista will present you with a list of newsgroup postings matching your search request (**Figure 5.5**). Scroll through the list and click on the ones that look promising. If necessary, go back to the Search form and revise your query.

✔ Tips

■ AltaVista offers two options for displaying search results: Detailed Form (the default for Web searches) and Compact Form (the default for newsgroup searches). In most cases, your best bet is to stay with the default (Standard Form) settings. To change the way results are displayed, use the drop-down menu (**Figure 5.6**).

■ The banner ads on the AltaVista home page change frequently. If you're like us, you'll quickly learn to mentally tune them out. Don't be surprised to find that an ad you see is directly related to your most recent AltaVista search!

■ Pay attention to the handy tips presented directly under the Search form on the AltaVista home page. They too change frequently. Before long, you'll be an AltaVista expert.

■ For more help with AltaVista Simple Search, click on Help in the Navigation bar (**Figure 5.7**).

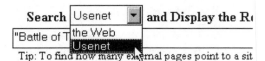

Figure 5.4 Click on Usenet to tell AltaVista that you want to search newsgroups instead of Web pages.

Figure 5.5 The results of a Usenet newsgroup search include the date, newsgroup name, sender's e-mail address, and the message's subject line.

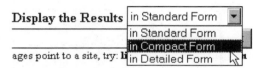

Figure 5.6 You can change the way AltaVista displays results using this menu. The Standard Form (or default) for Web results is Detailed Form. For Usenet newsgroup searches, the default setting is Compact Form.

Figure 5.7 Click on Help in the Navigation bar for all the latest information from AltaVista on how to use Simple Search.

Figure 5.8 The Simple Search Form on the AltaVista home page.

Creating Simple Search Queries

Most of the time, keying in a single word or phrase on the AltaVista Simple Search form (**Figure 5.8**) will not find the precise information you're looking for. You'll have to be creative in constructing your query. And you'll have to know how to use the tools that AltaVista provides.

We'll cover the basics here in step-by-step fashion. For a summary of all the Simple Search terms and rules for using them, see the AltaVista Simple Search Quick Reference.

Table 5.1

AltaVista Simple Search Quick Reference		
FOR THIS TYPE OF SEARCH:	DO THIS:	EXAMPLES:
Phrase	Type the phrase as a sequence of words surrounded by **double quotes**.	"Battle of Trafalgar"
Wildcard	Use an **asterisk** at the end of or within a word with at least three letters of the search term.	Brit* col*r
AND Search (multiple words and phrases, each of which *must* be present)	Use a **plus sign** in front of each word or phrase that must appear in the results.	+London +"art museum"
OR Search (multiple words and phrases, any one of which may be present)	Type words or phrases separated by spaces, without any special notation.	Stratford Shakespeare
NOT Search (to exclude a word or phrase)	Use a **minus sign** in front of word or phrase you want to exclude from results.	+python −monty
Proximity Search	Not available with Simple Search. Use Advanced Search.	
Nested Search	Not available with Simple Search. Use Advanced Search.	
Case-Sensitive Search	Use lowercase to find *any combination* of upper- and lower-case. Use capital letters to force an *exact match* of your search term. Example would match *Bath* but not *bath* or *BATH*.	Bath
Date Search	Not available with Simple Search. Use Advanced Search.	
Field Search	Type field-search keyword in lowercase, followed by a colon and your search word or phrase. (See page 43 for Web page field-search keywords; page 45 for newsgroup keywords.)	title:"Victoria and Albert Museum" host:cambridge.edu domain:com
Weighted Keyword Search	Not available with Simple Search. Use Advanced Search.	

To search for a single word or phrase:

1. Type the word or phrase in the Search text box. Phrases must be surrounded by double quotes: **"Tower of London"** (**Figure 5.9**).

2. Use an asterisk (*) at the end of (or within) a word to do a wildcard search. Be sure to use at least three letters of the search term or AltaVista will ignore the request. Using **Brit*** as a search term will find references to *Britain*, *British*, and *Britannia*, among others (**Figure 5.10**).

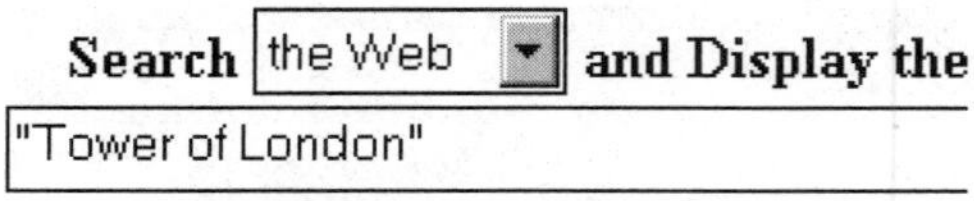

To search for multiple words or phrases:

1. Type them one after the next in the Search box, with a space between them. For example, to look for sites with references to either the *Battle of Trafalgar* or *Nelson*, use the search: **"Battle of Trafalgar" Nelson** (**Figure 5.11**).

2. To specify that a particular word or phrase must be present in every document retrieved by the search, put a plus sign (+) in front of it: **+London +"art museum"** (**Figure 5.12**).

3. Use a minus sign (−) in front of any word or phrase you want to *exclude* from the search results. To find London museums other than the Victoria and Albert, use the search: **+London +museum −"Victoria and Albert"** (**Figure 5.13**).

Search `the Web ▼` and Display the
`"Tower of London"`

Figure 5.9 To tell AltaVista to search for a phrase, enclose it in double quotes.

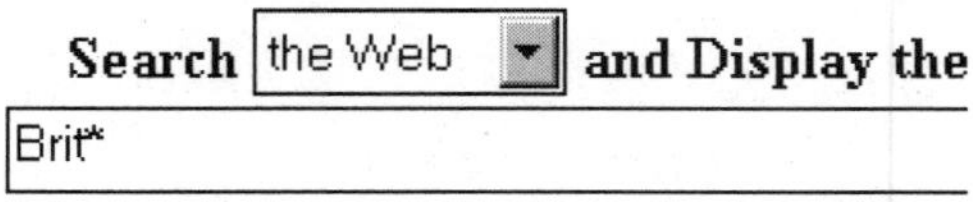

Search `the Web ▼` and Display the
`Brit*`

Figure 5.10 To do a wildcard search, use an asterisk at the end of or within a word.

Search `the Web ▼` and Display the
`"Battle of Trafalgar" Nelson`

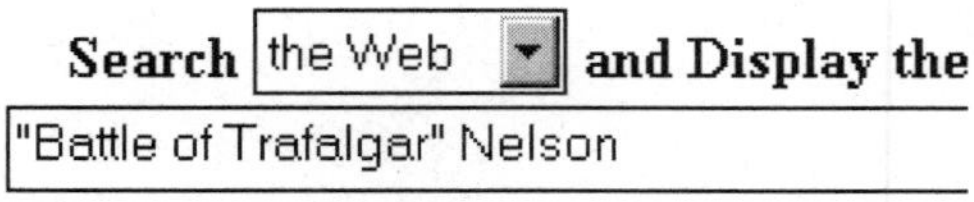

Figure 5.11 To find sites with references to either term but not necessarily both, type two words or phrases separated by a space.

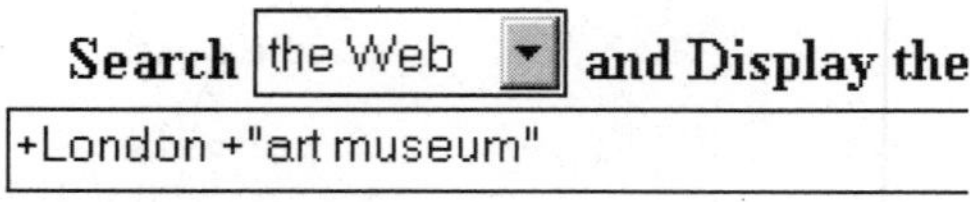

Search `the Web ▼` and Display the
`+London +"art museum"`

Figure 5.12 To find sites with references to both terms, use the plus (+) sign. This search would find sites that include the terms *London* and *art museum*.

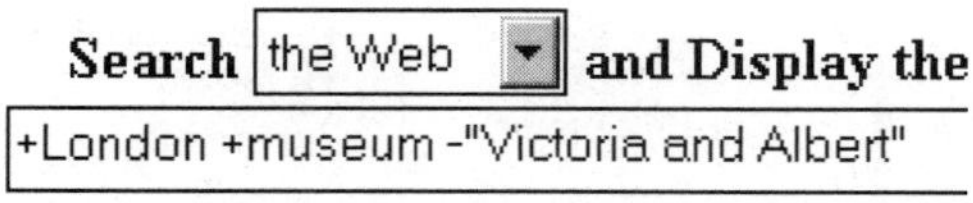

Search `the Web ▼` and Display the
`+London +museum -"Victoria and Albert"`

Figure 5.13 To search for information on London museums other than the Victoria and Albert, put a minus (−) sign in front of the phrase *"Victoria and Albert"*.

To make your search case-sensitive:

1. Use initial caps or all caps as appropriate to search for a proper name or an acronym: **Bath** to search for the town of that name; **BBC** to find sites featuring the British Broadcasting Company.

2. Remember that if you use *any* capital letters in a search request, AltaVista will perform a case-sensitive search. If, on the other hand, you enter your search terms in lowercase, you'll find all references to the term, regardless of case. The search term **bath**, for example, will find references to *bath*, *Bath*, and *BATH*.

✔ Tips

■ When in doubt, enter your AltaVista search terms in lowercase. (If you're a two-finger typist who routinely turns on Caps Lock and pecks away, you'll have problems with your AltaVista searches.)

■ Case-sensitive searching comes in handy when you're looking for a company name that also happens to be a common word or phrase. Searching for **"next inc"** will return thousands of hits. But a case-sensitive search for **"NeXT Inc"** will help you zero in on sites dealing with the company founded by Steve Jobs.

Improving Web search results with field search

One of the biggest problems you're likely to encounter with AltaVista's Simple Search is getting too many hits. It's not uncommon to enter a search request that returns hundreds, if not thousands, of Web pages, many of which have little or nothing to do with the information you're looking for.

When that happens, try adding one of AltaVista's *field-search* terms to your search strategy. Field-search terms allow you to limit your search to specific parts (or *fields*) of Web pages.

You'll find a complete list of Web field-search terms on page 43. The ones you are likely to find most useful are title:, host:, and domain:.

To limit your Web search to the titles of Web pages:

Add a title: field search to your query. Let's say your initial search for "John Lennon" results in too many hits. Try restricting your search to Web pages that include his name in the title: title:"John Lennon" (**Figure 5.14**).

To limit your Web search by company or organization:

Use a host: field search like host:beatlefest.com to find all the Web pages "hosted by" a particular company, educational institution, government agency, and so forth. To exclude all such pages, put a minus sign (–) in front of the field-search term, as we've done in **Figure 5.15**.

To limit your Web search by Internet domain:

Include a domain: field search in your search request (**Figure 5.16**). **Table 5.2** shows how to search for the most common Internet domains.

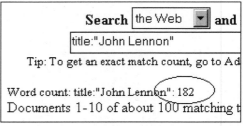

Figure 5.14 By limiting the John Lennon search to sites with his name in the title, AltaVista returned just 182 sites, a very manageable number.

Figure 5.15 A search like this would find Beatles sites other than those associated with the Beatlefest company, whose host name is **beatlefest.com**.

Figure 5.16 To look for Beatles information at college and university Web sites (the *edu* domain), you might try a search like this.

Table 5.2

Common Internet Domains	
DOMAIN TYPE	FIELD-SEARCH TERM
Commercial	domain:com
Educational	domain:edu
Government	domain:gov
Military	domain:mil
Network	domain:net
Non-Profit	domain:org

```
Naoto's Page (Beatles and Macintosh)
    English and Japanese available. Under Construction. English only. - Update Information -
    Red Capitals - Beatles page updates Blue Capitals - Macintosh...
    http://naoto.vampire.co.uk/ - size 1K - 10 Jan 97

The Beatles Companies
    The Beatles Companies. NORTHERN SONGS. Formed in February 1963 with directors
    Brian Epstein and Dick James. Initial share capital of £ 100 in £ 1 shares...
    http://www.rockmine.music.co.uk/Beatles/BeatleCo.html - size 18K - 4 Oct 96

London Beatles Fan Club, latest news, mailorder, walking tours.
    London Beatles Fanclub Hope Page, Club info, OFF THE BEATLE TRACK magazine,Fab
    Four news, London Beatles Walks,Clubs List> http://www.lbfc.demon.co.uk/ - size 3K - 30
    Dec 96

Rockmine Archives: Beatles Memorabilia: Re-direction Notice.
    Europe's finest selection of rock related memorabilia. PLEASE NOTE This Page Has Moved
    To A New Directory. PLEASE ENSURE YOU BOOKMARK THIS NEW
    LOCATION...
    http://www.rockmine.music.co.uk/MemB.html - size 618 bytes - 8 Aug 96

The Beatles Charicatures
    The Beatles Charicatures by Jimmy Hall Thomson.
    http://www.rockmine.music.co.uk/Char.html - size 902 bytes - 17 Jul 96

Bootleg Beatles Homepage
    The Bootleg Beatles Homepages , the best Beatles cover band in the world
    http://www.lipa.ac.uk/~people/students/lpah/aul/bb.htm - size 8K - 14 Jan 97

Beatles fan clubs & magazines worldwide currently functioning
    Welcome! *** LBFC *** Off The Beatle Track *** What Goes On *** Beatles Walks
    *** Good Humour Records *** Links *** Selected articles. BEATLES FAN CLUBS...
    http://www.lbfc.demon.co.uk/list5.htm - size 22K - 3 Jan 97

London Beatles Walking Tours, Sightseeing, Attractions, Fan club
    Welcome! *** LBFC *** Off The Beatle Track. *** What Goes On *** Good Humour
    Records *** Fan clubs list *** Links *** Selected articles. Beatles Walks. THE.
    http://www.lbfc.demon.co.uk/walks.htm - size 4K - 19 Nov 96

A Beatles Who's Who
    A Beatles Who's Who.
    ----------------------------------------------------------
    This is a guide width for the...
    http://www.rockmine.music.co.uk/BeWhoE.html - size 4K - 17 Jul 96

Beatles
    nbsp;Home. Search. Order. Image. Converter. Email. BEATLES. All prices are in UK
    Pounds. BADFINGER BABY BLUE 7" P/S...
    http://www.rockofa.demon.co.uk/stock/beatles.html - size 24K - 16 Jan 97

        p. 1 2 3 4 5 6 7 8 9 10 11 12 13 14 15 16 17 18 19 20 [Next]
```

Figure 5.17 The addresses of all the Web sites in this list end in *uk*. That's because we specified **+domain:uk +Beatles** in our search request to limit our search to Beatles sites based in the United Kingdom.

To find Web sites that originate in a particular country:

Do a domain search for the country's two-letter country code. Adding **+domain:uk** to a Beatles search would limit the search to sites based in the United Kingdom (**Figure 5.17**).

✔ Tips

■ A domain search is also useful when you want to eliminate foreign-language sites from your search results. If you can't read French and want to refine your search to avoid French-language pages, for example, add this to your query (note the use of the minus sign): **–domain:fr**.

■ See Appendix B for a complete list of Internet domains and country codes.

Table 5.3

AltaVista Web Page Field Search Quick Reference		
FIELD	**DESCRIPTION**	**EXAMPLES**
title:	Limits search to the part of the Web page that the author labeled as the title.	title:"John Lennon"
host:	Searches just the *host name* portion of Web addresses.	host:beatlefest.com host:oxford.edu host:BBC
domain:	Searches Web addresses for a specific domain (com, edu, gov, net, org, etc.) or two-letter Internet country code. (See Appendix B for complete list.)	domain:edu domain:uk
applet:	Searches for names or addresses of Java applets (small programs embedded in a Web page). If you don't know the name of the applet, try combining an applet wildcard search with some other search term.	applet:beatles applet:*
image:	Searches Web pages for the filenames of images matching your search term.	image:ringo.gif image:*.gif
link:	Searches for hypertext links (URL) embedded in a Web page.	link:beatles.com
object:	Searches Web for ActiveX objects.	object:crescendo object:*
text:	Searches for text in the body of the Web page.	text:"Strawberry Fields"
url:	Searches for text in complete Web addresses (URLs).	url:beatles.html

Searching Usenet newsgroups for information in specific fields

ALTAVISTA: SEARCHING USENET BY FIELDS

All Usenet newsgroup messages include information on who posted the message, along with a subject line that, if you're lucky, will give you some idea of the contents of the message. AltaVista makes it possible for you to search these and other parts of newsgroup messages by providing you with several field-search terms specially designed for newsgroup searches.

To search for messages posted to a specific newsgroup:

1. Using the AltaVista Simple Search form with Search set to Usenet, type **newsgroups:** (plural) followed by the name of the newsgroup you want to search (**Figure 5.18**).

2. For a broader search of all the newsgroups in a particular category, do a wildcard search. In **Figure 5.19**, we looked for newsgroups in the *soc* category having something to do with Europe. The first few entries in the resulting list are shown in **Figure 5.20**.

✔ Tips

■ The most popular newsgroup categories include those shown in **Table 5.4**.

■ Don't be surprised if the list of newsgroups resulting from your **newsgroups:** search doesn't match your query. If a message was posted to multiple groups, AltaVista lists only one of them in the search results. When you click on the item, you'll see the names of all the groups to which it was posted.

Figure 5.18 If you've had good experience with a particular newsgroup and want to limit your search to just that group, do a **newsgroups:** field search like this one.

Figure 5.19 A wildcard search like the one shown here would find references to Europe in all the *soc* (social/cultural) newsgroups.

```
24.Mar  rec.travel.europe     regrep@iinet.net  L B Travel companion, Europe
29.Mar  rec.travel.europe     dapark@NMSU.Edu   L B Re: Travel companion, Eu
06.Apr  alt.sports.soccer.eur neorama@southern  L B Europe [R/T] pt2
06.Apr  alt.sports.soccer.eur neorama@southern  L B Europe [R/T]
14.Apr  alt.sports.soccer.eur neorama@southern  L B Re: Europe [R/T]
14.Apr  soc.genealogy.medieva sbald@auburn.cam  L B Re: Oldest Lineage In Eu
14.Apr  soc.genealogy.medieva taf2@po.cwru.edu  L B Re: Oldest Lineage In Eu
14.Apr  soc.genealogy.medieva rtung@merle.acns  L B Re: Oldest Lineage In Eu
14.Apr  soc.genealogy.medieva spencer@worldnet  L B Re: Oldest Lineage In Eu
15.Apr  soc.genealogy.medieva rtung@merle.acns  L B Re: Oldest Lineage In Eu
15.Apr  soc.genealogy.medieva P.Metcalfe@stude  L B Re: Oldest Lineage In Eu
15.Apr  soc.genealogy.medieva jaskew@yoyo.cc.m  L B Re: Oldest Lineage In Eu
15.Apr  soc.genealogy.medieva jaskew@yoyo.cc.m  L B Re: Oldest Lineage In Eu
15.Apr  soc.genealogy.medieva jaskew@yoyo.cc.m  L B Re: Oldest Lineage In Eu
```

Figure 5.20 The first few listings from the wildcard search shown in **Figure 5.19**. The first four items were probably posted to multiple groups, which is why the newsgroups column shows something other than *soc*.

Table 5.4

Popular Newsgroup Categories	
alt	Alternative newsgroups—everything from sexy stuff to the truly offbeat
biz	Business-related newsgroups, which welcome advertising and marketing messages
comp	Computer-related newsgroups
misc	Grab-bag category, including the popular **misc.jobs** and **misc.forsale**
news	Groups concerned with the Usenet network (not current affairs)
rec	Recreation and hobbies
sci	Science-related newsgroups
soc	Groups devoted to social issues, often related to a particular culture

Search `Usenet` ▼ **and Display the Re**

`from:jgparks@oxford.edu`

Figure 5.21 Here's how to search Usenet newsgroups for all the messages posted by a particular individual.

Search `Usenet` ▼ **and Display the Re**

`+from:royalfamily.com +"future of the monarchy"`

Figure 5.22 If you know the Internet domain name of a particular company or organization, you can use a search like this one to find postings by anyone whose e-mail address includes that domain name.

Search `Usenet` ▼ **and Display the Re**

`+subject:"bed and breakfast" +Yorkshire`

Figure 5.23 Newsgroup etiquette dictates that the subject line for all postings be clear and informative. Unfortunately, that's not always the case. But a **subject:** search like this one is at least worth a try.

To search the from field:

1. For messages posted by a particular individual, use **from:** followed by the person's e-mail address (**Figure 5.21**). If you don't know the exact e-mail address, you might get by with just the person's last name (or e-mail nickname), but only if it's fairly unusual.

2. For postings by anyone at a particular company, use **from:** followed by the company's domain name (**Figure 5.22**).

To search the subject field:

1. Type **subject:** followed by the word you'd expect to find in the subject line (**Figure 5.23**).

2. If you're searching for a phrase, be sure to follow the AltaVista convention of enclosing the words in double quotes.

✔ Tip

■ AltaVista provides two additional newsgroup field-search terms: **summary:** and **keywords:**. Unfortunately, most people don't take the time (or aren't given the option) to supply summary and keyword information for their postings, so these fields are usually empty.

Table 5.5

AltaVista Usenet Newsgroup Field Search Quick Reference		
FIELD	DESCRIPTION	EXAMPLES
newsgroups:	Allows you to limit your search to specific newsgroups or newsgroup categories (alt, comp, rec, news, etc.)	newsgroups:rec.music.beatles newsgroups:rec.*
from:	Searches the newsgroup message *from* field containing the sender's e-mail address and possibly also the sender's real name, nickname, and/or company name.	from:"Prince Charles" from:royalfamily.com
subject:	Searches the subject field of newsgroup messages for the text you specify.	subject:"Beatles Poster" subject:"for sale"
summary:	Searches the summary field. Of limited value, because most people don't bother to provide summary information for their postings.	summary:"Paul McCartney"
keywords:	Searches for keywords (if any) provided by the person who posted the message.	keywords:musician

Using AltaVista's Advanced Search

AltaVista's Advanced Search uses the same rules as Simple Search for defining words and phrases, wildcards, capitalization, and field searches. But the rules for *combining* words and phrases into search queries are different. Instead of plus (+) and minus (−) signs, you'll use the traditional Boolean operators AND, OR, and AND NOT.

Figure 5.24 Clicking on Advanced in the AltaVista Navigation bar will take you to the Advanced Search page.

Navigation Bar

Banner Ad

Search Form

Keyword Weighting

Date Search

Figure 5.25 AltaVista's Advanced Search page.

Advanced Search also offers several very useful features not available with Simple Search:

■ **Proximity Search.** You can use **NEAR** to find terms that appear within ten words of each other: **"Princess of Wales" NEAR Charles**.

■ **Nested Search.** You can group search words and phrases in parentheses in order to form more complex queries: **(Oxford OR Cambridge) NEAR University**.

■ **Date Search.** You can specify a date or range of dates to limit your search to a particular time period.

■ **Keyword Weighting.** You can specify that certain keywords be considered more important than others so that documents containing those words will be listed first in the search results.

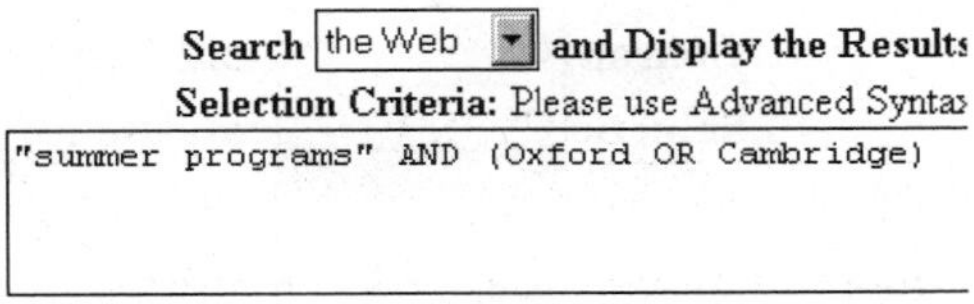

Search [the Web ▾] and Display the Results
Selection Criteria: Please use Advanced Syntax

```
"summer programs" AND (Oxford OR Cambridge)
```

Figure 5.26 Here's a sample Advanced Search query. We've used AND and OR as well as parentheses to combine words and phrases.

Results Ranking Criteria: Documents containing th

```
Oxford
```

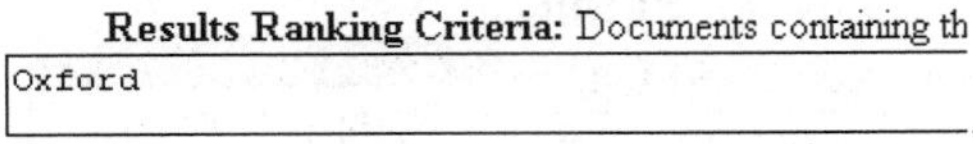

Figure 5.27 One of Advanced Search's special features is *keyword weighting*. Web pages or newsgroup postings containing the word or phrase you type in the Results Ranking Criteria box will be listed first in your search results.

Start date: [01/Jan/97] End date: [ ] e.g.
[Submit Advanced Query]

Figure 5.28 Advanced Search also gives you the opportunity to search based on the date a Web page was last updated, or a newsgroup message was posted. You can specify a single date or a range of dates.

Searching the Web and Newsgroups with Advanced Search

To get to AltaVista's Advanced Search page, point your Web browser at www.altavista.digital.com. That will take you to the AltaVista home page. From there, click on Advanced in the Navigation bar (**Figure 5.24**) and you'll find yourself at the Advanced Search page (**Figure 5.25**).

To search the Web using Advanced Search:

1. Type your search request in the area provided on the Search Form (**Figure 5.26**). Use AND, OR, and NEAR to combine words and phrases. To exclude a word, be sure to use AND NOT: Oxford AND NOT shoes. You can also use parentheses in your query to group words and phrases.

2. If there's any particular word or phrase that should be given greater weight in the presentation of search results, enter it in the Results Ranking Criteria box (**Figure 5.27**). We've requested that Web pages containing references to Oxford be listed first in our search results.

3. To limit your search to documents after a particular date, or within a range of dates, enter that information in the form DD/MMM/YY. Be sure to use a three-letter abbreviation (Jan, Feb, Mar, etc.) for the month (**Figure 5.28**).

4. Click on Submit Advanced Query to enter your search.

5. Review the results and refine your query if necessary.

To search Usenet newsgroups:

1. If you don't find what you're looking for on the Web, try searching Usenet using the same search request. Simply click on Usenet in the Search menu (**Figure 5.29**).

2. Then click Submit Advanced Query to enter your search.

✔ Tips

- Unless you request otherwise, AltaVista presents Web search results in Detailed Form and Usenet newsgroup search results in Compact Form. To change how results are presented (or to choose the special Advanced Search option of displaying just a *count* of the number of documents found), use the drop-down menu (**Figure 5.30**).

- The AltaVista Advanced Search Quick Reference includes a summary of all the Advanced Search features and how to use them.

- For more help with AltaVista Advanced Search, click on Help in the Navigation bar (**Figure 5.31**).

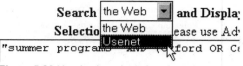

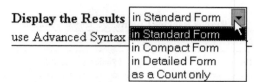

Figure 5.29 Use the drop-down Search menu to switch back and forth between Web and Usenet newsgroup searches.

Figure 5.30 You can change the way your search results are displayed by clicking on one of these options in the Display the Results menu.

Figure 5.31 Click on Help in the Navigation bar of the Advanced Search page to access the search engine's online help.

AltaVista: Advanced Search/Usenet

Table 5.6

AltaVista Advanced Search Quick Reference		
FOR THIS TYPE OF SEARCH:	DO THIS:	EXAMPLES:
Phrase	Type the phrase as a sequence of words surrounded by **double quotes**.	"Tower of London"
Wildcard	Use an **asterisk** at the end of or within a word with at least three letters of the search term.	bicycl*.
AND Search (multiple words and phrases, each of which *must* be present)	Use **AND** between words or phrases to specify that both must be present in the results.	Oxford AND Cambridge
OR Search (multiple words and phrases, any one of which may be present)	Use **OR** between words or phrases to specify that you want to find references to either or both items.	Oxford OR Cambridge
NOT Search (to exclude a word or phrase)	Use **AND NOT** in front of the word or phrase you want to exclude from the query.	Oxford AND NOT Cambridge
Proximity Search	Use **NEAR** to find words or phrases that appear within 10 words of each other. The example would find *bed and breakfast* as well as *bed & breakfast* and *breakfast in bed*.	bed NEAR breakfast
Nested Search	Use **parentheses** to group search expressions into more complex queries. The example would find *Prince of Wales* as well as *Prince and Princess of Wales*.	(Prince OR Princess) NEAR "of Wales"
Case-sensitive Search	Use lowercase to find *any combination* of upper- and lowercase. Use capital letters to force an *exact match* of your search term, as shown in the example.	"Round Table"
Date Search	Type the date or range of dates you want to search in the Start Date and End Date boxes. Use the form DD/MMM/YY.	01/Jul/97
Field Search	Type field-search keyword in lowercase, immediately followed by a colon and your search word or phrase. (See page 43 for Web page field-search keywords; page 45 for newsgroup keywords.)	title:"Castle Howard" host:royalfamily.com domain:edu
Keyword Weighting	In the Results Ranking Criteria box, type the word or phrase that should be given the greatest weight. Web pages or newsgroup postings meeting your criteria will appear at the head of the list.	See page 47 for a sample search.

Refining Simple or Advanced Searches with LiveTopics

LiveTopics is a tool that helps you refine and analyze the results of an AltaVista search. The only way to access the feature is to actually submit a query using Simple or Advanced Search. If your query generates a substantial number of hits (more than 20 or so), you'll be offered the opportunity to use LiveTopics to:

- Select additional words for a query that's too broad or vague.

- Eliminate topics that are too numerous to be useful.

- Explore topics related to your search request.

LiveTopics takes your original search request, analyzes the documents identified by the search, and displays groups of additional words, called *topics*, that you can use in refining your query. Topics are presented in order of relevance, and words within a topic are listed by frequency of occurrence.

Figure 5.32 To get to LiveTopics, you must first key in a Simple or Advanced search request. We're using Simple Search to look for "Mary Queen of Scots".

Figure 5.33 Our search found about 1,000 documents, so we're offered the opportunity to use LiveTopics to refine it.

To access LiveTopics:

1. Point your Web browser at **www.altavista.digital.com** and enter a query on the Simple Search form (**Figure 5.32**). (Or click on Advanced to use the Advanced Search form.)

2. Click on Submit to enter your search.

3. If your search results in a large number of hits, you'll see a message like the one in **Figure 5.33**.

4. Choose a LiveTopics format based on the capabilities of your Web browser:

   • Way-cool topics map! (for Java-enabled browsers)

   • Tables (for JavaScript-enabled browsers)

   • Text-only (for all browsers)

✔ Tips

■ If you're not sure of your browser's capabilities, start with the first option—for Java-enabled browsers. AltaVista will tell you if your browser can't handle Java. In that case, try JavaScript. If neither of these options works for you, you can always use the Text-only version.

■ All three interfaces produce the same suggested topics and results. The only difference is in how the information is presented, and how you choose words to include and exclude.

Using the LiveTopics Java interface

If your Web browser supports Java, you can use the LiveTopics graphical interface to refine your AltaVista query.

To refine your query using the Java interface:

1. Click on "Way-cool topics map!" to select the Java interface (**Figure 5.34**).

2. Your original search request will be presented along with either a list of topics (Topic Words view) or a topics map (Topic Graph view).

3. Click on Topic Words to display a list of topics related to your search (**Figure 5.35**). The topics that are most likely to be relevant will be at the top of the list. Words within a topic are ordered by frequency of occurrence.

4. In this example, Monty (Topic 16) probably refers to a Monty Python skit, and Golfers (Topic 17) seems totally irrelevant. So we've double-clicked on each word in these topics to eliminate them from the search (**Figure 5.36**).

5. As you add or delete words, your search query will be altered to reflect the changes (**Figure 5.37**).

6. When you're finished, click Submit to enter your new search request. More than likely, you'll come up with a much more manageable number of hits.

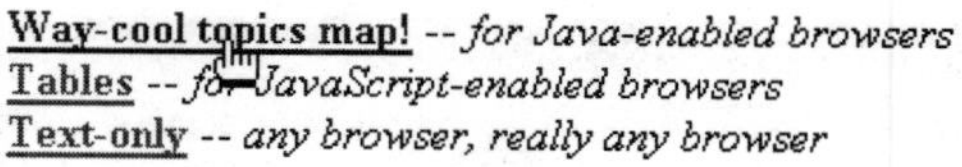

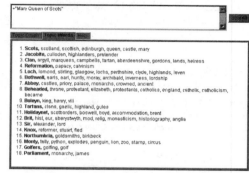

Way-cool topics map! -- *for Java-enabled browsers*
Tables -- *for JavaScript-enabled browsers*
Text-only -- *any browser, really any browser*

Figure 5.34 If your Web browser supports Java, click on "Way-cool topics map!" to get to LiveTopics.

Figure 5.35 Topic Words view provides the most information at-a-glance about topics that might be related to your search.

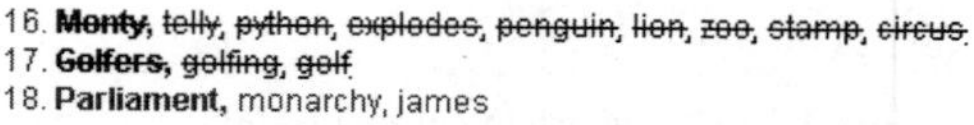

16. **Monty,** ~~telly, python, explodes, penguin, lion, zoo, stamp, circus~~
17. **Golfers,** ~~golfing, golf~~
18. **Parliament,** monarchy, james

Figure 5.36 Double click on any word you want to eliminate from your search. As you do so, a line will be drawn through the word.

Figure 5.37 As you click on words to add or delete from your search, your query will be altered to reflect the changes.

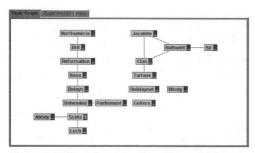

Figure 5.38 The information from **Figure 5.35** in Topic Graph view.

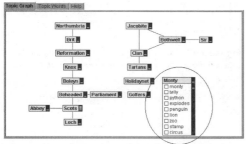

Figure 5.39 In Topic Graph view, you have to click on a topic to display the words associated with it.

Figure 5.40 When you delete a word in Topic Graph view, an X appears in the box next to it.

To see the same information in graphical form:

1. Click on Topic Graph in the upper left corner of Topic Words view to display a graphical representation of topics that might be related to your search (**Figure 5.38**).

2. A line connecting two topics indicates a strong relationship. The absence of a connecting line means that a particular topic almost never occurs in the same context with the other topics on the map.

3. Click on any topic to display the additional words associated with it (**Figure 5.39**). Then click once on any word you want to include, twice to exclude. We excluded all the words under Monty (**Figure 5.40**).

4. As words are added or deleted, your original query will be altered to reflect the changes.

5. Click Submit to enter the new search.

✔ Tips

- In Topic Graph view, the yellow bars to the right of each word indicate the probable relevance of that word to your search.

- To clear the mark from a word so that it's neither required nor prohibited, just continue clicking on it until the marking disappears.

Using the LiveTopics JavaScript and Text interfaces

Java is still somewhat new, and not all Web browsers support Java applications. If you click on "Way-cool topics maps!" and are told your browser can't handle Java, don't despair. You'll find that the JavaScript and Text interfaces work almost as well for refining search queries.

To refine a query using the JavaScript interface:

1. Click on Tables to select the JavaScript interface (**Figure 5.41**).

2. Your original search request will be presented, along with a set of topics presented in table form. **Figure 5.42** shows just the top portion of the table. Topics that are most likely to be relevant are at the head of the list. Words within a topic are ordered by frequency of occurrence.

3. Scroll down the page and click to place a check mark in the exclude column (marked with an X) for all the words under *Monty* and *Golfers* (**Figure 5.43**).

4. As words are added or deleted, the search query will be altered to reflect the changes (**Figure 5.44**).

5. When you're finished, click Submit to enter the new search request. Or click Reset to return to the original query and start over.

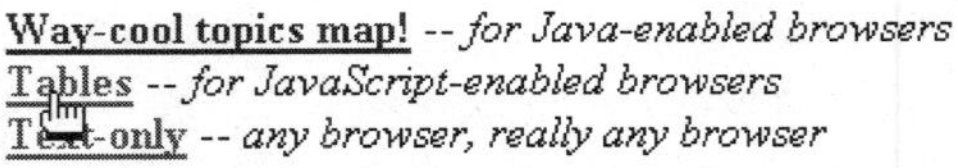

Way-cool topics map! -- *for Java-enabled browsers*
Tables -- *for JavaScript-enabled browsers*
Text-only -- *any browser, really any browser*

Figure 5.41 Click on Tables to use the JavaScript interface for LiveTopics.

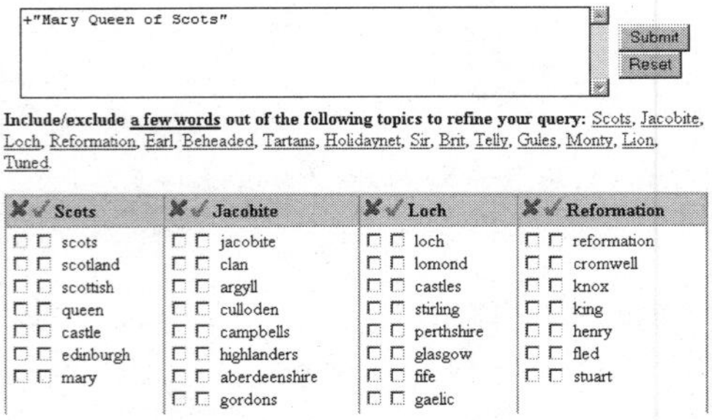

Figure 5.42 The first part of the table showing related topics for our "Mary Queen of Scots" search.

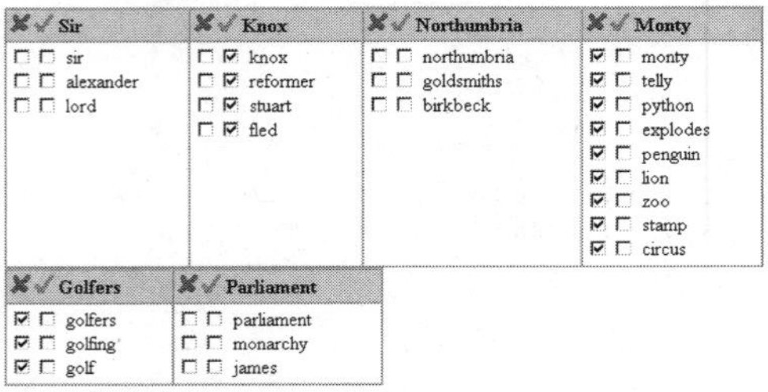

Figure 5.43 We scrolled down to the bottom of the table and clicked once in the exclude column next to each word under *Monty* and *Golfer*.

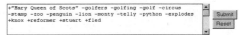

Figure 5.44 Here's what the search looked like once we were finished deleting and adding words.

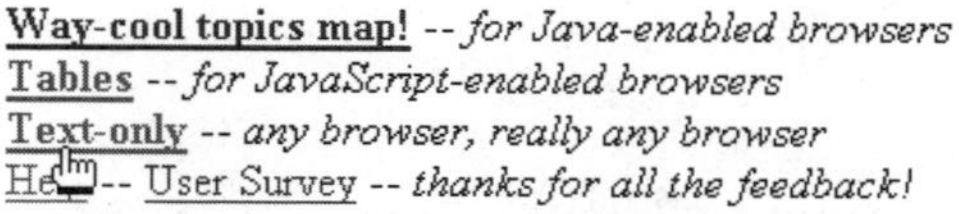

Way-cool topics map! -- *for Java-enabled browsers*
Tables -- *for JavaScript-enabled browsers*
Text-only -- *any browser, really any browser*
Help -- User Survey -- *thanks for all the feedback!*

Figure 5.45 The LiveTopics Text-only interface works with virtually any browser. But try the other two options first, since they do a much better job of displaying information.

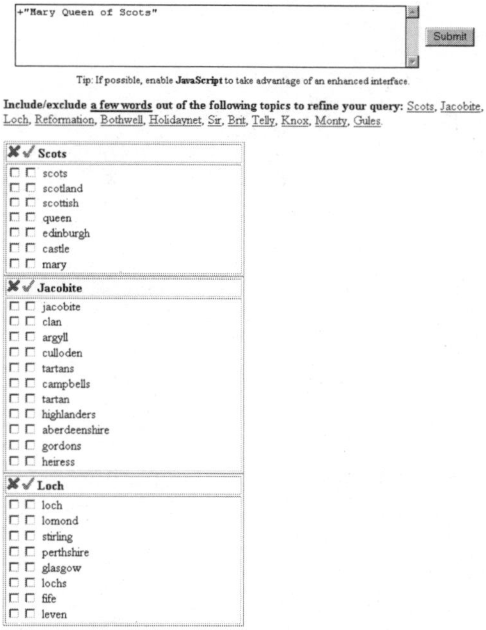

Figure 5.46 The first part of the LiveTopics Text-only display. Topics and words related to your search are presented in a single column. You may have to scroll down through many pages to reach the bottom of the list.

To refine a query using the Text interface:

1. Click on Text-only (**Figure 5.45**).

2. Your original search request will be displayed, with all the related topics and topic words in one long list (**Figure 5.46**).

3. Scroll down the page and click to put check marks in the appropriate column: exclude (X) or include (check mark).

4. Click on Submit when you're finished.

✔ Tips

■ With the Text interface, the Search text box does not get updated as you select words for inclusion or exclusion.

■ LiveTopics works best when the initial search returns 200 or more hits. When working with a smaller number of documents, the software may produce groupings that aren't too useful. Or it may fail to return any topics at all.

■ It's often best to start by excluding words that are clearly not related to your area of interest.

■ To make sure that you stay on track with your original search, resubmit your query after every couple of changes. You can always go back to LiveTopics and add or delete other topics.

EXCITE

www.excite.com

What you can search

- World Wide Web
- Web site reviews
- Usenet newsgroups
- Current news articles from more than 300 publications
- Travel guides for 5,000 cities

Contact information

Excite, Inc.
Mountain View, CA
415/943-1200
415/943-1299 (fax)
www.excite.com

If you're looking for a powerful search engine that's easy to master, along with the ability to quickly zero in on the *best* Web sites, Excite is the one to choose.

Excite's search engine uses a method called *concept-based searching* that allows you to enter your queries in plain English, without worrying about exact keywords and special punctuation. When you get your results and identify a site that's particularly good, you can search for similar sites with a single click on the "More Like This" option.

You can also limit your search to Web sites that have been selected by Excite's editors for inclusion in a special database of some 150,000 sites—about half of which are tagged with Excite ratings and include editors' reviews.

If you prefer to search the Net by topic, you can choose one of Excite's television-like *Channels*, which organize information into broad areas such as Business and Investing, Lifestyle, and Sports.

Two of our favorite Excite Channels are News and Travel. The News Channel, with its NewsTracker feature, allows you to search 300 newspapers and magazines and to set up your own personal clipping service. And the Travel Channel gives you access to a service

EXCITE

called City.Net, a searchable database of travel information for over 5,000 vacation and business travel destinations worldwide.

Excite's database is updated about once every seven to ten days, compared with AltaVista's daily updating. And its concept-based searching may take some getting used to if you're accustomed to doing precise keyword searches. Those considerations aside, Excite is a search tool that's well worth learning and using, especially when you want to focus on "the Best of the Net."

✔ Tips

- Like AltaVista, Excite is being used by a growing number of Web sites to provide visitors with the ability to search product catalogs and other information located at those sites. When you see the message "This site is powered by Excite," you can use what you've learned in this chapter (and especially the information in the Excite Quick Reference) to perform your search.

  For example, Peachpit's own site, (**www.peachpit.com**) uses Excite for its search functions. And America Online's NetFind search service for exploring the Internet is "powered by Excite."

- You can add Excite to your Netscape Navigator or Internet Explorer toolbar with a free software product called Excite Direct. Versions are currently available for Windows 95 and Windows NT. To download the software, click on Excite Direct on the Excite home page or go to **www.excite.com/direct**.

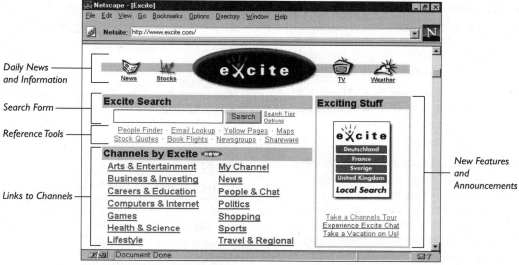

Daily News
and Information

Search Form

Reference Tools

Links to Channels

New Features
and
Announcements

Figure 6.1 The Excite home page.

Figure 6.2 Excite's Daily News and Information links.

Using Excite's main search page

To get to Excite, point your Web browser at **www.excite.com**. That will take you to the search engine's home page and main search form (**Figure 6.1**).

Excite packs a lot of information onto this page, and it can be a bit confusing at first. But once you learn what's here and how to use it, you may well decide to make the Excite home page your first stop whenever you venture onto the Web.

To explore the main features on the Excite home page:

1. Click on one or more of the Daily News and Information links (**Figure 6.2**) for easy access to the day's news headlines, stock quotes, TV listings, and weather—all of which you can customize to your particular interests and geographical location.

2. Type some words or phrases in the search form text box (**Figure 6.3**) and click on Search to submit your query. Don't worry about the syntax for now; we'll cover that later in the chapter.

3. Try Excite's Reference Tools (**Figure 6.4**). They provide links to some of the most popular *specialized* search services on the Web (**Table 6.1**).

4. Click on any one of Excite's 14 *Channels* (**Figure 6.5**) to go to a special page devoted to a single broad subject area. Each one offers a convenient collection of information: the best Web sites, organized by topic; news headlines, links to chat rooms and bulletin boards; and other special features. This is also the place to look for Excite's Web reviews—brief but informative descriptions of some of the best sites, prepared by Excite editors.

✔ Tips

- To complete your tour of the Excite home page, check out Exciting Stuff, where you'll find a regularly updated menu of announcements and special offers from Excite.

- Excite often provides at least two ways to access the same information. For example, clicking on Stocks next to the Excite logo (**Figure 6.2**) takes you to the same place as clicking on Stock Quotes in the Reference Tools (**Figure 6.4**).

- Take the time to visit all 14 Excite Channels to get a handle on the topics covered in each one. To create your own channel, click on My Channel and customize it to reflect your personal preferences.

- To get back to the Excite home page at any time, click on either the Home or Search button (**Figure 6.6**).

Figure 6.3 The Excite Search Form.

Figure 6.4 Excite's Reference Tools take you directly to some of the best specialized search services on the Web.

Table 6.1

Excite's Reference Tool Links

REFERENCE TOOL:	SEARCH SERVICE:
People Finder	WhoWhere?
Email Lookup	WhoWhere?
Yellow Pages	BigBook
Maps	City.Net
Stock Quotes	Quote.com
Book Flights	City.Net
Newsgroups	Deja News
Shareware	Download.com

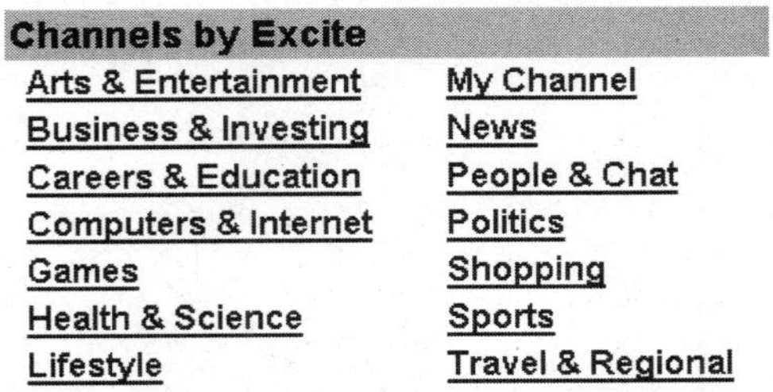

Figure 6.5 For the TV generation, Excite organizes the Web into 14 *Channels* that allow you to search for the best Web sites and other Internet resources by topic.

Figure 6.6 Clicking on Home or Search will always take you back to the Excite home page.

Figure 6.7 We've typed our search in the search form on the Excite home page.

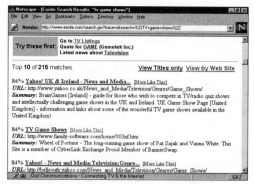

Figure 6.8 A sample of what your Excite search results will look like.

84% <u>TV Game Shows</u> [More Like This]
URL: http://www.family-softw...e.com/home/003nf.htm
Summary: Wheel of Fortune - The long-running game show of Pat Sajak and Vanna White. This Site is a member of CyberLink Exchange Proud Member of BannerSwap.

Figure 6.9 Excite's "More Like This" option helps you find other sites that might be of interest.

Try This Search on:	Current News Articles Selected Web Sites City.Net Travel Guide	Newsgroup Postings Magellan

Figure 6.10 Excite's search results page always includes recommendations for other search options.

Searching the Web with Excite

Excite makes it as easy and painless as possible for you to search the Web. It encourages you to enter your queries in plain English, without worrying about special punctuation and Boolean operators.

What's more, Excite doesn't take your query *literally*, as most search engines do. Instead, it uses a strategy called *concept-based searching*—to find not just what you asked for but also its best guess as to what you *really* want to know.

Believe it or not, it actually works quite well, especially when combined with Excite's "More Like This" feature for refining your initial search.

To search the Web:

1. Type your query in the text box of the Excite search form (**Figure 6.7**). You'll find this form on the Excite home page (www.excite.com) and on all the Excite Channel pages.

2. Click Search to submit your query. Within seconds, Excite will display your results, 10 to a page, with the best matches listed first (**Figure 6.8**). The percentages in front of each title are Excite's estimates of how well the site matches your search criteria.

3. Scroll through the first couple of pages, reading the titles and summary information. If you see a site that looks especially promising, click on the title to go to the site. Or click on "More Like This" (**Figure 6.9**) and Excite will perform a new search to find similar sites.

4. If you're not satisfied with the results of your initial search, rethink your query and try again. Or scroll down the page and try one of Excite's suggestions for other search options (**Figure 6.10**).

✔ Tips

- Excite often begins the list of search results with several sites next to the heading "Try these first." The search engine might also suggest some specific words for you to consider in order to narrow your search. Both features are worth a look, but don't be surprised if the suggestions are sometimes pretty far off the mark.

- To get a quick handle on your search results, click on one of the alternate display options (**Figure 6.11**). View Titles Only presents just the titles for the first 40 citations (**Figure 6.12**). View by Web Site organizes the titles by Web address (**Figure 6.13**)—a neat way to find out if there's a particular site that has lots of pages devoted to the information you're looking for.

View Titles only View by Web Site

Figure 6.11 To change the way your search results are presented, click on one of these options.

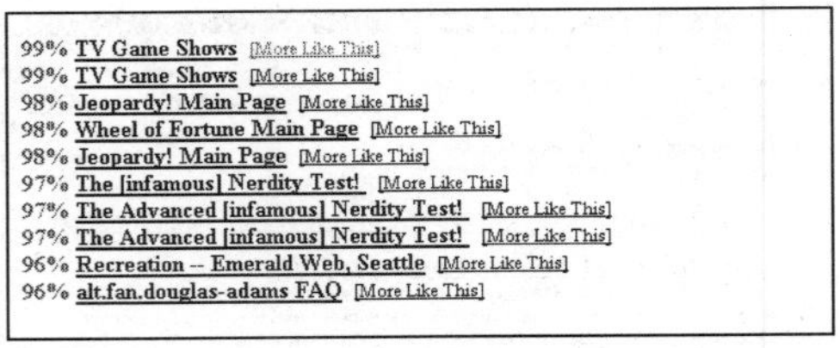

99% **TV Game Shows** [More Like This]
99% **TV Game Shows** [More Like This]
98% **Jeopardy! Main Page** [More Like This]
98% **Wheel of Fortune Main Page** [More Like This]
98% **Jeopardy! Main Page** [More Like This]
97% **The [infamous] Nerdity Test!** [More Like This]
97% **The Advanced [infamous] Nerdity Test!** [More Like This]
97% **The Advanced [infamous] Nerdity Test!** [More Like This]
96% **Recreation -- Emerald Web, Seattle** [More Like This]
96% **alt.fan.douglas-adams FAQ** [More Like This]

Figure 6.12 Excite's View Titles Only option lets you quickly scan your search results for relevant titles.

www.yahoo.co.uk
    84% Yahoo! UK & Ireland - News and Media:Television:Genres:G... [More Like This]
    82% Yahoo! UK & Ireland - Entertainment:Television:Genres:Ga... [More Like This]
www.family-software.com
    84% TV Game Shows [More Like This]
    82% Entertainment [More Like This]
bellsouth.yahoo.com
    84% Yahoo! - News and Media:Television:Genres:Game Shows [More Like This]
www.yahoo.com
    83% Yahoo! - News and Media:Television:Genres:Game Shows [More Like This]
www.labyrinth.net.au
    82% Television page [More Like This]
www.daily.umn.edu
    81% Untitled [More Like This]

Figure 6.13 Select View by Web Site when you want to find out if any one site offers a number of pages relevant to your query.

Creating Excite Queries

Excite is unique among the Web search engines in allowing you to look for *concepts* as well as specific keywords. If you submit a query like **"horse racing"**, Excite looks for that exact phrase, of course. But unless you "turn off" concept-based searching, Excite also broadens the query to include sites dealing with related subjects like jockey training, off-track betting, and veterinarians.

Table 6.2

Excite Quick Reference		
FOR THIS TYPE OF SEARCH:	DO THIS:	EXAMPLES:
Phrase	Type the phrase as a sequence of words surrounded by **double quotes**. Excite will search for that phrase *and* related concepts.	"Kentucky Derby"
Concept or idea	Simply type a phrase or question that expresses the idea or concept. Use as many words as necessary.	thoroughbred racing Kentucky Where can I find information about thoroughbred racing in Kentucky?
AND Search (multiple words and phrases, each of which *must* be present)	Use a **plus sign** in front of each word or phrase that *must* appear in the results.	+racing + "Churchill Downs"
	Alternatively, you can use **AND** (all caps) between the words or phrases. Using AND tells Excite to turn off its concept-based searching.	racing AND "Churchill Downs"
OR Search (multiple words and phrases, any one of which may be present)	Type words or phrases separated by a space, without any special notation. Excite will search for either term *and* for related concepts.	Derby Preakness
	Alternatively, you can use **OR** (all caps) between each word or phrase. (If you use OR, Excite will turn off concept-based searching and return just those sites containing references to at least one of the search terms.)	Derby OR Preakness
NOT Search (to exclude a word or phrase)	Use a **minus sign** in front of a word or phrase you want to exclude from results.	"horse race" –Derby
	Or use AND NOT (all caps) in front of the word or phrase you want to exclude. (Concept-based searching will be turned off.)	"horse race" AND NOT Derby
Nested Search	Use **parentheses** to group search expressions into more complex queries.	racing AND (horse OR thoroughbred)
Query by Example	Click on "More Like This" next to any item on the search results page.	

To search for ideas and concepts:

1. Type your query in the Search text box of any Excite search form, being as specific as possible about what you want to find. To search for a phrase, be sure to enclose it in double quotes: **"Churchill Downs"** (**Figure 6.14**). Otherwise you're likely to find Winston Churchill and the Rams' first downs among your results.

2. Use a plus (+) sign in front of a word or phrase that must appear in the results. Use a minus (-) sign to exclude a word or phrase. To find information on the 1997 Kentucky Derby winner while avoiding merchants of sterling silver jewelry, try a search like this: **+"Silver Charm" –jewelry** (**Figure 6.15**).

✔ Tip

■ If you prefer to express your query as a question, go ahead. The Search text box looks small, but you can actually type 'til your heart's content. We tried the query **What horse races make up the Triple Crown?** and found the answer (**Figure 6.16**) in the second item on the results page.

Figure 6.14 To search for a phrase, be sure to enclose it in double quotes.

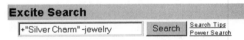

Figure 6.15 Use plus and minus signs to identify words or phrases you want to include (+) or exclude (–).

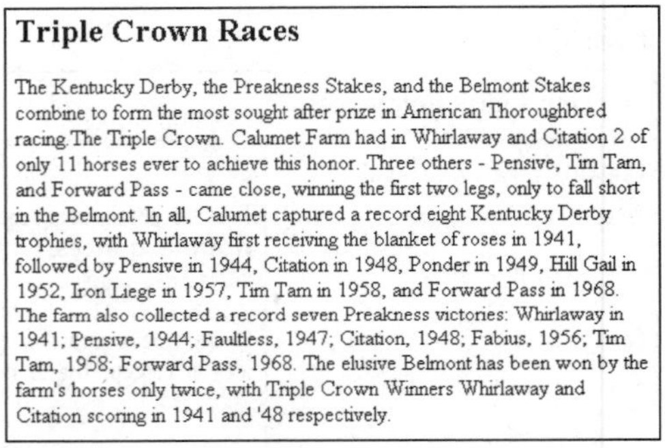

Triple Crown Races

The Kentucky Derby, the Preakness Stakes, and the Belmont Stakes combine to form the most sought after prize in American Thoroughbred racing, The Triple Crown. Calumet Farm had in Whirlaway and Citation 2 of only 11 horses ever to achieve this honor. Three others - Pensive, Tim Tam, and Forward Pass - came close, winning the first two legs, only to fall short in the Belmont. In all, Calumet captured a record eight Kentucky Derby trophies, with Whirlaway first receiving the blanket of roses in 1941, followed by Pensive in 1944, Citation in 1948, Ponder in 1949, Hill Gail in 1952, Iron Liege in 1957, Tim Tam in 1958, and Forward Pass in 1968. The farm also collected a record seven Preakness victories: Whirlaway in 1941; Pensive, 1944; Faultless, 1947; Citation, 1948; Fabius, 1956; Tim Tam, 1958; Forward Pass, 1968. The elusive Belmont has been won by the farm's horses only twice, with Triple Crown Winners Whirlaway and Citation scoring in 1941 and '48 respectively.

Figure 6.16 Excite's answer to our question about which races make up horse racing's Triple Crown.

EXCITE: CREATING QUERIES

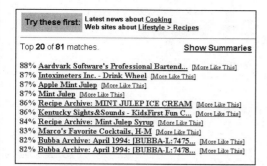

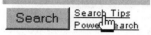

Figure 6.17 An AND search for **recipe AND "mint julep"** produced these results.

Figure 6.18 Click on Search Tips for more help, direct from Excite.

To turn off Excite's concept-based searching:

1. Use any of the traditional Boolean operators (AND, AND NOT, OR, and parentheses) in your query. That tells Excite to do a keyword search on your *exact* query instead of doing a concept-based search.

2. Combine words and phrases that *must* appear with AND. **Figure 6.17** shows the titles for our first 10 hits when we searched for **recipe AND "mint julep"**.

3. To find sites that include references to at least one of your search terms, use OR: **"Triple Crown" OR Preakness**.

4. To exclude a word or phrase, use AND NOT: **Derby AND NOT England**.

5. To group search terms into more complex queries, use parentheses: **"Silver Charm" AND (jockey OR trainer OR owner)**.

✔ Tips

■ You *must* use full caps for the Boolean operators AND, AND NOT, and OR. But Excite doesn't care whether you use upper- or lowercase for your search terms.

■ Don't worry if your Excite query returns a huge number of matching sites. Take a look at the first 10 or 20. Then use the More Like This feature. Or refine your query by adding more specific words.

■ For a summary of Excite search terms and the rules for using them, see the Excite Quick Reference on page 63.

■ For more information about using Excite, including new features that may have been added, click on Search Tips next to the Search button **Figure 6.18**.

Zeroing in on the best Web sites

So far, we've been using Excite to search the entire World Wide Web. But what if you want to do a more limited search of just the *best* sites? Or perhaps you'd like to read what Excite's editors have to say about several Web sites before taking the time to visit them. That's what we'll cover next.

To limit your search to selected Web sites:

1. Click on Power Search next to the Search button on the Excite search form (**Figure 6.19**). (You'll find the search form on the Excite home page and on all the Channel pages.) That will take you to Excite's Power Search page (**Figure 6.20**).

2. Use the "I want to search" drop-down menu and choose Selected Web Sites from the list (**Figure 6.21**).

3. Type your search terms in the appropriate text boxes to indicate words your search results *must*, *must not*, or *can* contain. To look for a name or phrase instead of a single word, use the drop-down menu (**Figure 6.22**).

4. Click on the Search button and Excite will do a targeted search of about 150,000 Web sites that have been visited and evaluated by the search engine's editors.

5. Your results will look like the example shown in **Figure 6.23**. They'll include the site's Title, URL (Internet address), the Excite Topic under which it is categorized, and a brief review.

6. Click on the site's Title to go directly to the site. Or click on its Topic link to locate other sites in that particular category.

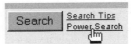

Figure 6.19 To search selected Web sites, click on Power Search.

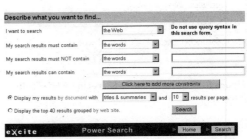

Figure 6.20 The Power Search page lets you create a query using drop-down menus and text boxes. You can also specify how you want your results displayed.

Figure 6.21 To search Web sites selected and reviewed by Excite's editors, click on Selected Web Sites.

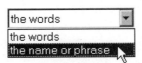

Figure 6.22 You can search for a name or phrase rather than a single word using this menu.

EXCITE: ZEROING IN ON THE BEST WEB SITES

```
Documents 1-2                          View Titles only

80% Jeopardy! Main Page  [More Like This]
URL: http://www.spe.sony.com/Pictures/tv/jeopardy/jeopardy.html
Topic: /Entertainment/TV/Game Shows/
Review: Information and multimedia about the TV trivia show.

19% UltimateTV -- Interact -- Your Favorite ...  [More Like This]
URL: http://tvnet.com/guestbook/favshows.html
Topic: /Entertainment/TV/
Review: Open forum for discussion.
```

Figure 6.23 Your search results will include an Excite topic category and a review (sometimes quite brief like the ones shown here).

```
Home > Arts & Entertainment Channel > TV > Game Shows

  ★★★★  Mike's Home Page
  Simple title for a page that describes a herculean intellectual feat: Mike Dupee and
  Dave Sampugnaro describe how they trained hard and overcame butterflies, tough
  competition and the newly redesigned buzzer button to reach the 1996 Jeopardy
  Tournament of Champions. There are links to other contestant's pages, Jeopardy lore,
  and a stack of study materials (some interactive) for other aspiring contestants.

  ★★★  Jeopardy Pro
  Are your friends always telling you should go on "Jeopardy"? Find out if that's true
  by playing this free, and probably unofficial, online version of the game. Anyone is
  welcome to play, and the top ten scorers are listed, but Alex Trebek is nowhere to be
  found.
```

Figure 6.24 Top-rated sites (those with 3- and 4-star ratings) typically have longer reviews like these.

✔ Tips

■ You can't use any punctuation or query operators (AND, AND NOT, OR) on the Excite Power Search form. If you want to specify additional words or phrases for your search, click on the bar labeled "Click here to add more constraints."

■ The Web reviews shown in **Figure 6.23** are very short, indicating that they were not among the Excite editors' favorites.

■ To find similar sites with higher ratings, click on the site's Topic. That will lead you to Web sites that merited Excite's 3- or 4-star ratings, like the ones shown in **Figure 6.24**.

EXCITE: ZEROING IN ON THE BEST WEB SITES

Searching by topic for the best Web sites

We've just stepped through the process for using Excite's Power Search form to limit your search to the database of selected Web sites. But what if you'd like to narrow your search even further by exploring just those sites within a particular topic?

The best way to do that is by using Excite Channels.

To find Web sites by topic using Channels:

1. Click on one of the Channels (**Figure 6.25**) on the Excite home page at www.excite.com.

2. You'll be presented with a list of topics for that Channel. We clicked on Sports and then Other Sports to get to the topics shown in **Figure 6.26**.

3. Next we clicked on Equestrian and were presented with a long list of rated sites, a portion of which is shown in **Figure 6.27**.

4. By clicking on Editor's Review next to any listing, you'll be taken to a page containing all the Web reviews for that topic. See **Figure 6.28** for a sample.

5. To get back to the main Excite search page from Channels, click on Home or Search (**Figure 6.29**).

Channels by Excite

Arts & Entertainment	My Channel
Business & Investing	News
Careers & Education	People & Chat
Computers & Internet	Politics
Games	Shopping
Health & Science	Sports
Lifestyle	Travel & Regional

Figure 6.25 The Channels menu on the Excite home page is your gateway to finding selected Web sites by topic.

Home > Sports Channel > Other Sports

Archery	Mountain Biking
Badminton	Orienteering
Billiards	Polo
Bowling	Raquetball
Boxing	Rodeo
Cricket	Rugby
Croquet	Running
Cycling	Shooting
Dog Racing	Skateboarding
Equestrian	Skydiving
Fencing	Softball
Field Hockey	Squash
Football (Australian)	Table Tennis
Gymnastics	Tennis
Handball	Triathlon
Lacrosse	Volleyball
Martial Arts	Walking
Miscellaneous	Weightlifting

Figure 6.26 You can tell from the top line that Excite's selected Equestrian sites are located in the Sports Channel under Other Sports.

★★★★ **Churchill Downs** *editor's review*
The official home page for this famous race track is ...
★★★★ **Electronic Zoo/NetVet - Horses** *editor's review*
Looking for equestrian sites on the Web? Look no further. ...
★★★★ **Grand Prix Discount Tack Store** *editor's review*
For those who don't run in horsey circles, "tack" means ...
★★★★ **Horse Racing Information** *editor's review*
A great site for horse sense and mailing lists. Winning ...
★★★★ **Horse Resources** *editor's review*
Whoa, Nelly, is there a stable of horse links at this site ...

Figure 6.27 These are just a few of the top-rated sites we discovered when we clicked on Equestrian. Note that each includes a link for an editor's review.

★★★★ **Churchill Downs**
The official home page for this famous race track is sponsored by Kentucky Tourism:
The Sun Shines Bright on My Old Kentucky Home! Link to Hugh Finn's Horse Racing
News.

★★★★ **Electronic Zoo/NetVet - Horses**
Looking for equestrian sites on the Web? Look no further. Here you find links, more
links, and then more links to horse sites of all shape and size.

★★★★ **Grand Prix Discount Tack Store**
For those who don't run in horsey circles, "tack" means equestrian equipment, and this
online catalog has an extensive selection of blankets, boots, barn items, clothing
helmets and saddles. Order via 800 number.

Figure 6.28 Here's a sample of the reviews for a few of the top-rated equestrian sites.

Figure 6.29 Clicking on Home or Search will always take you back to the Excite home page.

Guided Web Tours

- Little League
- Baseball Fan Pages
- Improve Your Golf Game
- Fantasy Sports Leagues
- Fresh-water Fishing
- Tennis Everyone?

Figure 6.30 Look for Guided Web Tours on Excite's Channel pages for links to the best sites on a particular topic. These are some of the tours you'll find on the Sports Channel.

✔ Tips

- Another good way to search the Web by topic is to take an ExciteSeeing Tour. You'll find interesting and informative tours on dozens of subjects: "Mystery Book Lovers' Tour," "Dr. Ruth on Safe Sex," "Windows 95 Shareware," to name just a few. Look for tour links under the heading Guided Web Tours on the Excite Channel pages. (**Figure 6.30** lists the tours available on the Sports Channel.)

- For a complete list of tours, visit the ExciteSeeing page at **tours.excite.com**.

Searching Usenet newsgroups

When you search Usenet newsgroups with Excite, you're actually using another very powerful search engine designed exclusively for newsgroups. It's called Deja News, and we'll have more to say about it in Chapter 11.

What's important for you to know at this point is that Deja News allows you to search more than two years' worth of Usenet newsgroup postings—going back to early 1995. And you can access the service right from the Excite search form.

To search newsgroup postings:

1. Go to the Excite home page (**www.excite.com**) and click on Newsgroups on the search form (**Figure 6.31**).

2. That will take you to Excite's Search Newsgroups form (**Figure 6.32**). Type your query in the text box and click on the Search button to submit it.

3. Your search results will be displayed 20 to a page, with the most relevant listed first (**Figure 6.33**). For each message, you'll see the date it was posted, the subject, the newsgroup it was posted to, and the author.

4. Click on the Subject link of any message to view the entire text.

5. To look at other messages or to post a reply, click on one of the buttons across the top of the message page (**Figure 6.34**). Clicking on Current Results will take you back to your original search results page (**Figure 6.33**).

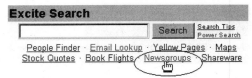

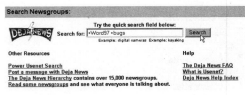

Figure 6.31 To search newsgroups, click on the Newsgroups link on the Excite search form.

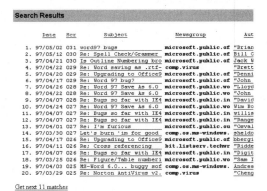

Figure 6.32 Excite's newsgroup search form is very simple. Just type your query in the space provided and click on Search.

Figure 6.33 Your newsgroup search results will look like this.

Figure 6.34 The Deja News navigation buttons are at the top and bottom of each newsgroup message page.

Figure 6.35 For more sophisticated newsgroup searches, click on Power Usenet Search.

✔ Tips

■ Newsgroups are a great place to look for advice and timely information on virtually any subject—car maintenance, hardware and software problems, travel tips, you name it. Think of them as an extension of your circle of friends and acquaintances.

■ To find out more about the author of a particular message—so that you know whether to trust the person's advice—click on the Author Profile button (**Figure 6.34**) or on the Author link on the Search Results page. Deja News will tell you how many messages the person has posted and to which groups. It's not foolproof, of course, but it will give you some idea of the person's activities and interests.

■ Deja News offers more sophisticated features—creating a query filter, for example, and targeting your search to a specific newsgroup. To try them, go back to your Search Results page and click on Power Usenet Search (**Figure 6.35**).

Searching for current news with Excite

One of our favorite Excite features is NewsTracker, which gives you the power to search more than 300 of the Web's best newspapers and magazines (including *The New York Times*, *Business Week*, and *TV Guide*) for up-to-the minute headlines and complete articles on virtually any topic.

Let's say you're listening to the radio on your way to work and catch the tail end of some brief report about PC mail-order companies. You've been thinking about buying a new system, so you check your local newspaper for the story, but it isn't there.

Your next thought might be to search the Web. But what's the likelihood of finding an early-morning news story there, given the fact that most Web pages and search engine databases aren't updated on a daily basis?

Your best bet is to go to the Excite home page (www.excite.com) and use the News Channel to search for the article with NewsTracker.

To search for current news articles:

1. Click on News in the Excite Channels menu (**Figure 6.36**).

2. When you get to the News Channel page, type your query in the search form text box and click on News Search (**Figure 6.37**).

3. Your results will be displayed 10 to a page, with the title of the article, news source, summary, date, and links to related articles (**Figure 6.38**).

4. Click on the title of an article to read the full text.

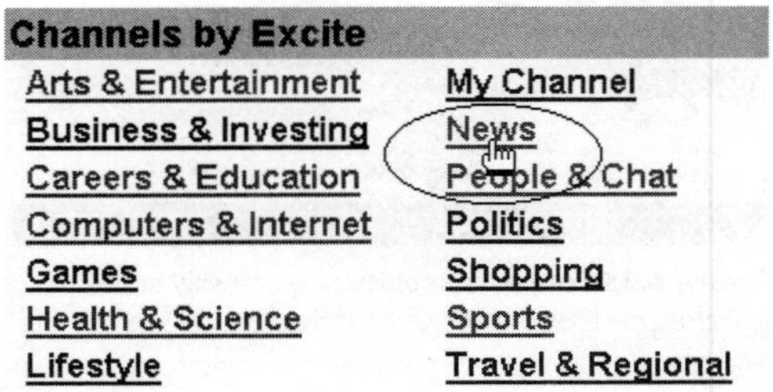

Figure 6.36 To do a news search, click on News in the Excite Channels menu.

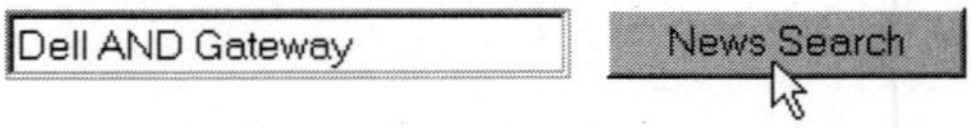

Figure 6.37 Type your query and click on News Search to submit it.

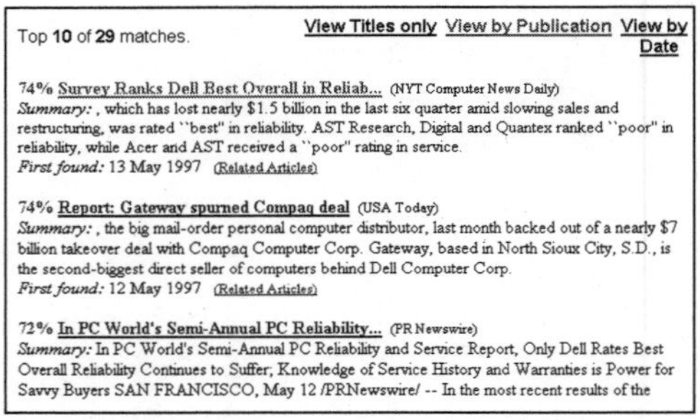

Figure 6.38 Our search for **Dell AND Gateway** turned up 29 matches, the first three of which are shown here.

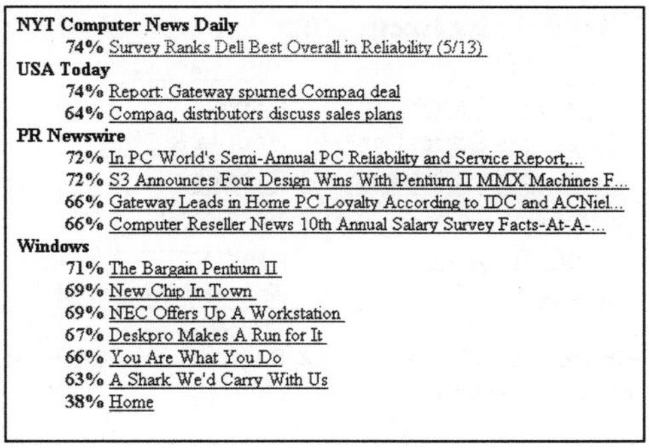

```
NYT Computer News Daily
    74%  Survey Ranks Dell Best Overall in Reliability (5/13)
USA Today
    74%  Report: Gateway spurned Compaq deal
    64%  Compaq, distributors discuss sales plans
PR Newswire
    72%  In PC World's Semi-Annual PC Reliability and Service Report,...
    72%  S3 Announces Four Design Wins With Pentium II MMX Machines F...
    66%  Gateway Leads in Home PC Loyalty According to IDC and ACNiel...
    66%  Computer Reseller News 10th Annual Salary Survey Facts-At-A-...
Windows
    71%  The Bargain Pentium II
    69%  New Chip In Town
    69%  NEC Offers Up A Workstation
    67%  Deskpro Makes A Run for It
    66%  You Are What You Do
    63%  A Shark We'd Carry With Us
    38%  Home
```

Figure 6.39 Click on View by Publication to see the same results organized according to the magazine or newspaper they appeared in.

Personalize your News
Click here to create your own
NewsTracker Topics!

Figure 6.40 To set up a customized news clipping service, click on this link on the News Channel page. You can track as many as 20 different topics.

NewsTracker   Change
Help | Sources | Lost my topics!

Figure 6.41 For a list of all the magazines and newspapers included in a NewsTracker search, click on Sources.

✔ Tips

■ If you'd prefer to see just article titles, or to have your search results sorted by publication or date, click on one of Excite's alternate views: View Titles Only, View by Publication, or View by Date. **Figure 6.39** shows news search results sorted by publication.

■ The News Channel is set to display headline news and articles in eight categories: Top Stories, Business, Sports, Entertainment, Science and Technology, Nation, World, and Lifestyle. You can create your own topics—in effect, setting up your own personalized *clipping service*—using the Personalize Your News feature (**Figure 6.40**).

■ For a complete list of all the publications covered by NewsTracker, click on Sources on the News Channel page (**Figure 6.41**).

■ News headlines and articles are a standard feature on all Excite Channels. To look for articles about personal computers, for example, click on the Computers & Internet Channel.

■ You can also search the NewsTracker database using Excite's Power Search form. Click on Power Search on the Excite home page and select Current News from the "I want to search" drop-down menu.

Using Excite to find travel information

If you've ever tried searching the Web for travel information, you know how difficult and time-consuming—if not completely impossible—it can be to find really good information about a particular vacation spot or business travel destination.

What's Bermuda's weather like in April? What are the best restaurants in Cleveland? You could try these queries using Excite's search form, and you just might find the answers. But if it's travel information you want, make your first stop Excite's City.Net Travel feature.

To search for travel information:

1. Go to the Excite home page (www.excite.com) and click on Travel & Regional in the Channels menu (**Figure 6.42**).

2. That will take you to the City.Net Travel page (**Figure 6.43**).

3. You can click on City.Net's world map to explore a particular region. But in most cases, you'll probably just type your destination in the search form and click on Take Me There (**Figure 6.44**).

4. If your chosen destination is one of the 5,000 or so in the City.Net database, you'll be presented with a well-organized and informative guide to help you plan your trip (**Figure 6.45**).

5. Click on Travel Reservations to access City.Net's service for checking flight information and making reservations for airline tickets, hotels, and car rentals. Or click on Change Location to go back to the City.Net search form (**Figure 6.46**).

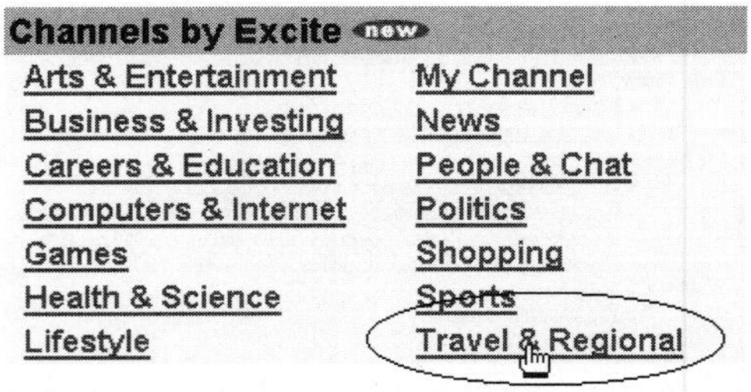

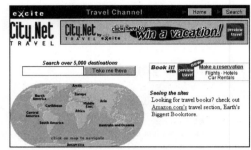

Figure 6.42 Click on Travel & Regional in the Channels menu to get to Excite's travel features.

Figure 6.43 The Travel Channel is also the home page for City.Net Travel.

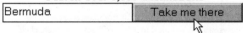

Figure 6.44 The best way to get travel information is to type a destination in the search form and click on Take Me There.

Bermuda

Travel Tools

Air, Car, Hotel Reservations	People Finder
Maps	Yellow Pages

Web Sites

Country Information	Newspapers
Culture and Language	Other Guides
Education	Parks and Gardens
Food and Drink	Relocation Information
Lodging	Travel and Tourism
Maps	Weather

Figure 6.45 Here's a sample of City.Net's guide for Bermuda.

Figure 6.46 Click on one of these buttons to choose another destination or to check flights and make reservations.

✔ Tips

- We prefer using a travel agent to actually book flights. After all, they're the pros, and tickets cost the same whether you book them yourself or use the services of an agent. But we often check City.Net prior to calling our travel agent to get an idea of schedules and fares. It's like having our own *Official Airline Guide* for free.

- Searching City.Net Travel is by far the best way to find travel information with Excite. But the Travel & Regional Channel also includes guides organized by geography. To use them, click on Travel & Regional on the Excite Channels menu, scroll down to the bottom of the page, and click on Web Guide Travel or Web Guide Regional.

- You can also search City.Net Travel from the Excite Power Search page. Click on Power Search on the Excite home page and choose City.Net Travel Guide from the "I want to search" drop-down menu.

- To go directly to City.Net's flight information and reservation service, click on Book Flights on the Excite home page.

- If you live in Europe or are planning a trip there, take a look at Global Excite—foreign language editions for France, Germany, Sweden, and the United Kingdom. You can use Global Excite to limit your searches to Europe or any one of these four countries. Look for Global Excite on the search engine's home page or choose one of the countries from the "I want to search" menu on the Power Search form.

HotBot

www.hotbot.com

What you can search

- World Wide Web

- Usenet newsgroups

Contact information

HotBot
HotWired, Inc.
San Francisco, CA
415/276-8400
415/276-8499 (fax)
www.hotwired.com

Inktomi Corp.
Berkeley, CA
510/883-7300
510/883-7399 (fax)
www.inktomi.com

HotBot is a joint venture of HotWired (of *Wired* magazine fame) and Inktomi, a company that makes high-end computer workstations. The *Wired* connection helps explain HotBot's bilious lime-green background. (If you've ever read—or *tried* to read—the magazine, you know what we mean.)

Nevertheless, you'll love the ease and speed with which you can search using HotBot—even if you've never tried a search engine before. Instead of typing your queries with special punctuation marks and Boolean operators, you can click on drop-down menu selections and radio buttons to conduct even the most complex searches.

Within about a second, you'll have your results, sorted according to how well they match your search criteria. If you don't find exactly what you're looking for, you can easily refine your search using one of HotBot's tools for adding more terms or limiting the search by date, location, or media type.

HotBot's Wired Source feature provides a relatively small collection of interesting and useful Web sites organized by topic, but the search engine's main focus is its lightning-fast search capability. If subject-matter organization is important to you, you'll want to look to one of the other search engines, like Excite or Yahoo!. But for sheer speed and ease of use, HotBot is a real winner.

✔ Tips

■ Slurp, the HotBot spider, searches the Web continuously for new or changed documents. When it finds one, it scans every word in the document—not just the header, keywords, and the first few lines—and adds the information to the HotBot database. If your search doesn't locate a Web site you know exists, it may be that the site is new and Slurp simply hasn't found it yet. (It takes a week or more for the spider to visit the entire Web.) Other possibilities are that the site's server is down or that links are broken or missing.

■ If you use Netscape Navigator and share our dislike for HotBot's lime-green background, you can easily change it. With Netscape Navigator 3.0, click on Options, then General Preferences, and then Colors. Set Background to Custom and choose a color (we prefer white). Then click on Always Use My Colors. With Netscape Navigator 4.0, the sequence is Edit, then Preferences, and then Colors. Remove the check mark in the Use Windows Colors box. Then click on Background and choose your preferred background color. Click on OK and then on Always Use My Colors. The next time you visit the HotBot home page (or any Web site that uses weird background colors or patterns), your chosen custom color will appear instead.

■ If you use Microsoft's Internet Explorer, you'll have to live with HotBot's green background. Internet Explorer lets you choose your own background color, but it will only be applied to Web pages for which the designer has not specified a color—which isn't the case with HotBot.

HotBot

Using HotBot's basic search form

As we've said, searching with HotBot could hardly be easier, even for first-time searchers. Point your Web browser at **www.hotbot.com** to get to the HotBot home page and search form (**Figure 7.1**).

HotBot's basic search form allows you to direct your query to either the Web or news-groups (or both), using drop-down menus to create your search request. Additional tools—labeled Modify, Date, Location, and Media Type—help you refine your search if you're not successful the first time around. You can save and reload your search settings using the buttons across the bottom of the page.

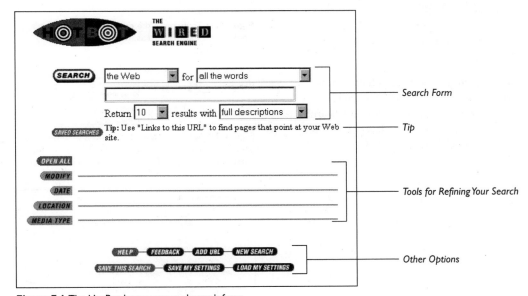

Figure 7.1 The HotBot home page and search form.

To search the Web
or Usenet newsgroups:

1. Type your query in the Search Form text box (**Figure 7.2**).

2. By default, HotBot performs an AND search, looking for *all* the words in your query. To change that, use the drop-down menu (**Figure 7.3**). Other options include searching for: *any* of the words (OR search), an exact phrase, a person, links to a URL (Internet address), or a Boolean expression.

3. You can also change how your results are displayed. The default is 10 to a page with full descriptions. Use the drop-down menus (**Figures 7.4** and **7.5**) to increase the number, and to choose brief descriptions or URLs only.

4. Click on Search. **Figure 7.6** shows a sample of HotBot search results with full descriptions.

5. To perform the same search on newsgroups, click on Revise Search and use the drop-down menu next to the Search button to select Usenet News or Web & Usenet (**Figure 7.7**). Then click on Search.

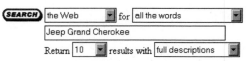

Figure 7.2 Here's a basic HotBot search request for information on the Jeep Grand Cherokee with the default settings.

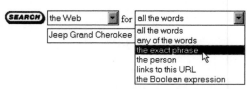

Figure 7.3 For a phrase search, use the drop-down menu to select "the exact phrase."

Figure 7.4 To increase the number of results displayed from the default of 10 to as many as 100, use the Return menu.

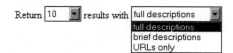

Figure 7.5 You can change the amount of detail presented with your search results using this menu. Most of the time you'll probably want full descriptions.

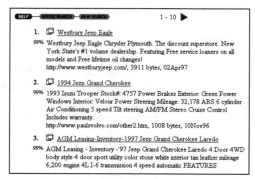

Figure 7.6 HotBot search results with full descriptions look like this. The percentage figure next to each item represents HotBot's confidence in the match.

Figure 7.7 For newsgroup searches, simply click on Usenet News on this drop-down menu.

Tips:

■ For best results with HotBot, use at least two or three search terms and be as specific as possible. To search for a phrase, select "the exact phrase" from the drop-down menu or put it in double quotes.

■ In general, you'll get the fastest results with an "all the words" search. Choosing "any of the words" takes longer, and "the exact phrase" longer still.

■ When looking for information about a person, be sure to specify that in the Search drop-down menu. Doing so tells HotBot to look for *near matches* to your query. Typing *Lee Iacocca*, for example, will find references to that exact name as well as *Iacocca, Lee*.

■ If you have your own Web site, you can find out how popular it is using HotBot's "links to this URL" option. Just type the site's URL in the Search Form text box and choose the "links" option on the Search drop-down menu. You can do the same for any site on the Web, of course.

■ Power searchers who prefer creating queries with AND, OR, NOT, and parentheses can do just that and then select "the Boolean expression" in the Search drop-down menu.

■ If you find yourself changing HotBot's default settings on a regular basis, why not save the changes? Make all your selections using the Search Form's drop-down menus. Then click on "Save My Settings" to store the changes.

Refining your HotBot searches

HotBot provides several very powerful tools to help you refine your searches. If you aren't successful the first time—you get too many hits, for example, and you don't want to take the time to wade through them—your best bet is to click on Open All (**Figure 7.8**) on the HotBot home page to get access to these additional tools. (You can also click on each tool individually to open just that tool.)

To refine your original search:

1. Use the Modify tool (**Figure 7.9**) to focus your search more precisely by including or excluding terms. A drop-down menu allows you to specify words your search results must, should, or must not contain. Another menu lets you tag your search terms as words, a phrase, a person, or a URL. Click on the small plus (+) button to copy the form so that you can add up to 20 modifiers to your search.

2. Use the Date tool (**Figure 7.10**) to look for documents created or modified within a certain time frame (days, months, or years) or before or after a specific date.

3. Use the Location tool (**Figure 7.11**) to limit your search by Web site. By default, HotBot searches the entire Web (Anyplace). But you can click on the CyberPlace radio button and type, say, **consumer.org** in the search box to focus on Web pages hosted by Consumers Union. Adding that to our query on the Jeep Grand Cherokee would be a good way to eliminate dealer sites and focus instead on safety and reliability issues.

   You can also use the Location tool to define CyberPlace as one or more of the

Figure 7.8 To access HotBot's tools for refining your searches, click on Open All.

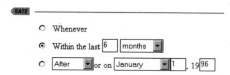

Figure 7.9 The Modify tool lets you specify additional words or phrases to help narrow your search. Click on the plus (+) sign to add more search forms (up to 20). Click on minus (–) to remove extra forms you've created.

Figure 7.10 The Date tool can be set so that your search only retrieves information from sites that have been added or changed within a particular time frame, or before or after a certain date.

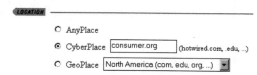

Figure 7.11 HotBot's Location tool makes it easy to limit your search to a specific Web site or Internet domain.

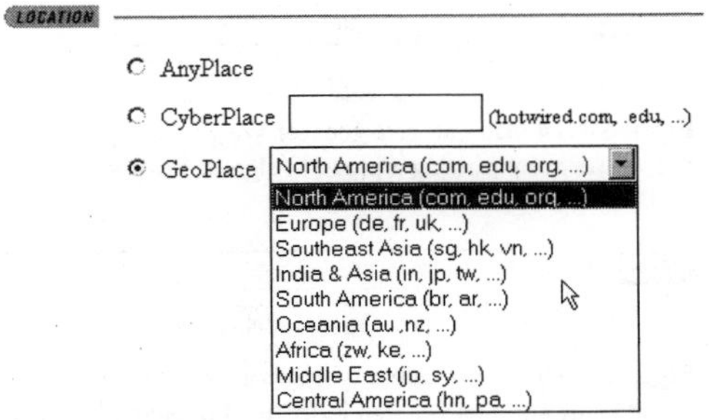

Figure 7.12 The Location tool can also be used to limit a search by geography. Make your selection from the drop-down menu shown here.

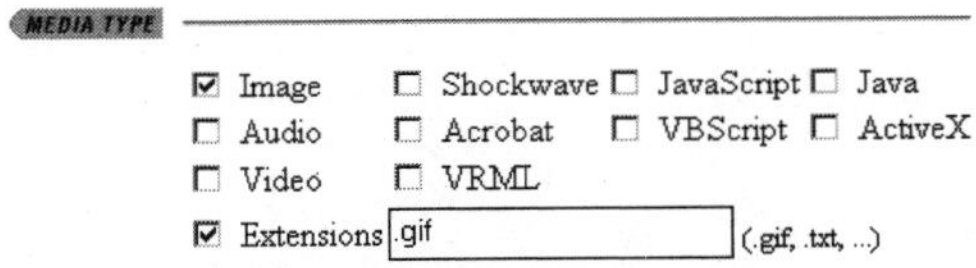

Figure 7.13 The Media Type tool helps locate sites offering special types of files. You can click on as many items as you wish, and specify one or more file extensions as well.

Internet domains: **.com** (companies), **.edu** (colleges and universities), **.org** (non-profits), etc. To exclude domains, use a minus (–) sign: **–.gov –.org**, for example, would prevent both government and non-profit sites from appearing in your results.

The GeoPlace option lets you search by geography. Click on the GeoPlace button and choose from the menu (**Figure 7.12**).

4. Use the Media Type tool (**Figure 7.13**) to zero in on Web sites offering special files like graphics, sound, video, Java applets, and others. Click on multiple entries to find sites with *all* the specified types.

✔ Tips

- The Location panel makes it easy to look for (or exclude) foreign language Web sites. To find sites with information presented in Spanish, for example, try setting GeoPlace to Central or South America.

- To target a particular country, use the Location panel's CyberPlace option. You'll need the country's two-letter Internet code (.CL for Chile, .ES for Spain, .MY for Malaysia, etc.). For a list, see Appendix B.

- If you find yourself using one or more of the HotBot panels for most of your searches, set things up so that they appear automatically whenever you visit HotBot. For example, to make Date and Location available, open them, choose your settings, and then click on Save My Settings.

HotBot: Refining Your Searches

Advanced searching with HotBot

The HotBot features we've described so far will probably take care of most of your searching requirements. But there are a few additional techniques that might come in handy from time to time.

To further refine searches for "all the words":

1. Use a plus (+) sign in front of a word or phrase that should be given greater weight. A search like the one shown in **Figure 7.14**, for example, would find references to sport utility vehicles. The sites with "buyer's guide" information as well would be ranked higher in the list.

2. Put a minus (–) sign in front of a word or phrase you want to specifically exclude from your search, as we did in **Figure 7.15**, to look for sport utility vehicles other than Jeeps.

To do a case-sensitive search:

- HotBot ignores case most of the time, so a search for jeep will find Jeep and JEEP as well as jeep. However, words that have unusual combinations of upper- and lowercase (like the company names HotWired and NeXT) have what HotBot refers to as "interesting case." The search engine can find such words for you if you type them with the exact combination of upper- and lowercase letters you're looking for.

Figure 7.14 You can give greater weight to a particular search term by putting a plus (+) sign in front of it.

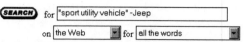

Figure 7.15 To exclude a word from your search results, put a minus (–) sign in front of it. A search like this would find Web sites dealing with sport utility vehicles other than Jeeps.

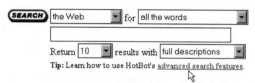

Tip: Learn how to use HotBot's advanced search features.

Figure 7.16 The tips just below the HotBot search form provide a mini-tutorial on using the search engine.

Figure 7.17 Click on the Help button for access to all the latest information on using HotBot's search features.

To search for specific types of information:

■ You can incorporate one or more of HotBot's Meta Words (special search terms) in your queries. For a complete list of Meta Words, see page 87. For the most part, they duplicate search capabilities provided by HotBot's main search form. But power searchers may on occasion prefer to incorporate the Meta Words in Boolean expressions.

✔ Tips

■ The "date search" Meta Words (**after:**, **before:**, and **within:**) work correctly only if used as part of a Boolean expression, without plus (+) and (−) signs in front of them.

■ You'll find a different tip for using HotBot each time you visit the search engine's home page. Look for it right below the Search Form (**Figure 7.16**). Often the tip will include a link that takes you to detailed information in the HotBot Help feature.

■ For more advice on using HotBot, click on the Help button at the bottom of the home page (**Figure 7.17**).

Table 7.1

HotBot Quick Reference	
FOR THIS TYPE OF SEARCH:	**DO THIS:**
Phrase Search	Type the phrase without any special punctuation and select **"the exact phrase"** on the drop-down menu.
	Alternatively, you can type phrases as a sequence of words surrounded by **double quotes** (" ") and select **"all the words"** or **"any of the words"** from the drop-down menu.
AND Search (multiple words and phrases, each of which *must* be present)	Type words or phrases and select **"all the words"** from the drop-down menu.
	You can also combine words and phrases with **AND** and select **"the Boolean expression"** from the menu.
OR Search (multiple words and phrases, any one of which may be present)	Type words or phrases separated by spaces and select **"any of the words"** from the menu.
	Alternatively, combine words and phrases with **OR** and choose **"the Boolean expression"** from the menu.
NOT Search (to exclude a word or phrase)	Use a **minus sign** (−) in front of a word or phrase you want to exclude from the results.
	Or use **NOT** in front the word or phrase and specify **"the Boolean expression."**
Nested Search	Combine search terms with **parentheses** and select **"the Boolean expression"** from the menu.
Case-Sensitive Search	Use lowercase to find *any combination* of upper- and lowercase. Use the correct combination of upper- and lowercase letters (for example, HotWired or NeXT) to force an *exact match* of your search term.
Date Search	Open the **Date tool** and select a time frame (days, months, or years) or a specific "before" or "after" date.
Location Search (Web site, domain, country, or geography)	Open the **Location tool** and choose CyberPlace to search for a specific Web site, Internet domain (.com, .edu, .gov, etc.), or country. Choose GeoPlace to search by geography.
Field Search (Media Type)	Open the **Media Type tool** and choose the file types and/or file extensions you want to find.
Field Search (Other)	See HotBot **Meta Words** on page 87.
Weighted Keyword Search	Put a **plus sign** (+) in front of a word or phrase that should be ranked higher in the results and select "all the words" or "any of the words" from the menu.

Table 7.2

HotBot Meta Words*	
META WORD FORMAT	WHAT IT DOES
domain:*name*	Restricts search to the domain name selected. Domains can be specified up to three levels: **domain:com domain:ford.com domain:www.ford.com**
depth:*number*	Limits how deep within a Web site your search goes. To go three pages deep, use **depth:3**.
linkdomain:*name*	Restricts search to pages containing links to the domain you specify. For example, **linkdomain:edmunds.com** finds pages that point to the Edmund's Car Guides Web site.
linkext:*extension*	Restricts search to pages containing embedded files with a particular extension. For example, **linkext:ra** finds pages containing RealAudio files.
scriptlanguage:JavaScript	Allows you to search for pages containing JavaScript.
scriptlanguage:VBScript	Allows you to search for pages containing VBScript.
newsgroup:*newsgroup name*	Restricts Usenet newsgroup searches to articles that have been posted to the specified newsgroup.
feature:*name*	Limits your query to pages containing the specified feature.
feature:embed	Detects plug-ins
feature:script	Detects embedded scripts
feature:applet	Detects embedded Java applets
feature:activex	Detects ActiveX controls or layouts
feature:audio	Detects audio formats
feature:video	Detects video formats
feature:acrobat	Detects Acrobat files
feature:frame	Detects frames in HTML documents
feature:table	Detects tables in HTML documents
feature:form	Detects forms in HTML documents
feature:vrml	Detects VRML files
feature:image	Detects image files (GIF, JPEG, etc.)
after:*day/month/year*	Restricts search to documents created or modified after a specific date: **Explorer AND after:30/09/97**.
before:*day/month/year*	Restricts search to documents created or modified before a specific date: **"buyer's guide" AND before:01/01/97**.
within:*number/unit*	Restricts search to documents created or modified within a specific time period. *Unit* can be *days*, *months*, or *years*: **Jeep AND within:3/months**.

*Note: The words shown in italics are variables. You'll find examples of the terms you can use for each of these variables in the column labeled "What It Does."

Exploring the Web by topic

HotBot currently gives very little emphasis to its topic-category organization of the Web. Our guess is that that may change as the search engines compete for visitors (and thus advertising dollars). But right now, the fact is that unless you know to look for it, you could easily miss Wired Source, HotBot's topic guide to some of the best Web sites.

Assembled by the editors of *Wired* magazine, Wired Source makes no pretense of being an exhaustive guide. Instead, it's a small but carefully selected collection of some of the Web's best and most useful resources, organized into five broad categories:

- Reference

- Business

- Culture

- SciTech

- Politics

Under Reference, for example, you'll find a searchable ZIP Code directory, various people-finding tools like Four11 and WhoWhere?, English and foreign language dictionaries, and currency converters.

The Business category provides links to *The Wall Street Journal Interactive Edition*, the business section of *The New York Times*, PR Newswire, and a number of other Web sites that carry business news.

Additional categories like Travel and Jobs are in the works and may have been added by the time you read this.

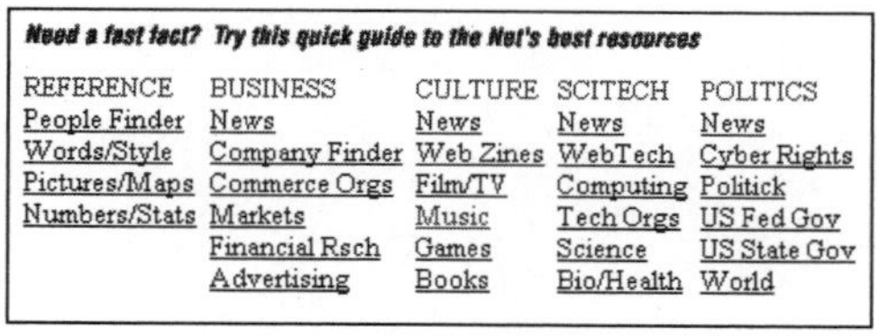

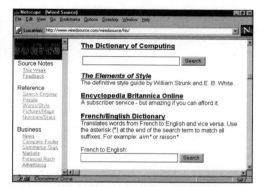

Figure 7.18 Wired Source, HotBot's small but carefully selected directory of Web sites, is presented at the bottom of the search engine's home page.

Figure 7.19 A few of the offerings you'll find in Wired Source's Reference category under the topic Words/Style.

To access Wired Source:

1. Point your Web browser at the HotBot home page (**www.hotbot.com**).

2. Scroll down to the bottom of the page and click on any one of the Wired Source links (**Figure 7.18**). We clicked on Words/Style under Reference to get to the page shown in **Figure 7.19**.

3. You can scroll through the offerings, read brief descriptions, and in many cases, perform a search by typing information in a search text box.

✔ Tip

■ Take the time to visit each of the Wired Source categories and read through the offerings to get a better idea of what's there. You'll find lots of great research and reference tools that you might never come across otherwise—tools that could help you zero in on some particular type of information that might elude even the most sophisticated search query.

8

INFOSEEK

www.infoseek.com

We'll never forget our first encounter with Infoseek, way back in 1995, shortly after the service was introduced. We had read that with Infoseek, you could type a question in plain English and search some 200,000 Web pages for the answer. Sign on, get the information, and sign off—that sounded pretty neat to us.

Naturally, we went straight to Infoseek and typed our first query: Where can we find information about getting tickets for the 1996 Olympics? Sure enough, Infoseek had the answer—and we were hooked. The company's slogan, "Proof of intelligent life on the Net," rang true for us from that very first experience.

Today, Infoseek is not only one of the most popular Internet search engines, it ranks right up there with the most heavily visited sites on the Web. Its search capabilities rival those of powerhouse AltaVista, but the interface is so clean and simple that even first-time users can often find what they're looking for with ease.

In addition to searching Infoseek's Web database (now covering some 50 million pages according to company literature), you can also search for e-mail addresses, company profiles, and FAQs (Frequently Asked Questions), right from the main Infoseek search form. Or you can explore the Net by topic using the service's 12-category Web directory. For Usenet newsgroup searches, Infoseek provides access

INFOSEEK

to the Internet's premier newsgroup search engine, Deja News.

Infoseek offers two slightly different search services: the full-featured Ultrasmart service and Ultraseek (for more experienced searchers). The Ultrasmart search page is where you'll find Infoseek's Web directory and recommendations for related topics and sites to consider.

One of our favorite Infoseek features is *set searching*—performing an initial search and then narrowing the focus by searching again within just those sites returned by the original query. It's a great way to zero in on Web sites containing just what you need, without having to wade through lots of irrelevant information.

Experienced searchers may be disappointed to find that they can't use common Boolean operators (AND, OR, NOT, NEAR) with Infoseek (although the service does support several good field-search terms and the use of plus (+) and minus (−) signs for including and excluding words). On the other hand, if the engine is good enough to find what you're looking for without requiring you to construct complicated queries, who cares?

✔ Tip

- Watch for sites labeled "powered by Infoseek." (CNET's Search.com at **www.search.com** is one example.) You can use the information in this chapter, especially the Infoseek Quick Reference, to construct queries using the search form at any site that is "powered by Infoseek."

- For a behind-the-scenes look at the Infoseek hardware and software, go to the search engine's home page (**www.infoseek.com**) and click on Ultraseek. When you get to the Ultraseek page, click on the link labeled "How we did it."

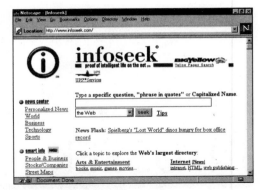

Figure 8.1 The Infoseek home page.

INFOSEEK

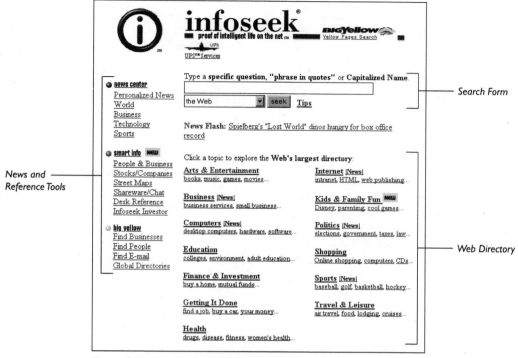

Search Form

News and Reference Tools

Web Directory

Figure 8.2 Infoseek's Ultrasmart search form and Web directory.

Click <u>Ultraseek</u> to hide directory topics for advanced, streamlined searching.

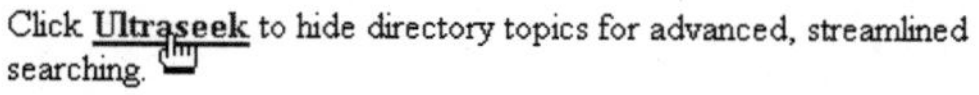

Figure 8.3 Infoseek's Ultraseek service is designed for more advanced searchers.

Using Infoseek's main search page

To get to Infoseek, point your Web browser at **www.infoseek.com**. That will take you to the search engine's home page and main search form (**Figure 8.1**), which they call their Ultrasmart service. With Ultrasmart, you can look for information by typing a query in the search form or browsing a directory of Web sites organized by topic (**Figure 8.2**).

Power searchers who prefer not to be bothered with the Web directory can hide it by clicking on Ultraseek (**Figure 8.3**). The Ultraseek search form is very similar to the one on Infoseek's home page, but search results are handled a bit differently. Ultraseek also provides links to some additional search tools not found on the Ultrasmart page.

To explore the main features on Infoseek's home page:

1. Type a question or some words or phrases in the Search Form text box (**Figure 8.4**). Use the drop-down menu (**Figure 8.5**) to choose whether you want to search the Web, newsgroups, or one of Infoseek's other collections of information. Click on Seek to submit your query.

2. Browse some of the topics presented in Infoseek's Web directory. First, click on one of the 12 main headings, like Arts & Entertainment or Business. You'll be presented with a whole page of subtopics like the one shown in **Figure 8.6**. You can work your way through the directory by clicking on links. Or use the form at the bottom of the page to search just that part of the directory.

3. Take a look at Infoseek's News Center (**Figure 8.7**), where you'll find headline news organized by category. You can customize the news so that you'll be presented with the topics that interest you most, including local weather and TV listings. You can also search news from Reuters, Business Wire, PR News Wire, and other major news organizations.

4. Try Smart Info and Big Yellow (**Figure 8.8**), a set of reference tools for finding e-mail addresses, stock quotes, company profiles, street maps and driving directions, shareware software, Chat rooms, and more.

Type a **specific question, "phrase in quotes"** or **Capitalized Name**.

Where can I find a biography of Jerry Seinfeld?

the Web ▾ | seek | Tips

Figure 8.4 If you prefer, Infoseek queries can be expressed as a question.

the Web ▾
the Web
Usenet Newsgroups
News Wires
Premier News
Industry News
E-mail Addresses
Company Profiles
Web FAQs

Figure 8.5 To choose the database you want to search, use the search form's drop-down menu.

Arts & Entertainment Topics

Amusement parks	Magazines
Animation	Movies
Architecture	Museums & parks
Books	Music
Celebrities	News
Dance	Performing arts
Digital art	Photography
Fashion & style	Radio
Festivals & events	Restaurants
Fine arts	Science fiction, fantasy, horror
Games	Television
Humor & fun	Writing

Figure 8.6 Clicking on Arts & Entertainment in the Infoseek Web directory takes you to this page of subtopics.

● news center
Personalized News
World
Business
Technology
Sports

Figure 8.7 Infoseek's news offerings are grouped together in the News Center.

● smart info
People & Business
Stocks/Companies
Street Maps
Shareware/Chat
Desk Reference
Infoseek Investor

● big yellow
Find Businesses
Find People
Find E-mail
Global Directories

Figure 8.8 You'll find some excellent tools for locating people, companies, and other information on Infoseek's Smart Info and Big Yellow menus.

✔ Tips

■ Clicking on the links for Smart Info's People & Business and BigYellow's Find People and Find E-mail all take you to the same place—a search form you can use to look up phone numbers, e-mail, and street addresses.

■ You'll find links on the Infoseek home page for several country-specific versions of the search service: France, Germany, Italy, Japan, and United Kingdom. Try them if you live in one of these countries or simply want to practice your foreign language skills. They also come in handy when you want to limit your Infoseek searches to sites located in a particular country.

■ Infoseek makes it easy to find sites that want to sell you something. Click on Shopping in the Web directory, or try the link for Infoseek Ultrashop.

■ To add an Infoseek button and search box to your browser, click on the link for Quickseek and download the software for your system (Windows 95/NT, Windows 3.1, or Power Mac).

Basic Web searching with Infoseek

Like Excite, Infoseek encourages you to enter your queries in plain English, without worrying about special punctuation and Boolean operators. You can type a question as a complete sentence in the Search Form text box: **Where can I find a directory of lawyers in Florida?** Or think of your query as the completion of the fill-in-the-blank sentence "Find me information on…", in which case you might simply type a series of words like **lawyers practicing in Florida.**

Your search results will be presented, often with a list of related topics you may want to explore. If you get too many hits, you can easily narrow your search by adding words and then telling Infoseek to look *just* at the results from your original search—instead of the entire Web. (This kind of searching is often referred to as a *set search.*)

To search the Web:

1. Go to the Infoseek home page (**www.infoseek.com**) and type your query in the text box of the Ultrasmart search form (**Figure 8.9**). We'll give you some tips for more effective searching later in the chapter. For now, just type your query in plain English.
2. Infoseek offers a drop-down menu of databases you can search (**Figure 8.10**). In this case, we'll use the default setting to search the Web.
3. Click on Seek and your results will be displayed 10 to a page, with the best matches listed first (**Figure 8.11**). The percentage figure shown in bold to the left of each Web address is Infoseek's "confidence rating" for the site—a measure of how well it matches your query.

Type a specific question, "phrase in quotes" or Capitalized Name.
study abroad programs in France
the Web
seek
Tips

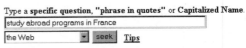

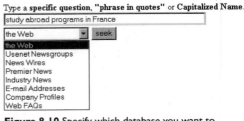

Figure 8.9 Infoseek's Ultrasmart search form allows you to search by typing a plain-English query.

Type a specific question, "phrase in quotes" or Capitalized Name.
study abroad programs in France
the Web
seek
the Web
Usenet Newsgroups
News Wires
Premier News
Industry News
E-mail Addresses
Company Profiles
Web FAQs

Figure 8.10 Specify which database you want to search using Infoseek's drop-down menu.

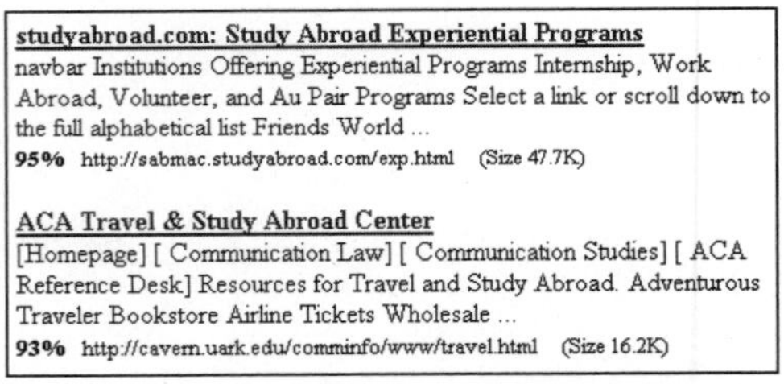

studyabroad.com: Study Abroad Experiential Programs
navbar Institutions Offering Experiential Programs Internship, Work Abroad, Volunteer, and Au Pair Programs Select a link or scroll down to the full alphabetical list Friends World ...
95% http://sabmac.studyabroad.com/exp.html (Size 47.7K)
ACA Travel & Study Abroad Center
[Homepage] [Communication Law] [Communication Studies] [ACA Reference Desk] Resources for Travel and Study Abroad. Adventurous Traveler Bookstore Airline Tickets Wholesale ...
93% http://cavern.uark.edu/comminfo/www/travel.html (Size 16.2K)

Figure 8.11 Infoseek's search results include title, brief summary, confidence rating, Web address, and the size of the page.

Hide Summaries

Figure 8.12 To display just the titles for your search results, click on Hide Summaries.

You searched for **study abroad programs in France**

| Marseille | seek | Tips |

⦿ Search **only** these results ◯ Search **the whole Web**

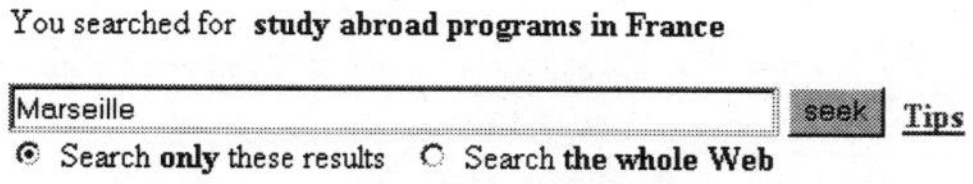

Figure 8.13 Use this search form to narrow your search by adding more terms and, if you wish, limiting the new search to just those sites identified by your initial query.

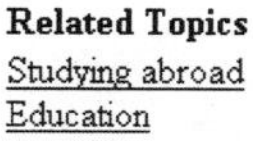

Related Topics
Studying abroad
Education

Figure 8.14 Infoseek will often recommend additional topics related to your search request.

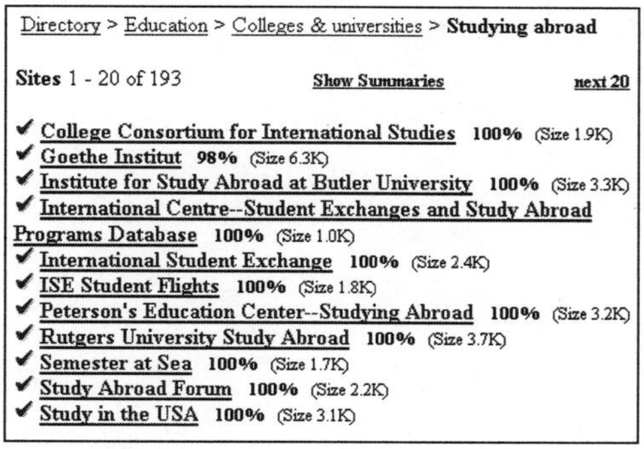

Directory > Education > Colleges & universities > **Studying abroad**

Sites 1 - 20 of 193   **Show Summaries**   **next 20**

✔ **College Consortium for International Studies** 100% (Size 1.9K)
✔ **Goethe Institut** 98% (Size 6.3K)
✔ **Institute for Study Abroad at Butler University** 100% (Size 3.3K)
✔ **International Centre--Student Exchanges and Study Abroad Programs Database** 100% (Size 1.0K)
✔ **International Student Exchange** 100% (Size 2.4K)
✔ **ISE Student Flights** 100% (Size 1.8K)
✔ **Peterson's Education Center--Studying Abroad** 100% (Size 3.2K)
✔ **Rutgers University Study Abroad** 100% (Size 3.7K)
✔ **Semester at Sea** 100% (Size 1.7K)
✔ **Study Abroad Forum** 100% (Size 2.2K)
✔ **Study in the USA** 100% (Size 3.1K)

Figure 8.15 The top line of this Related Topics page tells you where to look in Infoseek's Web directory for more information. Recommended sites are listed first and designated by a check mark.

4. Scroll through the first page or so, reading the titles and summary information. If a site sounds promising, click on the title to go there.

5. To display your search results in a more concise format, click on Hide Summaries (**Figure 8.12**). That way you'll be presented with just the titles, making it possible to quickly scan a larger number of sites (20 per page) to identify the ones that might be of interest.

6. If you get too many hits, go down to the bottom of the page and type one or more additional search terms in the form presented there (**Figure 8.13**). You're given a choice this time of searching the entire World Wide Web or limiting the search to your original results—a neat feature not found in most search engines.

✔ Tips

■ Be sure to take a look at Infoseek's suggestions for Related Topics. You'll find them near the top of the page, right before your search results. See **Figure 8.14** for an example.

■ Clicking on one or more of these topics will help you find Web sites recommended by Infoseek. They'll be listed first and designated by a check mark (**Figure 8.15**). You'll also find out where to look in the Infoseek Web directory for other sites that might be of interest. In this example, we learn that information about studying abroad can be found by clicking on Education and then Colleges & Universities in Infoseek's Web directory.

INFOSEEK: BASIC WEB SEARCHING

Creating more effective queries

With Infoseek, you can often find what you're looking for with a simple, plain-English query. Sure, you may get thousands of hits. But chances are, the ones near the top of the results page—or in Infoseek's Related Topics—will provide just the information you need.

That being the case, you might as well start most of your searches by simply typing whatever question or phrase comes to mind. When you get your results, look them over. Check the Related Topics. If necessary, search again within that set of results using the search form provided at the bottom of the Search Results page.

Still no joy? Then it's time to try some of Infoseek's special query operators and syntax. That's what we'll describe here. You'll also find this information summarized in the Infoseek Quick Reference on page 102.

To refine Infoseek queries:

1. Do a phrase search (**Figure 8.16**) by enclosing the words in double quotes. Or put hyphens between the words that must appear together.

2. Use a plus (+) sign in front of a word or phrase that must appear in the results. A search like the one shown in **Figure 8.17** would find sites that mention both Michael Flatley and his "Lord of the Dance" show. Without the pluses, Infoseek would find sites that mention one or the other, but not necessarily both.

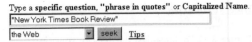

Type a **specific question, "phrase in quotes"** or **Capitalized Name**.

"New York Times Book Review"

the Web ▾ | seek | Tips

Figure 8.16 Here's an example of an Infoseek phrase search using double quotes.

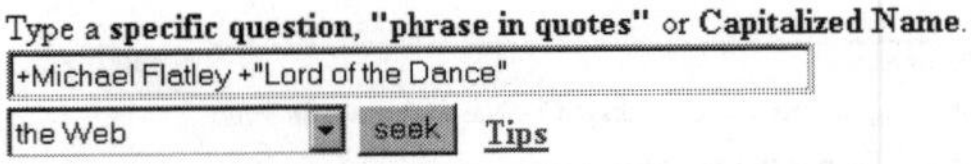

Type a **specific question, "phrase in quotes"** or **Capitalized Name**.

+Michael Flatley +"Lord of the Dance"

the Web ▾ | seek | Tips

Figure 8.17 Use a plus (+) sign in front of any word or phrase you want to be sure to find in your search results. Without the plus signs, Infoseek will treat your request as an OR search.

Type a **specific question, "phrase in quotes"** or **Capitalized Name**.

| Longfellow, Henry Wadsworth Longfellow |
| the Web ▾ | seek | Tips |

Figure 8.18 Search for multiple names by separating them with commas.

Infoseek Home

Figure 8.19 Click on the Infoseek Home icon to go back to the home page and start a new search.

Figure 8.20 The Tips button next to the Infoseek search form will lead you to lots of good information about Infoseek features and search techniques.

3. To exclude a word or phrase, put a minus (−) sign in front of it. A search for **dalmatians −Disney** would help you avoid *101 Dalmatians* sites.

Although undocumented, minus signs work in the main Ultrasmart and Ultraseek search forms. But in Ultrasmart's "Search only these results" form, using the minus sign produces a "No Results Found" message.

4. Always capitalize the first letter of proper names. That tells Infoseek to treat the words as a single name. (For names, it's not necessary to enclose the words in quotes.) If you don't use initial caps, the words will be treated like any other group of words. A search for **tiger woods**, for example, will find sites dealing with big-game hunting and Woods Hole Oceanographic Institute, along with those featuring the golf champion.

5. To search for several names, or multiple versions of the same name, use commas to separate them (**Figure 8.18**).

✔ Tips

■ To go back to the Infoseek home page and enter a new query, click on the Infoseek Home button (**Figure 8.19**). The search form will be blank when you get there.

■ If, on the other hand, you want to modify your original query, use your Web browser's Back feature to get back to the Infoseek home page. That way, your original query will be preserved and you can make whatever changes are necessary.

■ Click on Tips (**Figure 8.20**) to access Infoseek's Help information. We've done our best to give you everything you need in this chapter, but you may want to check to see if new features have been added.

Field searching with Infoseek

One of the best ways to limit your Web searches and zero in on specific information is to perform a *field search*. Typing a query like "movie review", for example, is likely to result in hundreds of thousands of hits. But if you tell Infoseek to focus on just the *titles* of Web documents, you'll find sites that *feature* movie reviews—as opposed to simply mentioning the phrase.

Infoseek offers four field-search terms that you can use in your queries: title:, url:, link:, and site:.

To search Web page titles:

Use a title: field search in your query: title:"movie review" (**Figure 8.21**). Your results will all include the phrase *movie review* in their titles (**Figure 8.22**).

To search URLs (Web addresses):

- Do a url: field search like, say, url:dinosaur (**Figure 8.23**) and you'll find Web documents with the word *dinosaur* anywhere in the Web address.

To search for hypertext links on Web pages:

- Put a link: field search in your search request: link:larrysworld.com. This comes in handy for measuring the popularity of a Web site—as indicated by the number of other sites that offer links to it. To avoid finding the site's own links, add a URL term with a minus (–) sign (**Figure 8.24**).

Type a specific question, "phrase in quotes" or Capitalized Name.
title:"movie review"
the Web
seek
Tips

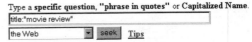

Figure 8.21 A **title:** field search like this one would find sites that feature movie reviews.

Movie Review: Star quality 39% (Size 4.5K)
EW Movie Review: Homebard 39% (Size 5.9K)
Metro Movie Guide: Write a Movie Review 39% (Size 2.8K)
EW MOVIE REVIEW 39% (Size 9.6K)
EW MOVIE REVIEW -- The Crow: City of Angels 39% (Size 5.3K)
EW Movie Review: Get Shorty 39% (Size 8.3K)
EW Movie Review: Four Rooms 39% (Size 6.3K)
EW MOVIE REVIEW 39% (Size 6.9K)

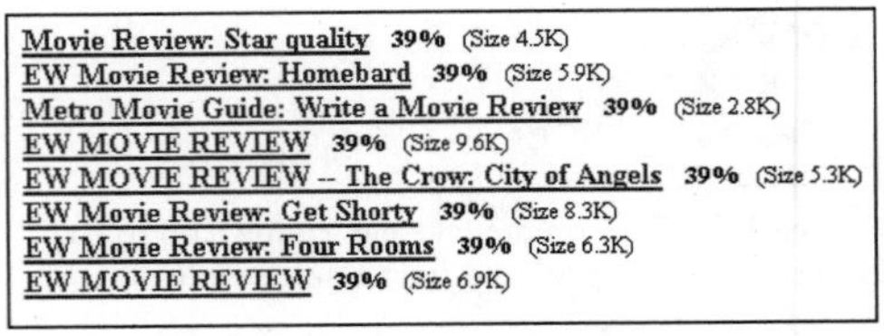

Figure 8.22 Here's a sample of the results from our "movie review" search. We've hidden the summaries to display more titles on the results page.

Type a specific question, "phrase in quotes" or Capitalized Name.
url:dinosaur
the Web
seek
Tips

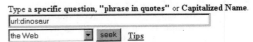

Figure 8.23 A **url:** search will find all the Web addresses containing your search term.

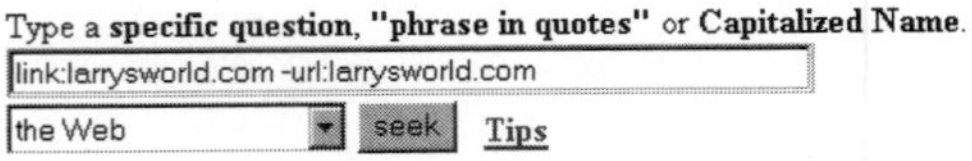

Type a specific question, "phrase in quotes" or Capitalized Name.
link:larrysworld.com -url:larrysworld.com
the Web
seek
Tips

Figure 8.24 To find all the *external* links to a particular Web site, you can combine a **link:** search with a **–url:** search. In this example, we'd find all the links to Larry Magid's Larry's World Web site, except those that he's put on his own Web page.

Type a **specific question**, **"phrase in quotes"** or **Capitalized Name**.

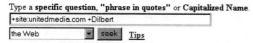

the Web ▼ | seek | Tips

Figure 8.25 Putting plus (+) signs in front of each search term as we've done here would find United Features Syndicate Web sites that cover Dilbert.

● **Imageseek**
  Site Search
  Link Search
  URL Search
  Title Search

Figure 8.26 For even easier field searching, go to the Ultraseek search page and click on one of these links to get to the Special Searches page.

Site Search

When you use the **site** special search, Infoseek will restrict the search to pages from a particular web site. You must put a + (plus sign) before each term in your search, and you must not put a space between the colon and the web site name.

+site: | seek | reset

+site:travelocity.com +Miami will find all the pages on the Travelocity web site that mention Miami.

Figure 8.27 The Ultraseek Special Searches page includes a fill-in-the-blank form like this one for each of the Infoseek field-search terms.

To search the site portion of a Web address:

■ Use a **site:** field search. To find all the Web sites for United Feature Syndicate, for example, try **site:unitedmedia.com**. To look for a specific word on all such pages, put a plus (+) sign in front of both search terms, as shown in **Figure 8.25**.

✔ Tips

■ The **site:** search term allows you to limit your search to a particular *type* of organization (based on its three-letter Internet domain), or to sites that originate in a particular country. To focus on government sites, for example, use the search term: **site:gov**. For sites in Australia, use: **site:au**.

■ Here are the **site:** search terms for the most common Internet domains. See Appendix B for a complete list of domains and country codes.

Commercial	**site:com**
Educational	**site:edu**
Government	**site:gov**
Military	**site:mil**
Network	**site:net**
Non-Profit	**site:org**

■ For fill-in-the-blank field searching, click on Ultraseek on the Infoseek home page. Then click on any one of the field-search links (**Figure 8.26**) to get to the Infoseek Special Searches page. There you'll find search boxes (like the one in **Figure 8.27**) for the four field searches described here, plus Imageseek for finding graphics files.

INFOSEEK: FIELD SEARCHING

Table 8.1

Infoseek Quick Reference		
FOR THIS TYPE OF SEARCH:	**DO THIS:**	**EXAMPLES:**
Plain-English Question	Simply type a phrase or question that expresses the idea or concept. Use as many words as necessary.	Where can I find information about "study abroad" programs in France?
Phrase Search	Type the phrase as a sequence of words surrounded by **double quotes**. Or put **hyphens** between the words that must appear together.	"youth hostel" study-abroad-program
AND Search (multiple words and phrases, each of which *must* be present)	Use a **plus sign** in front of each word or phrase that must appear in the results.	+Princeton +"financial aid"
OR Search (multiple words and phrases, any one of which may be present)	Type words or phrases separated by spaces, without any special punctuation.	grants scholarships loans
NOT Search (to exclude a word or phrase)	Use a **minus sign** in front of word or phrase you want to exclude from results.	"Shirley Temple" —cocktail
Case-Sensitive Search	Use lowercase to find *any combination* of upper- and lowercase. Use upper- and lowercase to force an exact match. The example would find *Java* but not *java* or *JAVA*.	Java
	Use initial caps to search for a person's name. To search for several names (or two versions of the same name), separate them with commas.	Steven Spielberg Hitchcock, Alfred Hitchcock
Field Search (title, URL, Web link, Web site)	Type field-search keyword in lowercase, followed by a colon and your search word or phrase.	title:"Jurassic Park" url:www.travelocity.com link:mrshowbiz.com site:disney.com
	To search a specific Web site for a word or phrase, you must put a plus (+) sign in front of each search term.	+site:disney.com +Dalmatian
Image Search	Click on Ultraseek, then Imageseek, and type your search term in the Search text box.	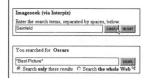
Set Search	Using the main (Ultrasmart) search form, do your first search. Scroll down to the bottom of the page, add one or more new search terms, and use the "Search Only These Results" feature to perform a new search.	
	Using the Ultraseek search form, add a **pipe symbol** (|) and another search term or phrase to your original query. Then click on Seek to look for the new term within your previous set of search results.	Oscars	"Best Picture"

Type a **specific question**, **"phrase in quotes"** or **Capitalized Name**.

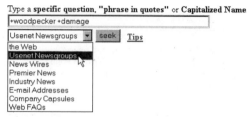

Figure 8.28 For a newsgroup search, use the drop-down menu in the Infoseek Search Form and click on Usenet Newsgroups.

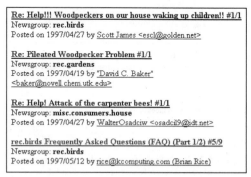

Figure 8.29 Here's an excerpt from our newsgroup Search Results page. Click on the subject line to display the full text of any message.

Figure 8.30 Newsgroup messages are displayed along with the Deja News navigation buttons.

Searching Usenet newsgroups

Infoseek's newsgroup search capability is "powered by Deja News," a service designed exclusively for searching Usenet newsgroups. The Deja News database includes more than two years' worth of newsgroup postings—going back to early 1995.

We'll cover Deja News in more detail in a later chapter. For now, let's take a look at the steps for doing basic newsgroup searches from the main Infoseek search form.

To search newsgroup postings:

1. Go to the Infoseek home page (**www.info seek.com**). Type your search request just as you would for an Infoseek Web search. Then use the drop-down menu to specify that you want to search Usenet news-groups (**Figure 8.28**).

2. Click on the Seek button to submit your query. Your results will be displayed 10 to page (**Figure 8.29**). For each message, you'll see the subject line, newsgroup it was posted to, date, and author.

3. Click on the Subject link of any message to view the entire text (**Figure 8.30**).

4. The Deja News navigation bar at the top of the page (**Figure 8.31**) makes it easy to look at other messages, view the *message thread* (other messages associated with this one), check the author profile, and post your own messages.

Figure 8.31 The navigation buttons help you move back and forth among messages, view threads and author profiles, and post your own messages and replies.

5. To try some of the more advanced Deja News features—query filters, targeted newsgroup searches, date searches, etc.—scroll down to the bottom of the page and click on Power Search (**Figure 8.32**). For an explanation of the Deja News search language, click on Help.

6. To get back to your original Search Results, click on Current Results in the Deja News navigation bar.

✔ Tips

■ You can find out more about a message's author by clicking on the Author link (e-mail address and name) provided with the message, or on the Author Profile button in the navigation bar (**Figure 8.31**). Deja News will tell you how many messages the person has posted and to which groups (**Figure 8.33**).

■ If your first newsgroup search is unsuccessful or returns too many hits, go to the bottom of the Search Results page and try a new query in the form you'll find there (**Figure 8.34**). Notice that your original query is presented in bold right above the search form, but the form itself is blank.

■ To add additional terms, you'll have to first type the original query and then add the new terms. (Infoseek doesn't allow you to do a *set search* of your newsgroup results. That capability is limited to Web searches.)

■ The Deja News search language includes Boolean operators (AND, OR, NOT, NEAR), wildcards, parentheses, and special field-search terms. Once you learn to use them, you can put them in your Infoseek newsgroup queries—even though they are not part of the official Infoseek search language. That's because when you specify a Usenet newsgroup search, Infoseek simply passes your request along to Deja News.

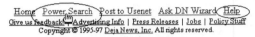

Figure 8.32 For more sophisticated newsgroup searches, click on Power Search. Click on Help for detailed information from Deja News on how to use their search language.

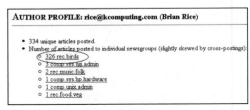

Figure 8.33 From his author profile, we can tell that this person is an active contributor to the **rec.birds** newsgroup.

Figure 8.34 You'll find a form like this one near the bottom of your Search Results page. Unlike Infoseek's Web results page, this one doesn't offer a "Search only these results" option.

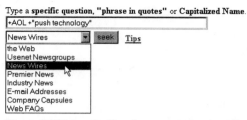

Figure 8.35 Infoseek offers three news-related search options on its main search form.

Figure 8.36 If you don't find anything with your initial search, you can easily choose one of the other Infoseek news options—right from the No Articles Found page.

Figure 8.37 Once you find an article that looks promising, click on its subject line to display the full text, as shown here.

Searching for current news with Infoseek

So far we've covered Web site and Usenet newsgroup searching with Infoseek. But what about news headlines and articles, for those times when you need more current information than you're likely to find on most Web sites and newsgroups? Infoseek offers three news-related databases you can explore from the main search form:

- **News Wires**, including Reuters, Business Wire, and PR Newswire.

- **Premier News** from seven national news organizations: the *Chicago Tribune*, CNN, the *Los Angeles Times*, MSNBC, the *New York Times*, the *San Jose Mercury News*, *USA Today*, and the *Washington Post*.

- **Industry News** from a broad range of newspapers and magazines reporting on business matters.

Start by going to the Infoseek home page (www.infoseek.com). Then simply type your query in the Search Form text box and use the drop-down menu to choose the database you want to search.

To search for current news articles:

1. Type your query and click on one of the Infoseek News options—News Wires, Premier News, or Industry News (**Figure 8.35**).

2. Click on Seek to submit it. If your first attempt is unsuccessful, you'll be given the opportunity to try one of the other news databases, or to search the World Wide Web (**Figure 8.36**).

3. When you find an article that's of interest, you can click on the subject line to display the full text (**Figure 8.37**).

✔ Tips

- For more news services, click on News Center on the Infoseek home page. There you'll find news headlines organized by category. You can also customize the news page so that it presents just the information you'd like to see on a regular basis—including local weather, TV and movie listings, cartoons, and so forth.

- If you find yourself looking for the same types of news stories on a regular basis, use the Infoseek News Center to set up a personalized "clipping service." You can choose to have your news delivered by e-mail or straight to your desktop with BackWeb.

- One of the drawbacks of Infoseek's news search service is that there's no way to sort articles by date. If you need that capability, try the Excite search engine's News Channel or News Tracker feature (nt.excite.com).

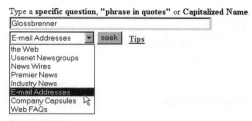

Figure 8.38 You can search for e-mail addresses right from the main Infoseek search form, as long as the name is fairly unusual.

Figure 8.39 If you're lucky, your e-mail search will return just a handful of matches.

Searching other Infoseek databases

Let's look briefly at three additional databases you can search from the Infoseek search form:

- **E-mail Addresses** from a database of over 12 million listings.

- **Company Capsules**, profiles of over 45,000 leading public and private companies in the U.S.

- **Web FAQs** (Frequently Asked Questions) on subjects ranging from hobbies and sports to computer hardware and software issues. Actually, calling these documents *Web* FAQs is a misnomer. They are more accurately described as *Usenet newsgroup* FAQs, which are available on the Web.

To search for e-mail addresses:

1. Type the person's name (first and last, or last name only) and choose E-mail Addresses from the drop-down menu (**Figure 8.38**). Then click on Seek to forward your request to the Four11 directory service.

2. Click on any entry in the resulting display (**Figure 8.39**) to get the person's e-mail address. The listing may also include land address, business and club affiliations, and so forth.

✔ Tip

- For more common names, your best bet is to go directly to Four11 (**www.four11.com**). Or use one of the Smart Info/Big Yellow options on the Infoseek home page (People & Business, Finding People, or Finding E-mail). With both Four11 and Smart Info/Big Yellow, you'll be prompted to supply additional information (city, state, country, etc.) that will help to narrow your search.

To search for company profiles:

1. Type the company name and choose Company Capsules from the drop-down menu (**Figure 8.40**).

2. Click on Seek to submit your query. The information that's displayed (**Figure 8.41**) is provided by Hoover's Online.

✔ Tip

- For more company information, click on Smart Info's Stocks/Companies link. Resources there include ticker symbol and stock quote look-ups, IPO and Internet stock information, currency exchange rates, and links to job listings and career information.

Type a **specific question, "phrase in quotes"** or **Capitalized Name**.

Amazon.com

Company Capsules ▾ | seek | Tips

the Web
Usenet Newsgroups
News Wires
Premier News
Industry News
E-mail Addresses
Company Capsules
Web FAQs

Figure 8.40 Choose Company Capsules to search Infoseek for company profiles.

Company Capsule brought to you by **Infoseek** and **HOOVER'S ONLINE**

Amazon.com, Inc.

Billed as the "earth's biggest bookstore," Amazon.com is an Internet version of a bookstore. It offers 1.5 million in-print titles and another million of the most popular -- but hard-to-find -- out-of-print books. It also sells CDs, videos, and audiotapes. Customers can search the company's online catalog by author, title, subject, or keyword. Sold at discounts of up to 40%, books are ordered directly from distributors or publishers after the customer selects a particular book; most are delivered within 2 to 3 days, although more obscure titles can take up to 6 weeks. One of the most popular Web sites, Amazon.com also offers free e-mail notification services of new books or recommendations for specified genres or subjects.

Address:	Amazon.com, Inc. 1516 Second Ave., 4th Fl. Seattle, WA 98101
Web Site:	http://www.amazon.com
Phone:	206-622-2335
Fax:	206-602-2405
CEO:	Jeffrey P. Bezos
CFO:	Joy D. Covey
HR:	Sheryl Peterson
Fiscal Year End:	12/31
Sales Year:	1996
Sales (millions $):	15.7
1-Yr. Sales Change:	3040.0%

Figure 8.41 Here's a sample company profile for the online bookseller, Amazon.com.

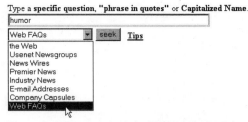

Type a **specific question, "phrase in quotes"** or **Capitalized Name**.

Figure 8.42 You can search for FAQs by choosing this option from Infoseek's drop-down menu.

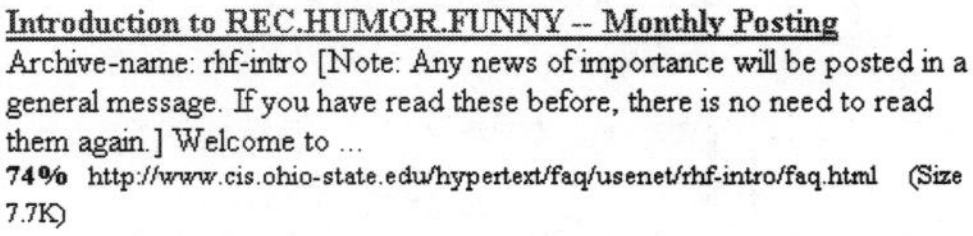

Introduction to REC.HUMOR.FUNNY -- Monthly Posting
Archive-name: rhf-intro [Note: Any news of importance will be posted in a general message. If you have read these before, there is no need to read them again.] Welcome to ...
74% http://www.cis.ohio-state.edu/hypertext/faq/usenet/rhf-intro/faq.html (Size 7.7K)

Figure 8.43 To read the complete text of a FAQ (like this one for the newsgroup **rec.humor.funny**), all you have to do is click on the title in the top line.

To search for newsgroup FAQs:

1. Type your search term and choose Web FAQs from the drop-down menu (**Figure 8.42**).

2. Your results will be displayed in the standard Infoseek format, with a subject line, summary, and Web address (**Figure 8.43**). Click on the subject line to display the FAQ.

✔ Tips

■ Most newsgroups publish a FAQ for new users. Before posting your first message to a particular newsgroup, do a Web FAQ search on the group's name (**rec.humor.funny**, for example) to locate the new user FAQ.

■ FAQs are often quite long, and you can't always tell from their titles whether they are going to contain the information you want. Before printing a FAQ, use your browser's Find feature to search for a couple of keywords. You'll save yourself time (and paper) in the long run.

INFOSEEK: SEARCHING OTHER DATABASES

Power searching with Ultraseek

As we mentioned at the beginning of this chapter, Infoseek offers a service for more experienced searchers called Ultraseek. It looks and acts a lot like the search service on the Infoseek home page (Ultrasmart). But with Ultraseek, the Web directory isn't displayed unless you specifically ask to see it.

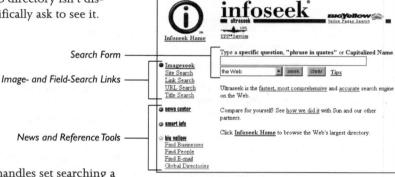

Search Form

Image- and Field-Search Links

News and Reference Tools

Figure 8.44 The Ultraseek search page.

In addition, Ultraseek handles set searching a bit differently than Ultrasmart. And it's on the Ultraseek search page that you'll find Infoseek's links for doing image and field searches using fill-in-the-blank forms.

To search using Infoseek's Ultraseek service:

1. Go to the Infoseek home page (www.infoseek.com) and click on Ultraseek to get to the main Ultraseek search page (**Figure 8.44**).

2. Type your query in the Ultraseek Search Form (**Figure 8.45**) just as you would for an Ultrasmart search. The one difference you'll notice is the presence of a Clear button, which you can use to remove—with a single click—anything you've typed in the Search Form text box.

3. Your search results will be presented 10 to a page (**Figure 8.46**), just as they are for an Ultrasmart search.

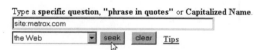

Figure 8.45 Ultraseek's Search Form looks just like the one on the Infoseek home page, except for the presence of a Clear button you can use to wipe the slate clean.

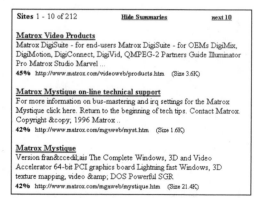

Figure 8.46 Here's an excerpt from our Ultraseek search for Matrox.com Web sites.

You searched for **site:matrox.com**

| site:matrox.com | seek | **Tips** |

Figure 8.47 Your Ultraseek Search Results page will include a form like this one for doing a follow-on search.

You searched for **site:matrox.com**

| site:matrox.com|drivers | seek | **Tips** |

Figure 8.48 Ultraseek doesn't offer a "Search only these results" button for doing set searches. Instead, you must use a pipe symbol (|) followed by the word or phrase you want to add to your query.

Sites 1 - 10 of 29   **Hide Summaries**   **next 10**

Matrox Millennium Windows 95 drivers and utilities
Click here to return to /millennm /win95/ Millennium Windows 95 Drivers
1677_341.exe 1.27 MB - Mar. 17/97 Millennium Win 95 driver Version
3.41 These are the latest Win 95 ...
56% http://www.matrox.com/mgaweb/ftp_mw95.htm   (Size 4.5K)

Figure 8.49 Our Ultraseek set search helped us reduce the number of hits from over 200 to just 29, including this one that offered exactly what we needed.

● **Imageseek**
Site Search
Link Search
URL Search
Title Search

Figure 8.50 For easy, fill-in-the-blank image and field searching, click on one of these links on the Ultraseek search page.

To refine your Ultraseek queries:

1. If you get too many hits, scroll down to the bottom of the Search Results page, where you'll find an abbreviated version of the Ultraseek Search Form (**Figure 8.47**). Your original query will be shown in bold above the Search Form, and it will also be displayed in the text box.

2. To search again, looking at just those sites identified by your initial query (set searching), put a pipe symbol (|) right after your original request, followed by an additional word or phrase. In **Figure 8.48**, we've chosen to search our original results looking for the word *drivers*. That helped us zero in on just the site we needed (**Figure 8.49**), within the first 10 items of a very manageable 29-item list.

✔ Tip

■ With Ultraseek, you can search fields by putting one of the field-search terms (**site:**, **link:**, **url:**, or **title:**) in your query, as we did in **Figure 8.45**. Or click on any image- or field-search link (**Figure 8.50**) to get to Infoseek's Special Searches page, where you can do image and field searches using fill-in-the-blank forms.

LYCOS

What you can search

- World Wide Web
- Reviews of top-rated Web sites
- Multimedia database (graphics, photo, video, and sound files)
- Travel guides for over 800 cities
- Personal home pages
- E-mail directory
- Stock quotes and market news
- Road maps and driving directions

Contact information

Lycos, Inc.
Framingham, MA
508/424-0400
www.lycos.com

One of the oldest Internet search engines, Lycos, was developed by Michael "Fuzzy" Mauldin at Carnegie Mellon University in 1994. The name comes from the Latin word for wolf spider, a creature Mauldin has long admired for its tenacity at searching for and finding its prey.

Now a commercial enterprise, Lycos bills itself as "Your Personal Internet Guide" whose mission is to take the confusion and chaos out of the Internet. That's the gentle, avuncular side of the search engine's persona. The hipper, less sympathetic side suggests (throughout the Web site and in a recent ad campaign) that you "Get Lycos or get lost." A search engine with an attitude!

Fortunately for those who are new to the Net and to search engines, the "Uncle Lycos" personality is the one that comes through most of the time. The basic Lycos search page does indeed make the Net less confusing, with its 18 topic guides and very simple search form. You have to dig deep into the help information (or use the more sophisticated Lycos Pro with Java Power Panel) to find any mention of Boolean operators and search syntax.

Lycos doesn't currently offer newsgroup searching, so you'll have to look to Deja News or one of the other search engines for that capability.

✔ Tips

- One of the best reasons to use Lycos is to access its ratings and reviews of exceptional Web sites, known as the Lycos Top 5%. Prepared by a staff of 25 Web-savvy editors, the ratings cover site content, design, and overall appeal. The reviews are generally informative and well written, and they give you a good place to start exploring a specific topic.

- Lycos is also an excellent choice for locating multimedia files. You can easily search for graphics, video, and sound files using a drop-down menu on the Lycos search form. With a properly equipped Web browser, you can even view or listen to the files as they are being downloaded to your computer.

- To customize your Web browser for Lycos, click on Free Software on the Lycos home page. You'll find information and links for downloading Lycos QuickSearch, as well as plug-ins and other Web browser tools.

- If you pay attention to the banner ads on Lycos, you'll notice that they're often related to the search terms you typed for your latest query. Lycos has one of the online industry's most sophisticated ad targeting capabilities. Of course, they're not always right. We did a search for Cat Stevens and the next banner ad to appear featured a pet cat Web site!

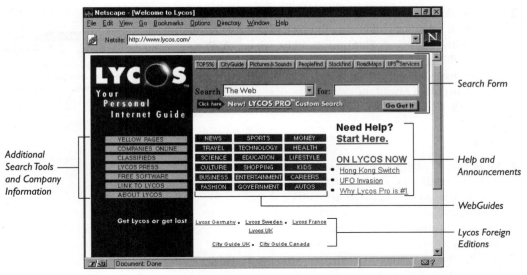

Figure 9.1 The Lycos home page.

Search Form

Additional Search Tools and Company Information

Help and Announcements

WebGuides

Lycos Foreign Editions

Using the main Lycos search page

Before doing any real searching, let's take a look at how the Lycos home page (**Figure 9.1**) is organized. To get there, point your Web browser at **www.lycos.com**. For your first visit, the key features to zero in on are the search form and the topic-specific WebGuides.

To use the search form:

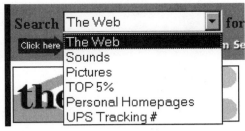

Figure 9.2 To search a database other than the Web, use the search form's drop-down menu.

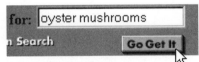

Figure 9.3 The search form text box and submit button.

1. Choose a database from the drop-down menu (**Figure 9.2**). Most of the time, you'll use the default setting to search the Web. Other options include the Lycos multimedia databases (Pictures and Sounds), reviews of top-rated Web sites (Top 5%), personal home pages, and, for frequent shippers, the UPS (United Parcel Service) package-tracking database.

2. Type some search terms in the search form text box and click on Go Get It to submit the search (**Figure 9.3**).

3. Your results will be presented 10 to a page. Scan the descriptions and, if necessary, try another search. This time, in addition to adding or changing terms, you can specify that you want to look for All the Words instead of Any of the Words (**Figure 9.4**).

Figure 9.4 For a follow-up search, you can use this form. It includes a drop-down menu that allows you to specify All the Words or Any of the Words, a feature not offered on the Lycos home page.

✔ Tips

■ Lycos doesn't offer much in the way of tools for refining a query on the basic search form. According to the help information, you can search for phrases by enclosing words in quotation marks. And you can include or exclude words by putting plus (+) and minus (–) signs in front of them. But in our experience, you get mixed results when you use punctuation of any kind in the basic search form.

■ Your best bet is to search on two or three terms, being as specific as possible. To find information on identifying mushrooms, for example, try a search like **edible mushrooms** or **mycology poisonous**. If you don't find what you're looking for in the first couple of pages, try a Lycos Pro with Java Power Panel search (described later in the chapter) or use another search engine.

■ For a summary of Lycos search terms and syntax, see the Lycos Basic Search Quick Reference on page 118.

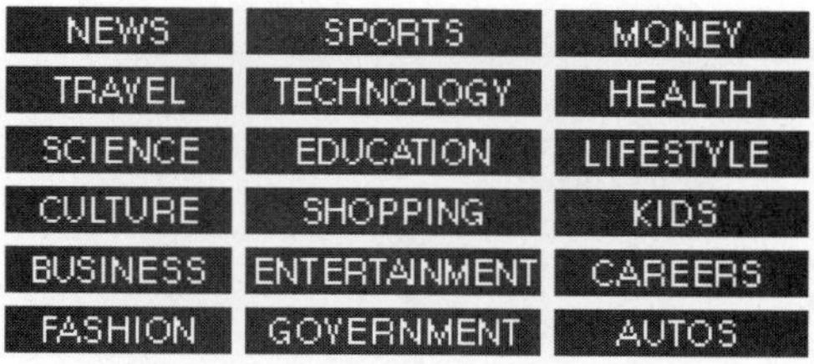

Figure 9.5 The Lycos WebGuide menu.

Figure 9.6 Here's the Fashion WebGuide. News headlines, Power Searches, mini-guides, and a Top 5% topic list are standard features of all Lycos WebGuides.

Fashion Sites

- Apparel
- Beauty & Cosmetics
- Fashion Accessories
- Fashion Advice
- Apparel Sites

Figure 9.7 To access reviews and ratings for the best sites, look for the Top 5% logo and topic list on WebGuide pages.

To search by topic using WebGuides:

1. Click on one of the 18 WebGuide topic buttons in the center of the Lycos home page (**Figure 9.5**).

2. Each WebGuide contains news headlines, one or more mini-guides on interesting subjects, and several pre-defined searches (called Power Searches) to help you get started exploring a topic. (See **Figure 9.6** for a sample WebGuide.)

3. Best of all, you'll find a mini-directory of top-rated sites (**Figure 9.7**). Click on any item in this list to locate the reviews and ratings for sites chosen by the Lycos editors—sometimes just a handful of sites, sometimes as many as 25. You may not always agree with the editors' selections and evaluations, but at least you'll have a manageable number of sites to explore when you begin researching a topic.

Table 9.1

Lycos Basic Search Quick Reference		
FOR THIS TYPE OF SEARCH:	DO THIS:	EXAMPLES:
Phrase Search	Type the phrase as a sequence of words surrounded by **double quotes**.	"oyster mushroom"
AND Search (multiple words and phrases, each of which *must* be present)	Use a **plus sign** in front of each word or phrase that must appear in the results.	"oyster mushroom" +recipe
OR Search (multiple words and phrases, any one of which may be present)	Type words and phrases separated by a space without any special punctuation. Lycos will search for documents containing either term.	mushrooms mycology
NOT Search (to exclude a word or phrase)	Use a **minus sign** in front of a word or phrase you want to exclude from the results.	magazine —computer
Plain-English Search	Not available on basic search form. Use Lycos Pro with Java Power Panel and choose The Natural Language Query option.	
Boolean Search (including Proximity Search)	Not available on basic search form. Use Lycos Pro with Java Power Panel and choose The Boolean Expression option.	
Multimedia Files	Choose Sounds or Pictures in the search form's drop-down menu. Or click on the Pictures & Sounds button at the top of the Lycos home page.	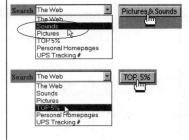
Web Site Reviews	To search for reviews, choose Top 5% in the search form's drop-down menu. To browse the directory of reviews, click on the Top 5% button at the top of every Lycos page.	

Figure 9.8 To get to the Topic Directory, click on the Top 5% button on the Lycos home page.

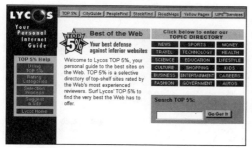

Figure 9.9 The Top 5% Topic Directory page.

Searching for the best Web sites

You may find another search engine you like better for day-to-day use, but when it comes to tracking down the *best* Web sites, Lycos is hard to beat. First of all, they make a selection for you and present no more than 25 sites on a given topic. Second, they provide ratings and reviews for the sites that are among the most thorough and detailed you'll find anywhere on the Internet.

There are three ways you can explore top-rated sites with Lycos:

- To search for the best sites relating to a specific search term, use the Top 5% option on the search form's drop-down menu.

- To find the best sites on a particular topic, select the appropriate WebGuide and use the Top 5% mini-directory presented there.

- To browse the entire Top 5% database by topic, use the Topic Directory.

We covered the first two methods earlier in this chapter. Here, we'll take a look at using the Lycos Top 5% Topic Directory to discover the "best of the Web."

To access the Top 5% Topic Directory:

1. Go to the Lycos home page (www.lycos.com) and click on Top 5% in the row of buttons across the top of the page (**Figure 9.8**).

2. That will take you to a page like the one shown in **Figure 9.9**. To read about the rating categories and selection process, use the Top 5% Help links on the left side of the page. To access the Topic Directory, click on one of the 18 topic categories on the right side of the page. (You can also do a Top 5% search using the search form just below the Topic Directory.)

3. Clicking on a topic category takes you to a set of subtopics like the ones for Government shown in **Figure 9.10**.

4. Choose a subtopic to get to the list of up to 25 recommended sites. **Figure 9.11** shows the first two sites from the U.S. Federal Government subtopic, with their ratings and the first three lines of their reviews.

5. To read the complete review, click on the site title. **Figure 9.12** shows the review for the Thomas Legislative Information site, which appeared farther down the list of recommended U.S. Federal Government sites.

✔ Tips

- If you'd like to actually visit a site after reading its review, use the link labeled "Click here to go directly to site."

- By default, Web site reviews are presented based on their *overall* ratings, with the highest-rated site listed first. To choose a different criterion, click on one of the other options presented at the top of the list: content rating, design rating, date reviewed, or alphabetic (**Figure 9.13**).

Government
Elections
International Politics
Political Parties & Organizations
Political Personalities
US Federal Government
US State & Local Government

Figure 9.10 Each of the 18 topics in the Topic Directory is broken down further into subtopics like these for Government.

Government→ US Federal Government

1) Army Tour
Uncle Sam wants you to be all you can be in his army, and he's got one heck of a Web site to talk you into it. It's not that there's any stunning information here -- just the usual lines about ...
Content: 64 Design: 88 Overall: 90

2) U.S. Postal Service Address Quality and Zip Code Lookup
Thanks to the U.S. Postal Service (derided all too casually by e-mail fanatics), you can now find most any zip code you like -- online! When we typed in America's most famous address, 1600 ...
Content: 88 Design: 52 Overall: 90

Figure 9.11 A sample of what you'll find for each subtopic—the first two recommended sites in a list of 25.

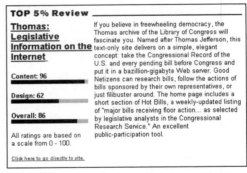

TOP 5% Review

Thomas: Legislative Information on the Internet

Content: 96

Design: 62

Overall: 86

All ratings are based on a scale from 0 - 100.

Click here to go directly to site.

If you believe in freewheeling democracy, the Thomas archive of the Library of Congress will fascinate you. Named after Thomas Jefferson, this text-only site delivers on a simple, elegant concept: take the Congressional Record of the U.S. and every pending bill before Congress and put it in a bazillion-gigabyte Web server. Good Netizens can research bills, follow the actions of bills sponsored by their own representatives, or just filibuster around. The home page includes a short section of Hot Bills, a weekly-updated listing of "major bills receiving floor action... as selected by legislative analysts in the Congressional Research Service." An excellent public-participation tool.

Figure 9.12 A typical review with ratings on the left and an informative review on the right.

Click one of the following to sort by:

Content Rating	Design Rating	Overall Rating	Date Reviewed	Alphabetic

Figure 9.13 To present the reviews in a different order, click on one of these options. The default is Overall Rating.

Search
The Web
for:
Botticelli Venus
Go Get It
The Web
Sounds
Pictures
TOP 5%
Personal Homepages
UPS Tracking #

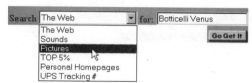

Figure 9.14 To search for images, be sure to select Pictures from the drop-down menu before submitting your query.

1) Birth Of Venus - Botticelli
http://stoner.eps.mcgill.ca/~bud/craters/images/b_venus.gif
(159k) [100%, 3 of 3 terms]

2) "Birth of Venus" Botticelli
http://www.datatamers.com/~blach/gallery/botticelli.gif
(0k) [96%, 3 of 3 terms]

3) Botticelli: The Birth of Venus
http://www.cs.helsinki.fi/~wikla/botticelli.gif
(196k) [95%, 3 of 3 terms]

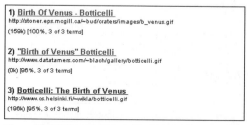

Figure 9.15 Your image search results will look like this.

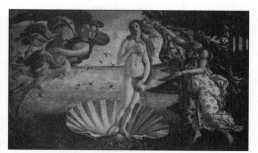

Figure 9.16 Finding this GIF file of Botticelli's "Birth of Venus" was a snap using the Lycos Pictures search option.

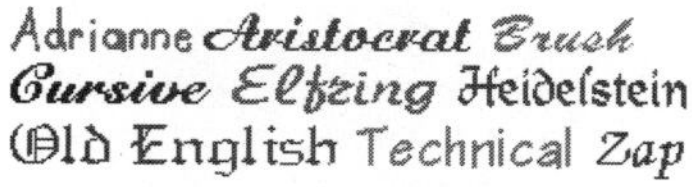

Adrianne Aristocrat Brush
Cursive Elfring Heidelstein
Old English Technical Zap

Figure 9.17 To search for interesting fonts like these, try a Pictures search on the phrase **"font collection."**

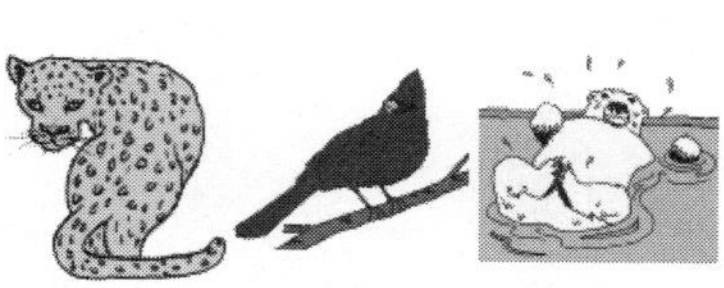

Figure 9.18 Clip art like this is easy to find with a Lycos Pictures search.

Searching for images and sounds

Lycos is a particularly good search engine to use for locating image and sound files—photos, fonts, clip art, videos, music, strange noises—you name it. You can find all of these types of files by searching the Web, of course, but Lycos makes the quest easier by providing a Pictures and Sounds database that you can explore right from the basic search form.

To search for images:

1. Go to the Lycos home page (www.lycos.com) and use the search form's drop-down menu to choose Pictures. Then type your search terms in the search form text box (**Figure 9.14**).
2. Click on Go Get It to submit your search. Your results will look like the ones in **Figure 9.15**. For each image, you'll be given the title, Web address, file size, and information on how well it meets your search criteria.
3. To display an image, click on its title. In this case, the very first item was an excellent rendering of Botticelli's "Birth of Venus" (**Figure 9.16**).

✔ Tips

- Use your Web browser's File/Save As option to name an image and save it to a particular location on your computer.
- To look for a specific type of graphics file, add that information to your search—**gif** or **jpeg**, for example. To locate video (MOV) files, include the phrase "**mov format**" in your query.
- To locate fonts or clip art like the examples shown in **Figures 9.17** and **9.18**, try a Pictures search on the phrase "**font collection**" or "**clip art collection**".

To search for sound files:

1. Click on Sounds in the search form's drop-down menu, type your query, and then submit the search by clicking on Go Get It (**Figure 9.19**).

2. Your results will look like the excerpt from our James Taylor search shown in **Figure 9.20**. You'll find the sound file's location and filename in the second line of each item on the list.

3. Click on any item to start the download process. A few seconds later, it will start playing through your system's speakers.

✔ Tips

■ You can search for a specific type of sound file (AU, MID, SND, WAV) by including that information in your query.

■ To actually go to one of the sites located by a Sounds search, use your Web browser's Copy and Paste function to put its URL in the browser's Location or Address box.

■ If you have trouble viewing or listening to files from the Pictures and Sounds database, you may be missing some of the special programs (called plug-ins) you need for multimedia. Click on the Pictures & Sounds button above the Lycos search form (**Figure 9.21**) to find out more about plug-ins and to download the ones you need.

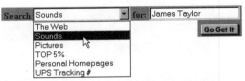

Figure 9.19 To find sound files for a favorite performer, choose Sounds from the drop-down menu.

Figure 9.20 The results of a Sounds search are quite brief. Click on the first line to play the sound. The second line tells you the filename and where to find it on the Web.

Figure 9.21 For help with plug-ins and other aspects of multimedia, click on Pictures & Sounds.

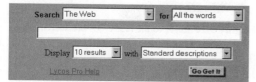

Figure 9.22 The Lycos Pro search form, accessible by clicking on Lycos Pro Custom Search on the Lycos home page.

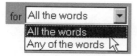

Figure 9.23 The main advantage of the Lycos Pro search form is that it lets you specify in advance whether you want to do an AND or OR search.

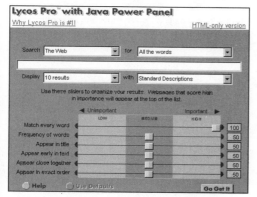

Figure 9.24 The more sophisticated Lycos Pro with the Java Power Panel search form.

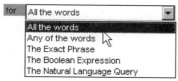

Figure 9.25 The Lycos Pro with Java Power Panel form gives you more search options: Phrase searching, Boolean expressions, and Natural Language (or Plain-English) queries.

Custom searching with Lycos Pro

If you're relatively new to online searching, you may well find that the search form on the Lycos home page provides all the capability you need for most of your searches. With experience, however, you're likely to want more advanced features—like Boolean searching or controlling the order in which your search results are presented. That's what Lycos Pro is all about. There are actually two Lycos Pro search forms:

Lycos Pro Custom Search (**Figure 9.22**) allows you to search the Web and other Lycos databases using a drop-down menu, just like the one on the basic search form. The "customizing" comes in the ability to specify up front whether you want to perform an AND (All the Words) or OR (Any of the Words) search—also from a drop-down menu (**Figure 9.23**). You can also tell Lycos how to display your results. The default is 10 per page with Standard descriptions, but you can request up to 40 per page with Brief descriptions or with URLs only (Just the Links).

Lycos Pro with Java Power Panel (**Figure 9.24**) includes all the features offered on the non-Java form, plus options for doing phrase searches, natural language (i.e., Plain-English) queries, or Boolean expressions (**Figure 9.25**). The Java Power Panel lets you give more or less weight to certain factors (and thus control the order in which your results are displayed).

Sophisticated searchers will probably find the Lycos Pro/Java Power Panel approach somewhat cumbersome and less intuitive than other search engines. But it's worth a look if you plan to do most of your searching with Lycos.

To search with Lycos Pro:

1. Click on Lycos Pro Custom Search (**Figure 9.26**) on the Lycos home page (www.lycos.com) to get to the first search form (**Figure 9.22**).

2. If you have a Java-enabled browser, continue on to the second form by clicking on Lycos Pro with Java Power Panel (**Figure 9.27**). (You may not use the Power Panel, but you'll appreciate the options for Phrase, Natural Language, and Boolean searching.)

3. Type your query in the text box. On the Java form, Boolean operators are allowed as long as you specify in the drop-down menu that you are doing a Boolean search (**Figure 9.25**). For details on search commands, see the Lycos Pro Quick References on pages 125–126.)

4. Use the drop-down menus to change the settings that tell Lycos what to search (Web, Pictures, Sounds, etc.) and how to display the results.

5. On the Java form, review the slider positions (**Figure 9.28**). The defaults give the greatest weight (100) to matching all the words, with the others set at medium (50). You can change that by using your mouse to move the sliders left or right.

6. Click on Go Get It to submit the query.

✔ Tip

- Changing the Java Power Panel settings has no effect on which sites are located by your search. It simply alters the order in which the results are displayed.

Figure 9.26 To get to the first Lycos Pro search form, click on this link on the Lycos home page.

Figure 9.27 For more powerful search options, continue on to Lycos Pro with Java Power Panel using this link.

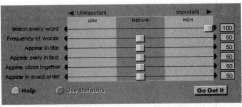

Figure 9.28 The Java Power Panel lets you control the order in which your results are displayed by moving the square sliders left or right.

Table 9.2

Lycos Pro Custom Search Quick Reference		
FOR THIS TYPE OF SEARCH:	**DO THIS:**	**EXAMPLES:**
Phrase Search	Type the phrase as sequence of words surrounded by **double quotes**.	"French table wines"
AND Search (multiple words and phrases, each of which *must* be present)	Type the words (or phrases in quotes) in the search form text box and choose All the Words from the drop-down menu.	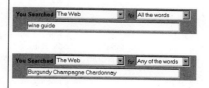
OR Search (multiple words and phrases, any one of which may be present)	Type the words (or phrases in quotes) in the search form text box and choose Any of the Words from the drop-down menu.	
NOT Search (to exclude a word or phrase)	Use a **minus sign** in front of a word or phrase you want to exclude from the results.	Chardonnay —California
Plain-English Search	Not available with Lycos Pro Custom Search. Use Lycos Pro with Java Power Panel and choose The Natural Language Query option.	
Boolean Search (including Proximity Search)	Not available with Lycos Pro Custom Search. Use Lycos Pro with Java Power Panel and choose The Boolean Expression option.	
Multimedia Files	Choose Sounds or Pictures in the search form's drop-down menu and type your query using any of the commands described in this Quick Reference.	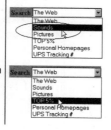
Web Site Reviews	Choose Top 5% in the search form's drop-down menu and type your query using any of the commands described in this Quick Reference.	

Table 9.3

Lycos Pro with Java Power Panel Quick Reference

FOR THIS TYPE OF SEARCH:	DO THIS:	EXAMPLES:
Phrase	Type the phrase in the search form text box and choose The Exact Phrase from the drop-down menu. Note that you don't need quotation marks if you specify The Exact Phrase.	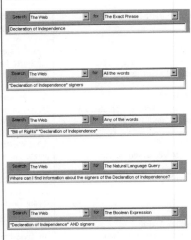
AND Search (multiple words and phrases, each of which *must* be present)	Type the words (or phrases in quotes) in the search form text box and choose All the Words from the drop-down menu.	
OR Search (multiple words and phrases, any one of which may be present)	Type the words (or phrases in quotes) in the search form text box and choose Any of the Words from the drop-down menu.	
Plain-English Search	Type your question in the search form text box and choose The Natural Language Query from the drop-down menu.	
Boolean Search	Type your query in the search form text box using Boolean operators and choose The Boolean Expression from the drop-down menu.	

You can use any of the following Boolean operators. (We've used uppercase, but lowercase works as well.)

- *Combine* terms with AND, OR, NOT.

  Leonardo AND Michelangelo
  Chico OR Zeppo
  Marx NOT Brothers

- *Require* or *exclude* terms with plus (+) or minus (−) signs. Produces much the same results as AND and NOT.

  Leonardo +Michelangelo
  Marx −Brothers

- For *phrases*, use quotation marks.

  "Panama hat"

- For more *complex queries*, group search terms with parentheses, or with [ ], < >, or { }. This is often referred to as a *nested search*.

  "clip art" AND (animals OR tiger)

- For *proximity searches*, use ADJ (words adjacent to each other in any order) or NEAR (within 25 words). Also available (but less useful) are FAR (at least 25 words apart), and BEFORE.

  car ADJ race
  "Jimmy Stewart" NEAR career

- For more precise proximity searches, add a forward slash (/) and any word count you choose: **NEAR/5**, for example, to look for search terms within five words of each other.

  "Men in Black" NEAR/5 review

Multimedia Files	Choose Sounds or Pictures in the search form's drop-down menu and type your query using any of the commands described in this Quick Reference.	
Web Site Reviews	Choose Top 5% in the search form's drop-down menu and type your query using any of the commands described in this Quick Reference.	

Using other Lycos search tools

Before leaving Lycos, we need to introduce you to several additional search tools that may come in handy from time to time. You'll find links for all of them on the Lycos home page (www.lycos.com) and on most other Lycos pages.

We encourage you to explore the tools on your own, but here's a quick rundown of what they are and how to reach them:

- **Classifieds**. The Internet provides a great meeting ground for buyers and sellers of used merchandise like computers, musical instruments, VCRs, and so forth. One of the most active sites for such transactions is Classifieds 2000, which you can reach by clicking on Classifieds on the Lycos home page.

  You can search the Classifieds 2000 database by category, or place your own ads for free. The site also provides information about services like Trade-Direct (www.trade-direct.com), which will act as an intermediary so buyers and sellers can trade with confidence.

- **Company Information**. You'll find two search tools for locating company information on the Lycos home page: Companies Online and Yellow Pages.

  Click on Companies Online to search Dun and Bradstreet's database of some 100,000 public and private companies. Searching is free, but you'll need to complete the online registration form to get access to information like annual sales, number of employees, and so forth.

  Click on Yellow Pages to locate businesses using GTE SuperPages Interactive Services. You can search by business name, category,

keyword, city, state, Zip code, or phone
number. Or you can look for businesses
within a certain distance of a location
you specify.

- **Maps and Driving Directions**. Click on
RoadMaps for this Lycos feature offering
"custom maps" and driving directions.
The maps will never replace the full-size,
folded ones you buy or get from your
automobile club. But we've used the driving directions on occasion to get a quick
handle on the best route to a particular
destination (maximum distance: 300
miles). For longer trips, try MapQuest
(www.mapquest.com) instead.

- **People-Finding Tools**. You can search for
phone numbers, land, and e-mail addresses
for anyone in the United States using a
simple, fill-in-the-blank form. To access the
form, look for the PeopleFind button.

- **Stock Quotes**. For stock quotes and market news, click on StockFind. Quotes are
provided by PC Quote with a 20-minute
delay.

- **Travel Guides**. Lycos currently offers
searchable guides to over 800 cities in the
U.S., Canada, Europe, and Australia. More
are planned for Africa, the Middle East,
and Oceania. Click on CityGuide to search
for travel destinations.

- **United Parcel Service**. Track UPS ship-
ments, download software, and find your
nearest UPS drop-off location by clicking
on the UPS Services button.

2

Yahoo!

www.yahoo.com

What you can search

- World Wide Web
- Detailed Web directory
- Usenet newsgroups
- Current news articles
- Net events and chat
- E-mail directory

Contact information

Yahoo! Inc.
Santa Clara, CA
408/731-3300
408/731-3301 (fax)
www.yahoo.com

Yahoo! is often referred to as the granddaddy of directory-based Web search tools. It was developed in 1994 at Stanford University by David Filo and Jerry Yang, Ph.D. candidates in electrical engineering. At the time, they were simply interested in keeping track of their personal favorite sites on the Internet—mostly Gopher, FTP, and Telnet locations. (The World Wide Web wasn't much of a factor back then.) But before too long, word got out and they began getting hundreds of requests a day alerting them to wonderful sites that should be added to the Yahoo! directory.

Eventually the workload started interfering with their Ph.D.s, so Filo and Yang dropped out of school, raised a million dollars in venture capital, and turned their dorm-room project into one of the Internet's most popular (and successful) businesses.

From the very beginning, what has set Yahoo! apart from other search engines is its hierarchical approach to organizing the information that's available on the Internet and the World Wide Web. Its directory and classification system are far more detailed than those offered by rival services. The *San Jose Mercury News* has called Yahoo! "the closest in spirit to the work of Linnaeus, the 18th-century botanist whose classification system organized the natural world."

Yahoo!

4

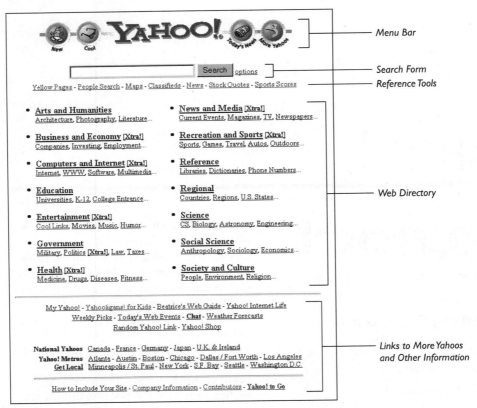

Figure 10.1 The Yahoo! home page.

Yahoo! is also more of a "hands-on" operation than other search engines. Instead of relying on automated search robots or spider programs, Yahoo! gets most of its information about new sites from human beings—Internet users and Web site creators who complete a form describing the site and recommending where it should be placed in the Yahoo! directory.

Certain rules apply. For example, commercial sites are limited to two categories and must be placed under Business and Economy. Personal home pages go in the Entertainment/People category. But none of this happens automatically. All submissions are reviewed by Yahoo! staffers, and the company reserves the right to make the final decision about how sites are

classified. Those found to be totally lacking in content might never find their way into the Yahoo! database.

Because of this hands-on approach, the Yahoo! database isn't as large as those offered by other search engines, and it may take longer for a site to get added to the database. Furthermore, Yahoo! doesn't index the full text of Web pages, so your search is limited to the site's topic category, title, and brief description entered in the database.

None of this is really a problem, however. Use Yahoo! when you want to explore in an organized fashion what the Internet has to offer on a topic, or when you want to identify a few really good sites on a particular subject.

YAHOO!

music boxes   Search options

Figure 10.2 The Yahoo! search form.

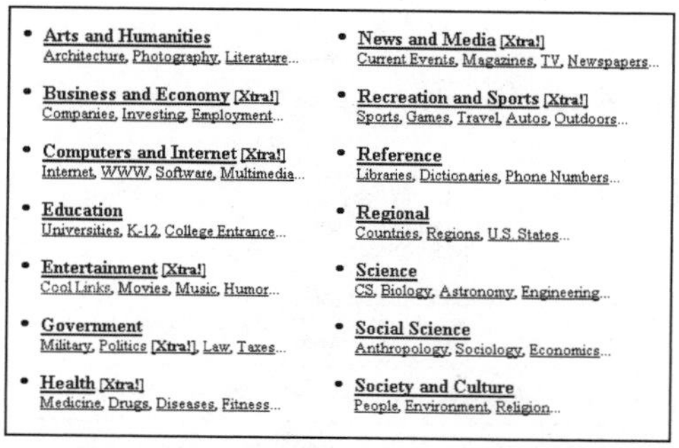

- **Arts and Humanities**
  Architecture, Photography, Literature...

- **Business and Economy [Xtra!]**
  Companies, Investing, Employment...

- **Computers and Internet [Xtra!]**
  Internet, WWW, Software, Multimedia...

- **Education**
  Universities, K-12, College Entrance...

- **Entertainment [Xtra!]**
  Cool Links, Movies, Music, Humor...

- **Government**
  Military, Politics [Xtra!], Law, Taxes...

- **Health [Xtra!]**
  Medicine, Drugs, Diseases, Fitness...

- **News and Media [Xtra!]**
  Current Events, Magazines, TV, Newspapers...

- **Recreation and Sports [Xtra!]**
  Sports, Games, Travel, Autos, Outdoors...

- **Reference**
  Libraries, Dictionaries, Phone Numbers...

- **Regional**
  Countries, Regions, U.S. States...

- **Science**
  CS, Biology, Astronomy, Engineering...

- **Social Science**
  Anthropology, Sociology, Economics...

- **Society and Culture**
  People, Environment, Religion...

Figure 10.3 Yahoo!'s Web directory. Each major topic leads to a detailed subject outline.

Keep in mind that Yahoo!'s directory and classification system is second to none, and well worth a place in your "searcher's toolkit."

✔ Tip

- For more about Yahoo! (including conflicting stories about the origin of the name and how to buy a Yahoo! T-shirt), click on Company Information on the Yahoo! home page.

Using Yahoo!'s main search page

To get to the Yahoo! home page, point your Web browser at **www.yahoo.com**. That's where you'll find the Yahoo! search form and Web directory, as well as links to other Yahoo! features and reference tools (**Figure 10.1**).

When you know exactly what you're looking for, your best bet is to use the Yahoo! search form (**Figure 10.2**). Just type some words or phrases in the text box (we'll cover search syntax later in the chapter) and click on the Search button.

Within seconds, you'll be presented with a list of Yahoo! topic categories and Web sites that match your request. If no matches are found, Yahoo! automatically performs a full-text search of the Web using AltaVista.

For those occasions when, instead of doing a targeted search, you want to explore the Web for information on a broad subject, use the Web directory (**Figure 10.3**). Click on one of the 14 major topic categories and then on the link labeled "Sub Category Listing." What you'll find is an exceptionally detailed outline (the one for Arts & Humanities, for example, is over 60 pages), with every entry leading to specific Web sites.

To explore other features on the Yahoo! home page:

1. Click on the icons in the Yahoo! menu bar (**Figure 10.4**) for these features:
   - **What's New**. Sites added to Yahoo! in the past week. Plus daily features like Dilbert, Letterman's Top Ten, and Net Events.
   - **What's Cool**. Yahoo!'s selections especially of amusing, unusual, or useful sites.
   - **Today's News**. Headline news, updated hourly.
   - **More Yahoos**. Special Yahoo! directories—Yahooligans! for Kids, Net Events & Chat, Yahoo! Metros (for major U.S. cities), and National Yahoos (for Asia, Canada, France, Germany, Japan, and the United Kingdom).

2. Try Yahoo!'s menu of Reference Tools (**Figure 10.5**):
   - **Yellow Pages**. Business lookups, plus maps and driving directions.
   - **People Search**. Telephone numbers, land, and e-mail addresses.
   - **Maps**. Custom maps and driving directions for U.S. locations (maximum distance: 300 miles).
   - **Classifieds**. Search by geography or product and place your own ads for free.
   - **News**. Daily news headlines. (Same as Today's News on menu bar.)
   - **Stock Quotes**. Stock market news, historical data, and quotes.
   - **Sports Scores**. All the major sports.

3. Scroll down to the bottom of the Yahoo! home page (**Figure 10.6**) for links to many of the same features found on the Yahoo! menu bar and Reference Tools menu.

✔ Tip

- To get back to the Yahoo! home page at any time, click on the Yahoo! logo at the top of the page, or look for the Yahoo Home button (**Figure 10.7**) found on some pages.

Figure 10.4 The Yahoo! menu bar.

Yellow Pages - People Search - Maps - Classifieds - News - Stock Quotes - Sports Scores

Figure 10.5 Yahoo!'s Reference Tools menu.

My Yahoo! - Yahooligans! for Kids - Beatrice's Web Guide - Yahoo! Internet Life
Weekly Picks - Today's Web Events - **Chat** - Weather Forecasts
Random Yahoo! Link - Yahoo! Shop

National Yahoos Canada - France - Germany - Japan - U.K. & Ireland
Yahoo! Metros Atlanta - Austin - Boston - Chicago - Dallas / Fort Worth - Los Angeles
Get Local Minneapolis / St. Paul - New York - S.F. Bay - Seattle - Washington D.C.

How to Include Your Site - Company Information - Contributors - **Yahoo! to Go**

Figure 10.6 You can access More Yahoos (National, Metro, Yahooligans!, etc.) and other information using these links at the bottom of the Yahoo! home page.

Figure 10.7 To get back to the Yahoo! home page, click on the Yahoo! logo or (in some cases) this button.

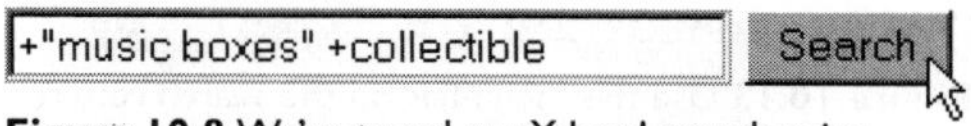

Searching with Yahoo!

Now let's try an actual Yahoo! search. We'll start from the Yahoo! home page (www.yahoo.com) and use the search form presented there.

To search with Yahoo!:

1. Type your query in the search form text box and click on the Search button to submit it (**Figure 10.8**). To search for a phrase, enclose the words in double quotes. Use plus and minus signs in front of words or phrases you want to include (+) or exclude (–) from the results.

2. Yahoo! will search its database for *topic categories* and *Web sites* that match your query and report the results. Category matches (if any) will be listed first, followed by site matches. **Figure 10.9** shows the first portion of the results from our search for +"music boxes" +collectible.

Note: If Yahoo! doesn't find any matching categories or Web sites in its database, it will automatically check AltaVista and report those results to you.

3. To explore any category or Web site on the results page, simply click on it. Web site links, of course, take you directly to the site. Category links (**Figure 10.10**) take you to the next level down in the topic outline (**Figure 10.11**), where you're given a chance to do another search or explore more links.

4. If you choose to do another search, you have the option of limiting it to the category you're currently exploring, shown in bold right above the search form. Just key in one or more search terms and click on the "Search only in…" radio button (**Figure 10.12**).

Figure 10.8 We've typed our Yahoo! search using double quotes to indicate a phrase and plus (+) signs to tell Yahoo! that both search terms must appear in the results.

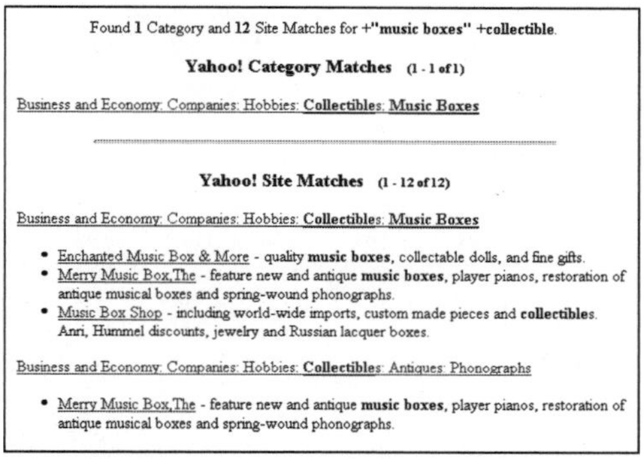

Figure 10.9 Here's how Yahoo! reports search results: number of matches, followed by category matches, and then site matches. Search terms are displayed in bold to make them easier to spot.

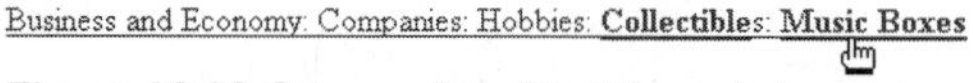

Figure 10.10 Category links like this one take you to the next level down in the topic outline, shown in Figure 10.11.

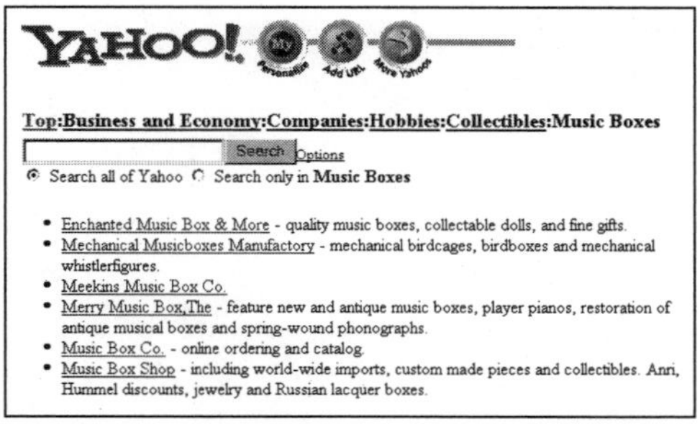

Figure 10.11 From here, you can click on a link to go to a specific site, or you can do another search.

Figure 10.12 Use the "Search only in…" option to do another search that's limited to the category you're currently exploring.

✔ Tips

- To look for news articles or Internet events that match your search request, click on Headlines or Net Events in the menu bar on the search results page (**Figure 10.13**).

- Case doesn't count with Yahoo!, so you can use upper- or lowercase (or a combination) and get the same results.

- To search for phrases, enclose the words in double quotes: **"Russian lacquer boxes"**.

- Yahoo! ignores the words AND, OR, and NOT. Therefore, to do an AND search, put a plus (+) sign in front of each word or phrase. For OR searches, type each word or phrase separated by a space. For NOT searches, put a minus (−) sign in front of the word or phrase you want to exclude.

- For wildcard searches, type at least three letters of the word followed by an asterisk: **classic***, for example, would find *classic*, *classics*, and *classical*.

- Yahoo! allows two types of field searches: titles and URLs. To limit your search to the titles of Web pages, use **t:** followed by a word or phrase: **t:antiques**, for example, to find Web pages with the word *antiques* in the title. The term **u:antiques** would find sites with that word anywhere in the URL.

- For Yahoo!'s online help (Quick Tips, Features, Frequently Asked Questions, etc.), click on Company Information at the bottom of the Yahoo! home page.

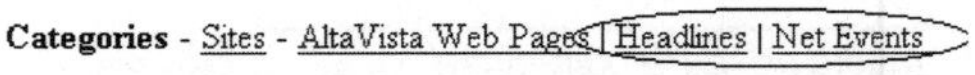

Categories - Sites - AltaVista Web Pages | Headlines | Net Events

Figure 10.13 Use this menu bar on the search results page to look for news headlines or Internet events related to your search request.

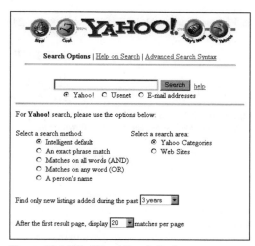

Figure 10.14 The Yahoo! Search Options page.

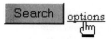

Figure 10.15 To get to the Search Options page, click on Options on the Yahoo! home page.

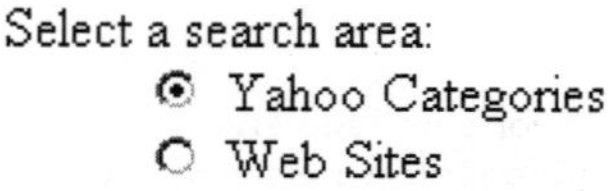

Select a search area:
- ⦿ Yahoo Categories
- ○ Web Sites

Figure 10.16 You can limit your search to Yahoo! categories *or* Web sites by clicking on the appropriate radio button.

Select a search method:
- ⦿ Intelligent default
- ○ An exact phrase match
- ○ Matches on all words (AND)
- ○ Matches on any word (OR)
- ○ A person's name

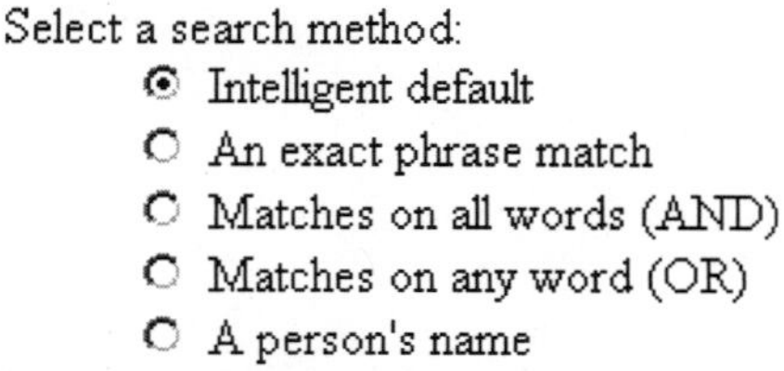

Figure 10.17 The Search Method menu lets you specify that you want to do a phrase, AND, OR, or name search.

Customizing your Yahoo! searches

Yahoo! offers a second search form on what it calls the Search Options page (**Figure 10.14**) that gives you a bit more control over what you can search and how your results are displayed. Let's say, for example, that you're really not interested in locating specific Web sites. What you want to know is, what *types* of information are available on the Web relating to a particular hobby or business interest? A good way to find out would be to use the Search Options page, where you can limit your search to Yahoo! *categories*.

For some searches, you might not be at all interested in topic categories. Instead, you might want to identify Web sites dealing with, say, Swiss watches—but you only want to look at the ones that have been added or updated within the past month. You can do that from the Search Options page as well.

To get there, click on the Options link (**Figure 10.15**) next to the Search button on the Yahoo! home page. Here's a quick overview of the features you'll find most useful.

To customize a Yahoo! search:

1. Limit your search to categories *or* Web sites by selecting the appropriate radio button (**Figure 10.16**).

2. When you type your Yahoo! search request, you can use double quotes to indicate a phrase search and plus and minus signs to include (+) or exclude (−) terms, in which case you'd leave Search Method set to Intelligent Default (**Figure 10.17**). Alternatively, you can use one of the other Search Method settings to do a phrase, AND, OR, or name search.

3. If you want to limit your search to categories or sites added or updated within a certain timeframe, use the drop-down menu (**Figure 10.18**) to select from choices ranging from one day to three years.

4. To change the number of matches displayed per page (after the first page, for which the layout is fixed), use the drop-down menu shown in **Figure 10.19**.

✔ Tip

■ When you get your results, you'll be given the opportunity to automatically use another search engine. Yahoo! warns, however, that "most of the options selected (on the Search Options page) will not be carried over to the other search engines."

To search Usenet newsgroups:

■ Type your query and click on the Usenet radio button (**Figure 10.20**). Then click on Search and your query will be directed to a database of newsgroup postings created and maintained by Deja News, a service that deals exclusively with newsgroups. (See the Deja News chapter for more on this service.)

To search for e-mail addresses:

■ Type the person's name (try first and last, or last name only) and click on the radio button labeled "E-mail addresses" (**Figure 10.21**). Then click on Search for a quick check of the Yahoo! "white pages" database, provided by a company called Four11. If you don't find the person you're looking for, you can go directly to Four11 (**www.four11.com**) or one of the other major people-finding sites, where you'll have more advanced search options at your disposal.

Figure 10.18 To find new or recently updated Yahoo! categories or Web sites, use this drop-down menu.

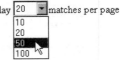

Figure 10.19 Yahoo! typically displays search results 20 to a page, but you can change that with this menu.

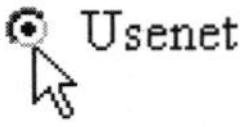

○ Usenet

Figure 10.20 You can search newsgroups from the Search Options page by clicking on the Usenet radio button.

○ E-mail addresses

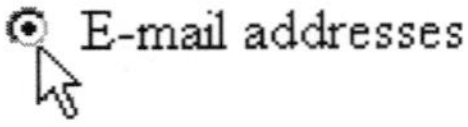

Figure 10.21 To search for e-mail addresses, make sure you click on this button before submitting your search.

Table 10.1

Yahoo! Quick Reference		
FOR THIS TYPE OF SEARCH:	**DO THIS:**	**EXAMPLES:**
Phrase Search	Type the phrase as a sequence of words surrounded by **double quotes**.	"Russian lacquer boxes"
AND Search (multiple words and phrases, each of which *must* be present)	Use a **plus sign** in front of a word or phrase that *must* appear in the results. The plus sign in front of the first word is not required, but we've found you get more precise results if you include it.	+antiques +18th-century
OR Search (multiple words and phrases, any one of which may be present)	Type words or phrases separated by a space, without any special notation.	"Carl Faberge" "Faberge egg"
NOT Search (to exclude a word or phrase)	Use a **minus sign** in front of a word or phrase you want to exclude from your results. To find software Easter eggs, for example, you might want to exclude the word *Fabergé*.	"Easter eggs" –Faberge
Wildcard Search	Use an **asterisk** (*) with at least the first three letters of your search term. The example would find references to *lacquer* as well as *lacquered* and *lacquerware*.	lacq*
Field Search	Use **t:** directly in front of a word or phrase to limit your search to *titles* of Web page documents. Use **u:** to search for the word or phrase in document URLs.	t:"oriental rugs" u:"oriental rugs"
Date Search	Click on Options to get to the Search Options page and use the drop-down menu to select a timeframe (1 day to 3 years).	Find only new listings added during the past 3 years 1 day 3 days 1 week 1 month 3 months 6 months 3 years

YAHOO!: QUICK REFERENCE

Using Yahoo!'s Web directory

As we've said before, when it comes to orga-nizing the Web by topic, no other search engine comes anywhere close to Yahoo! All the major engines offer Web directories. But for the most part, they're only two or three levels deep: topics, subtopics, and (possibly) sub-subtopics.

A topic in the Yahoo! Web directory, on the other hand, might be organized into five or more levels of subtopics and sub-subtopics. Think of Yahoo!'s directory as an incredibly detailed outline of what's available on the Web. And the outline itself, as well as 15- to 20-word site descriptions provided by the site creators, can be searched. So you can usually zero in on just the information you need, without having to wade through descriptions of hundreds, if not thousands, of irrelevant sites.

The best way to understand what we're talk-ing about is to simply go to the Yahoo! home page (**www.yahoo.com**) and choose a topic from the Web directory (**Figure 10.22**). Then explore (or "drill down," as Yahoo! aficiona-dos often say).

- **Arts and Humanities**
  Architecture, Photography, Literature...
- **Business and Economy** [Xtra!]
  Companies, Investing, Employment...
- **Computers and Internet** [Xtra!]
  Internet, WWW, Software, Multimedia...
- **Education**
  Universities, K-12, College Entrance...
- **Entertainment** [Xtra!]
  Cool Links, Movies, Music, Humor...
- **Government**
  Military, Politics [Xtra!], Law, Taxes...
- **Health** [Xtra!]
  Medicine, Drugs, Diseases, Fitness...
- **News and Media** [Xtra!]
  Current Events, Magazines, TV, Newspapers...
- **Recreation and Sports** [Xtra!]
  Sports, Games, Travel, Autos, Outdoors...
- **Reference**
  Libraries, Dictionaries, Phone Numbers...
- **Regional**
  Countries, Regions, U.S. States...
- **Science**
  CS, Biology, Astronomy, Engineering...
- **Social Science**
  Anthropology, Sociology, Economics...
- **Society and Culture**
  People, Environment, Religion...

Figure 10.22 The Yahoo! Web directory is organized into 14 major topic categories.

- ### Business and Economy [Xtra!]

Figure 10.23 Clicking on **[Xtra!]** next to
a topic takes you to related news headlines and articles.

✔ Tips

- If you have a subject in mind but aren't sure what topic to choose from the Web directory, do a Yahoo! search first. For example, a search on the word *collectibles* would direct you to three Yahoo! topics: Business and Economy, Recreation, and Regional.

- Some Yahoo! categories are followed by the clickable link **[Xtra!]**, as shown in **Figure 10.23**. As you might guess, that means there are current news headlines and stories related to the topic (as in "Extra! Extra! Read all about it!"). You'll find the same information if you click on the News link or the Today's News button on the Yahoo! home page.

- Yahoo!'s 14 main topic categories haven't changed in some time, but new subtopics and sub-subtopics are added quite frequently. Watch for the word **NEW!** on the topic lists as you explore the directory. (Web sites recently added to Yahoo! are designated the same way.)

Exploring the Web by topic:

You'll find Yahoo!'s Web directory to be pretty easy to use once you're familiar with the basic format and the terminology for certain key features. That's what we cover here.

To browse the Web by topic:

1. Click on one of the 14 topic categories on the Yahoo! home page (**www.yahoo.com**) to get to a page like the one shown in **Figure 10.24**.

2. The search form at the top of the page (**Figure 10.25**) gives you two options: Do a regular Yahoo! search by clicking on the radio button labeled "Search all of Yahoo." Or limit your search to the category you're currently exploring (shown in bold above the search form) by activating the "Search only in…" radio button.

3. Right below the search form you'll find a set of links (**Figure 10.26**) that varies from one topic to the next, but always includes this one:

   • **Sub Category Listing**. This is Yahoo!'s term for the complete, detailed outline associated with each of the 14 major topics. To get a bird's-eye view of an entire topic (instead of "drilling down" through the directory), click on Sub Category Listing and print the outline. Load plenty of paper, though, because it may take 60 pages or more.

   Other links you may find here include the following:

   • **Indices**. Links to major subject guides and topic-specific resources. Such guides are often prepared by experts in a particular field and made available on the Net as a convenience to their colleagues and anyone else who might be interested.

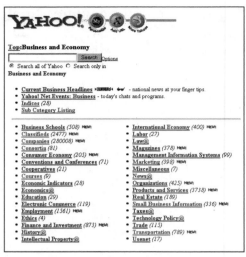

Figure 10.24 Click on any of Yahoo!'s 14 topic categories to get to a page like this one, which happens to be for Business and Economy.

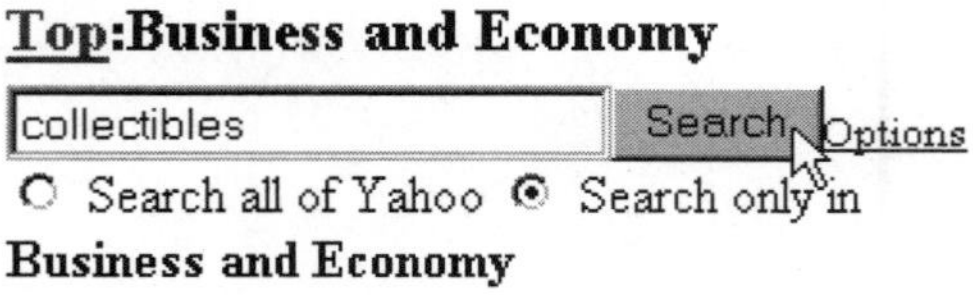

Top:Business and Economy

collectibles   Search Options

○ Search all of Yahoo ◉ Search only in
Business and Economy

Figure 10.25 The search form lets you search all of Yahoo! or just the current topic (as shown here).

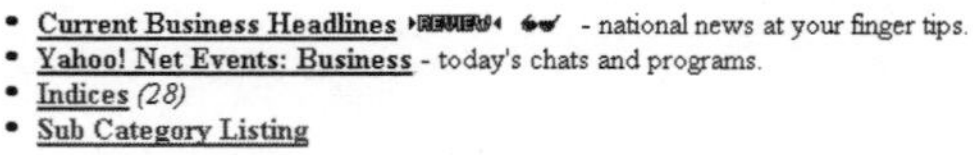

• Current Business Headlines - national news at your finger tips.
• Yahoo! Net Events: Business - today's chats and programs.
• Indices (28)
• Sub Category Listing

Figure 10.26 Most major topics include links like these. The ones for Indices and Sub Category Listing are especially useful.

Figure 10.27 Subtopics are presented alphabetically and include information on the number of entries you'll find under each one.

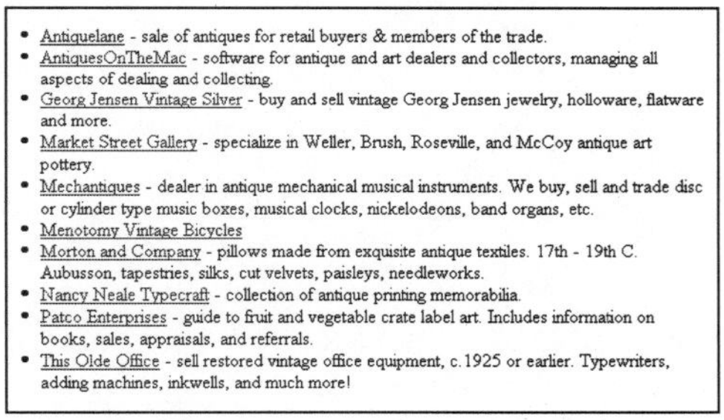

Figure 10.28 Links for specific Web sites include a very brief description (15–20 words) provided by the site's creator.

Top:Business and Economy:Companies:Hobbies:Collectibles

Figure 10.29 The top line here shows that we're on the Collectibles page, four levels down in the topic directory. To move up two levels, click on Companies.

They can often save you a lot of time by presenting just the best and most useful resources on a topic.

- **News Headlines**. National news stories related to the topic.

- **Net Events**. Today's chat sessions and other Internet events.

4. The lower portion of the Yahoo! topic page presents the next level of subtopics (**Figure 10.27**). The numbers in parentheses tell you how many entries are categorized under a particular subtopic. An @ symbol means that the topic appears in several places in the Yahoo! directory. (Clicking on one of these links will take you to the topic's primary location.)

5. As you work your way down through the Yahoo! directory, you'll eventually reach a page that includes a set of links for specific Web sites (**Figure 10.28**).

✔ Tips

- A pair of sunglasses next to a site means that it's considered "cool" (defined as "amusing, extraordinary, or especially useful") by the folks at Yahoo!

- When you see the word **REVIEW** in the Yahoo! Web directory, click on it to see what *Yahoo! Internet Life* (a Yahoo!/Ziff-Davis publication) has to say about the site.

- As you move around the Yahoo! directory, the category you're exploring will always be presented in bold right above the search form (**Figure 10.29**), with each level separated by a colon. You can go directly to any level by simply clicking on it.

PART 3

USING SPECIALIZED SEARCH ENGINES

Chapter 11: **Searching Newsgroups
with Deja News**   145

Chapter 12: **Searching Mailing Lists
with Liszt**   151

Chapter 13: **Searching Subject Guides
with the Argus Clearinghouse**   157

Chapter 14: **Searching for People
with Four11**   163

Chapter 15: **Searching for Businesses
with Zip2 Yellow Pages**   171

Chapter 16: **Searching for Everything
from Authors to ZIP Codes**   177

Using Specialized Search Engines

Good as they are, the all-purpose search engines presented in Part 2 of this book aren't the best tools for every job. Sometimes the fastest, easiest way to find a particular type of information is with a special-purpose search engine like the ones presented in these chapters:

Chapter 11   Searching Newsgroups
              with Deja News

Chapter 12   Searching Mailing Lists
              with Liszt

Chapter 13   Searching Subject Guides
              with the Argus Clearinghouse

Chapter 14   Searching for People
              with Four11

Chapter 15   Searching for Businesses
              with Zip2 Yellow Pages

Chapter 16   Searching for Everything
              from Authors to ZIP Codes

Chapters 11–15 each focus on a single search engine that's designed for a specific purpose: searching newsgroups, searching mailing lists, etc. You'll find step-by-step examples and Quick Reference guides, similar to the ones for the all-purpose search engines in Part 2.

Chapter 16 takes a slightly different approach. Here you'll find brief descriptions of 25 of the best *single-subject* search tools. In most cases, they are so specialized that using them is as easy as filling in the blanks. The most difficult thing about them is simply remembering to use them.

SEARCHING NEWSGROUPS WITH DEJA NEWS

www.dejanews.com

What you can search

- Usenet newsgroups (current postings)
- Usenet newsgroup archives (older postings, dating back to March 1995)

Contact information

Deja News, Inc.
Austin, TX
512/343-6397
www.dejanews.com

The World Wide Web gets most of the press coverage, but for many people, Usenet newsgroups are the best thing about the Internet. Think of them as "electronic-word-of mouth"—millions of people from all over the world sharing information, ideas, and personal experiences. There are some 35,000 newsgroups, each devoted to a specific topic. And unlike Web sites, nobody owns or controls newsgroups, so people are free to say anything they wish—rants, raves, and tirades included.

You have to take a lot of it with a grain of salt, of course. But the fact is, newsgroups can be an excellent source of information—especially if you use a search engine like Deja News to find the really good stuff. Deja News also makes it relatively easy to avoid the "Get Rich Quick," "Free Horoscope Reading," and other widely distributed junk-mail postings—generally known as *spam*—that have made browsing and subscribing to newsgroups virtually impossible.

Now as you may recall, with the exception of Lycos, all the search engines we've talked about so far give you the option of searching newsgroups as well as the Web. Excite, Infoseek, and Yahoo! actually use Deja News to handle newsgroup queries. So why bother learning more about Deja News? Why not simply master a couple of general-purpose search engines and rely on them whenever you want to explore newsgroups?

There are several very good reasons for visiting and learning your way around the Deja News Web site:

- **Newsgroup Archives**. Deja News has the largest collection of indexed, archived Usenet newsgroup postings available anywhere. You can search the current database for recent postings (about a month's worth). Or search the archives for older material dating back as far as March 1995.

- **Power Searching**. Deja News is *optimized* for searching newsgroups. You can do a Quick Search on a couple of keywords. But for even better results, try the Power Search and Search Filter options.

- **Query Language**. The Deja News query language is quite sophisticated and well documented, with all the standard types of searches (AND, OR, NOT) as well as more advanced features like proximity and field searching. They even publish their *stopwords*—common words that the search engine ignores (**Table 11.1**).

In short, the Deja News Web site is superb, and for serious newsgroup searching it just can't be beat.

✔ Tips

- The name *Deja News* is a pun on the phrase *déjà vu*—that odd sensation we all get from time to time of having heard or seen something before.

- The Deja News Author Profile feature (available on any search results page) can help you assess the reliability of a source. It's by no means foolproof, but it will give you a handle on the person's interests and activities.

- You won't find images, program listings, and other encoded binary files among Deja News postings. They're simply too large and can't be easily indexed.

Table 11.1

| **Deja News Stopwords** Quick Reference |

Stopwords are words that search engines ignore because they are too common and therefore don't really help to narrow a search. Here's the current list of Deja News stopwords.

1994	gmt	organization
1995	have	path
1996	i	re
a	if	references
an	in	s
and	is	sender
any	it	subject
are	jan	t
as	lines	that
be	may	the
but	message-id	there
can	newsgroups	this
date	nntp-posting-host	to
do	of	uuneo
for	on	with
from	or	you

DEJA NEWS

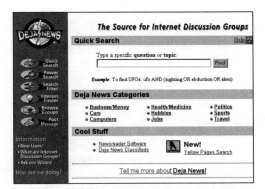

Figure 11.1 The Deja News home page and Quick Search form. The menu bar on the left gives you access to all major Deja News features.

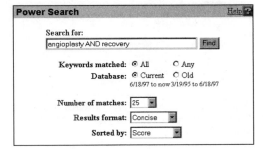

Figure 11.2 The Power Search form lets you control which database you search and how your results are displayed.

Using Deja News to search newsgroups

The Deja News Web site is so well designed and well documented that you'll have newsgroup searching mastered in no time. All the major features are accessible from the menu bar that appears on the left side of the home page (**Figure 11.1**). The menu bar is also the place to look for general information about the service.

You can use Deja News to browse groups by category and to post messages, but the real power lies in its newsgroup search features. That's what we'll focus on here, with a few suggestions for your first visit.

To search newsgroups:

1. Point your Web browser at **www.dejanews.com** to reach the Deja News home page (**Figure 11.1**).

2. You can use the Quick Search form on the home page, but you'll have no control over which database you search (recent postings vs. archives) or how your results are presented. Consequently, we recommend that you click on Power Search in the vertical menu bar on the left side of the page to go directly to the more sophisticated Power Search form (**Figure 11.2**).

3. With both Quick Search and Power Search, you can type a single word or create a more complex query using the search terms and operators summarized in the Deja News Quick Reference on page 149. Deja News ignores case, so you might as well type all your searches in lowercase.

4. When you complete the Power Search form, be sure to specify whether you want to search recent postings (Current) or the archives dating back to March 1995 (Old).

5. You may want to experiment with different settings for the Power Search display options. We usually leave the ones labeled "Number of matches" and "Sorted by" set to their defaults. But we change "Results format" from Concise to Threaded because we prefer reading complete newsgroup *message threads* (postings and replies) instead of individual messages taken out of context.

6. For even more control, click on Search Filter on the vertical menu bar on any Deja News page. Fill out as much of the Search Filter form (**Figure 11.3**) as you wish: Group (complete or partial newsgroup name), Author, Subject, and From/To (range of dates). Then click on Create Filter. Within a few seconds, Deja News will present a Filtered Search Form (**Figure 11.4**) that you can use for subsequent searches.

✔ Tips

- Each Deja News feature has its own Help page with well-written explanations, search tips, and examples. You can access Help for any feature by clicking on the Help button (**Figure 11.5**) in the top right corner of the page.

- The Deja News Interest Finder is a neat tool for identifying newsgroups that deal with your favorite topic (**Figure 11.6**). Once you have that information, you can focus your searches on just those groups using a Search Filter or the newsgroup field-search term (~g).

- For a guide to newsgroup topic categories (or *hierarchies*), see Appendix C.

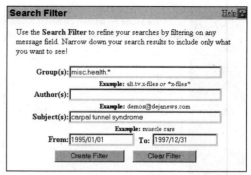

Figure 11.3 The Search Filter gives you even more control. You can search specific *fields* in newsgroup postings.

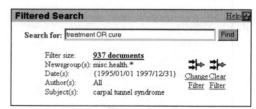

Figure 11.4 Once you've created a Search Filter, the Filtered Search form appears. It stays in effect until you change or clear it.

Figure 11.5 You'll find a Help button like this one on every Deja News feature page.

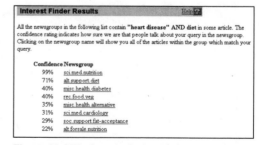

Figure 11.6 The Interest Finder is a handy tool for locating newsgroups (rather than specific articles) on a favorite topic. You can then use that information for a targeted search.

Table 11.2

Deja News Quick Search and Power Search Quick Reference		
FOR THIS TYPE OF SEARCH:	**DO THIS:**	**EXAMPLES:**
Phrase Search	Type the phrase as a sequence of words surrounded by **double quotes**. (Note: Deja News searches are *not* case sensitive.)	"forensic medicine"
	Restrictions: Wildcards cannot be used within phrases. Also, phrases must contain at least two words that are not Deja News *stopwords*. For a list of stopwords, see page 146.	
Wildcard Search	Use an **asterisk** (*) to search for wildcard characters. The example would find *therapeutic, therapist,* and *therapy.*	therap*
	You can also use **braces** to search for a range of words. The example would find all words that fall alphabetically between *therapeutic* and *therapy.*	{therapeutic therapy}
AND Search (multiple words and phrases, each of which *must* be present)	Use **AND** or & to connect two or more words or phrases. Or simply type the words or phrases separated by a space. All three of the examples would produce the same results.	cholesterol AND exercise cholesterol & exercise cholesterol exercise
OR Search (multiple words and phrases, any one of which may be present)	Use **OR** or | to connect two or more words or phrases. Both examples would find newsgroup postings that mention either fitness or nutrition.	fitness OR nutrition fitness | nutrition
NOT Search (to exclude a word or phrase)	Use **NOT** or &! in front of a word or phrase you want to exclude from your results. To look for postings about vitamins but not multi-level marketing deals, for example, you might want to exclude *mlm.*	vitamins NOT mlm vitamins &! mlm
Proximity Search	Use ^ to find words that appear in close proximity to each other. The default distance is 5 *characters*, but you can change that by including a number following the ^ symbol. The second example would look for the two words within 30 characters of each other.	infertility ^ treatment infertility ^30 treatment
	Restrictions: Phrases aren't allowed with Deja News proximity searches. Also, neither search term can be on the Deja News stopwords list. (See page 146 for stopwords.)	
Nested Search	Use **parentheses** to group search expressions into more complex queries. The example would find postings that mention a *clinical study* or *clinical trial.*	clinical & (study | trial)
Field Search	Use one of the **field-search operators** shown below in front of your search term to zero in on a specific field in newsgroup postings: Author: ~**a** Subject: ~**s** Group name: ~**g** Date Created: ~**dc** For even easier (fill-in-the-blank) field searching, use the Deja News Search Filter.	~a bjones ~s lyme disease ~g sci.med.diseases.* ~dc 1997/04/01

SEARCHING MAILING LISTS WITH LISZT

 Liszt, the mailing list directory

www.liszt.com

What you can search

- Directory of some 1,600 public, general-interest mailing lists organized by topic

- Directory of over 70,000 mailing lists (everything in the first directory, plus private, special-interest lists)

Contact information

Liszt, the Mailing List Directory
Scott Southwick
liszt@liszt.com
www.liszt.com

Internet mailing lists are groups of people who regularly exchange e-mail on a subject that interests them. As with newsgroups, there are tens of thousands of mailing lists covering every conceivable topic. The vast majority of them are private—university professors discussing scholarly subjects, clubs and associations communicating with their members, families doing genealogical research or planning reunions. But there are plenty of general-interest mailing lists that welcome subscribers. The trick is to find them.

Liszt, the mailing list directory, is designed to help you do just that. You can search the entire Liszt database of over 70,000 mailing lists, public and private. Or browse Liszt Select, some 1,600 general-interest lists, all of which are open to the public.

Once you find a list that sounds interesting, you can use the information you get from Liszt to subscribe (or to request more information if it's a members-only group for which you might qualify). From that point on, you'll receive all the group's postings automatically by e-mail.

Mailing lists aren't as freewheeling and interactive as newsgroups. It takes some effort to locate and subscribe to the right ones, and you have to deal with the postings as they come into your mailbox.

But on the plus side, they aren't nearly as likely to be polluted with advertisements and get-rich-quick solicitations—because many list owners go to the trouble of making sure that such junk never reaches your mailbox. Furthermore, people who have taken the time to seek out and subscribe to a particular mailing list are likely to be genuinely (perhaps passionately) interested in the subject, so they can be an incredible information resource.

Keep in mind that what you are searching for with Liszt is not the mailing list postings themselves, but a *directory of information* about the lists. Some groups maintain a searchable archive of previous postings, but that's the exception rather than the rule.

There are two other widely used and respected mailing list directories available on the Web: Stephanie da Silva's Publicly Accessible Mailing Lists, often referred to as just PAML (**www.neosoft.com/internet/paml/**); and Vivian Neou's List of Lists (**catalog.com/vivian/interest-group-search.html**). But neither is as comprehensive and easy to use as Scott Southwick's Liszt directory.

✔ Tips

- Mailing lists vary widely in what they offer and how they operate. As we've mentioned, some maintain searchable archives. Some give you the option of reading "digests" instead of complete messages. Some lists are quite interactive, while others are designed primarily to distribute a newsletter or magazine and do little to encourage interaction with or among members.

- Before joining or even sending an e-mail message to a mailing list, do your homework. Use Liszt to get a description of the mailing list (the list's *Info File*). It will tell you what the group is all about and whether new members are welcome.

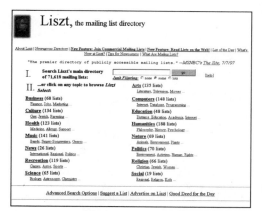

Figure 12.1 The Liszt home page includes a search form and a mailing list directory organized by topic.

Figure 12.2 Liszt's search form gives you the option of filtering out lists that aren't open to the general public. The middle setting is the one to use for most searches.

Using the Liszt directory

Liszt gives you two ways of accessing the information in its database. Starting from the Liszt home page at **www.liszt.com** (**Figure 12.1**), you can do a keyword search of over 70,000 mailing lists. Or you can browse Liszt Select, a tiny subset of the main directory (about 1,600 lists). Liszt Select is organized by topic and includes lists most likely to be of interest to the general public.

Browsing is fine, but the best way to use Liszt is to plunge right in with a directory search. That's what we'll focus on here.

To search for mailing lists:

1. Type your query in the text box on the Liszt search form (**Figure 12.2**). By default, Liszt does what's called a *string search*, meaning that it looks for a sequence of letters instead of a distinct word. A search on *lan*, for example, might find references to *landmarks* and *planets*, when what you really want is *local area networks* (LANs). To tell Liszt to search for a specific word, enclose it in double quotes.

2. Liszt's Junk Filtering option (right below the text box in **Figure 12.2**) is designed to help you screen out lists that aren't likely to be of interest. Set for the default (Some filtering), you can avoid lists whose descriptions include words like *association*, *members*, or *course*. The notion is that you probably don't want to be bothered with lists on subjects like "Bankers Association Golf Outing" and "Professor Smiley's Zoology 101 Course Syllabus." If you want to see all the results and make your own decisions about the lists, set Junk Filtering to None.

3. Your search results will be organized into three sections (**Figure 12.3**): matching Liszt Select *categories*, matching Liszt Select *lists*, and matching lists from the entire database.

4. Clicking on a mailing list name will take you to its description in the Liszt database. If you're lucky, what you'll find is the list's *Info File*. Prepared by the list owner, an Info File typically includes a brief description of the list (**Figure 12.4**) and details on how to subscribe, unsubscribe, communicate with the list owner, and access other features like archives and digests (**Figure 12.5**).

✔ Tips

- Mailing lists almost always have a special e-mail address to use for subscribing and unsubscribing. Don't make the classic new-user mistake of sending a subscription-related request to the list owner.

- Liszt uses a color code on its Search Results page to give you a clue as to how much information the directory contains on a particular mailing list. For list names highlighted in green, you'll find the group's official Info File. Yellow means that Liszt has some information but perhaps not the Info File. Red or white color coding means that Liszt has little or no information about the group and has tried contacting the list owner without success.

- The Liszt search language is based on a programming language called Perl. If you know Perl, you're all set. If not, refer to the Liszt Quick Reference on page 155 for help creating Liszt queries.

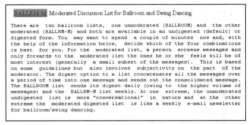

Figure 12.3 Search results are organized into three sections. The first two (Liszt Select categories and mailing lists) are the ones most likely to be of interest.

Figure 12.4 Info Files typically include a description of the mailing list. Here's a sample from the Info File for the BALLRM-M (Ballroom Dancing-Moderated) mailing list.

```
To subscribe to either list, you should e-mail the command(s) shown below
in the BODY of a message to LISTSERV@MITVMA.MIT.EDU

1. To subscribe to ballroom (UN-moderated, UN-digested):
        subscribe ballroom Yourfirstname Yourlastname

2. To add the (daily) digest option to ballroom, after your subscription
   has been confirmed:
        set ballroom digest

3. To subscribe to ballrm-m (moderated, UN-digested):
        subscribe ballrm-m Yourfirstname Yourlastname

4. To add the (weekly) digest option to ballrm-m, after your
   subscription has been confirmed:
        set ballrm-m digest

(Yourfirstname Yourlastname should  be replaced with your  real first and
last names,  of course.) You  will then get additional  information about
the list, including Submission policies, etc.

If you  have other questions  about the list, or  need to reach  the list
administrators directly for some reason, you may send e-mail to

               BALLRM-M-Request@MITVMA.MIT.EDU
```

Figure 12.5 Info Files also include details like this on how to subscribe, unsubscribe, and communicate with the list owner.

Table 12.1

Liszt Quick Reference		
FOR THIS TYPE OF SEARCH:	DO THIS:	EXAMPLES:
Word or Phrase Search	Enclose the word or phrase in **double quotes**. (Without the quotes, Liszt performs a *string search* and thus might find references to the Marshall family reunion as well as the planet Mars.)	"mars" "handwriting analysis"
Wildcard Search	Use an **asterisk** (*) to search for wildcard characters, or simply type a sequence of letters and Liszt will perform a string search. The first two examples would find both *dance* and *dancing*. The third would find *baseball* and *basketball*.	danc* danc b*ball
AND Search (multiple words and phrases, each of which *must* be present)	Use **and** (lowercase) to connect two or more words or phrases. Or simply type the words or phrases separated by a space, since AND searching is the default.	ballroom and swing ballroom swing
OR Search (multiple words and phrases, any one of which may be present)	Use **or** (lowercase) to connect two or more words or phrases.	bird or birding
NOT Search (to exclude a word or phrase)	Use **not** (lowercase) in front of a word or phrase you want to exclude from your results.	music not jazz
Nested Search	Use **parentheses** to group search expressions into more complex queries.	games and (board or card)
Case-Sensitive Search	Click on Advanced Search Options on the Liszt home page and activate the Case Sensitive radio button.	⦿ Case sensitive ○ Case insensitive

SEARCHING SUBJECT GUIDES WITH THE ARGUS CLEARINGHOUSE

The Internet's Premier Research Library
A Selective Collection of Topical Guides

The**Argus**Clearinghouse
www.clearinghouse.com

What you can search

■ Directory of subject-specific guides to Internet resources, prepared by subject-matter experts and reviewed and rated by Clearinghouse staff of information and library studies professionals

Contact information

Argus Clearinghouse
Argus Associates, Inc.
313/913-0010
clearinghouse@argus-inc.com
www.clearinghouse.net

We can't do a book about online searching without covering one of our all-time favorite information-finding resources, the Argus Clearinghouse. The quick handle on the Argus Clearinghouse is this: It's designed to make it as easy as possible for you to find "master" subject-specific Web sites or *guides*, as the Argus Clearinghouse calls them.

Guides are assembled and maintained by experts in a particular subject—not by robots and spider programs. They offer links—selected, organized, and annotated—to the most important Internet resources devoted to that subject.

To fully appreciate this incredible resource, a little history is in order. The Clearinghouse (its original name) was created in 1993 as an academic venture at the University of Michigan's School of Information and Library Studies (SILS). As part of their Master's Degree program, SILS students would choose a topic and prepare a comprehensive guide to Internet resources.

The guides were critiqued and evaluated by professors and fellow classmates, and the best ones were made available on the Internet. Graphical Web browsers like Netscape Navigator and Microsoft's Internet Explorer hadn't been invented yet, nor had Web search engines and directories like AltaVista and Yahoo!. So the Clearinghouse was a most welcome addition to the Internet. But it was simply a Gopher menu site and the guides were plain text files you could read or download.

Now the Clearinghouse has moved to the Web, of course. It's owned and operated by Argus Associates, a consulting firm that specializes in information architecture design for complex Web sites and Intranets. Students and graduates of the SILS Master's Degree program are still very much involved, but the guides are created by subject-matter experts from all over the world. Argus Clearinghouse staff members set rigorous standards and will only accept guides that rate high on content, design, and organization.

The Argus Clearinghouse doesn't claim to be comprehensive. You may or may not find the guide you need among its collection. But it's the perfect first stop for any in-depth Web research project.

✔ Tip

■ You'll find details on the Argus Clearinghouse rating system and guide submission procedures on the site's home page.

■ Another link on the Argus Clearinghouse home page that's worth checking is the Digital Librarian's Award. It's sort of a Clearinghouse Hall of Fame—guides recognized by the staff as being truly exceptional in design and organization.

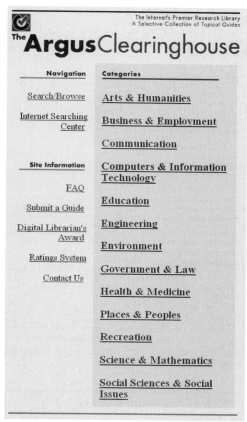

Figure 13.1 The Argus Clearinghouse home page includes a menu of 13 major subject categories.

Search/Browse

Figure 13.2 The Search/Browse link located in the upper left corner of the home page takes you to the search form and a more detailed subject outline.

Search

children AND literature

submit search

Figure 13.3 Here's the Argus Clearinghouse search form with a sample query you might use to locate guides dealing with children's literature.

Finding subject guides

To experience the Argus Clearinghouse for yourself, point your Web browser at **www.clearinghouse.net**. That will take you to the site's home page (**Figure 13.1**), where you're given a choice of clicking your way through menus or searching for guides by keyword.

The menu system organizes Clearinghouse guides into 13 major categories (Arts & Humanities through Social Sciences & Social Issues). Click on any one of them and you'll be presented with a half dozen or so subcategories that lead, in turn, to a set of keywords. Click on a keyword and you'll be presented with all the guides for that subject.

By all means, take a walk through the menus. But if you have something specific in mind, you may find it's faster to use the keyword search feature. That's what we'll step through here.

To search for guides by keyword:

1. Click on Search/Browse (**Figure 13.2**) on the Argus Clearinghouse home page to get to the search form shown in **Figure 13.3**.

2. Type your query in the search form text box. Coming up with the right search terms might take some trial and error. Keep in mind that what you are searching is a directory of guide descriptions (the Clearinghouse calls them *information pages*), not the guides themselves.

   Each information page includes the guide's title, Web address, author and professional affiliation, scores on five Argus Clearinghouse criteria, and some descriptive keywords. It's the title and keywords, obviously, that you want to try to match.

3. Your search results (**Figure 13.4**) will tell you the name of each guide, along with its associated keywords and overall rating (one to five check marks).

4. Click on the name of any guide to display its information page (**Figure 13.5**). From there you can click on the Web address to view the guide itself (**Figure 13.6**).

✔ Tips

■ You can search for a single word or phrase, or use some very basic search operators: AND, OR, parentheses, and wildcards. Searches are *not* case sensitive. (See the Argus Clearinghouse Quick Reference on page 161 for search syntax and examples.)

■ Your best bet with the Argus Clearinghouse is to try to think of a very general search word or phrase that's likely to appear on the guide's information page. Searching for **Dr. Seuss AND Beatrix Potter** would be a great way to find children's literature Web pages with a search engine like AltaVista or Excite, but *not* with the Argus Clearinghouse. For a Clearinghouse search, you'll have better luck with terms like **children AND books** or **teenagers AND literature**.

Search Results

The query "**children AND literature**" retrieved 5 guides.

Guides

1. <u>Children's Literature Nook</u>   *(not rated yet)*
keywords: **children's literature, authors**

2. <u>Children's Literature Web Guide</u>   ✔✔✔✔✔
keywords: **children's literature**

3. <u>The Compleat Bellairs Other Spooky Links</u>   ✔✔✔
keywords: **children's literature, mysteries**

4. <u>Young Adult Literature</u>   ✔✔✔
keywords: **children's literature, young adult literature, teenagers**

5. <u>Electronic Resources for Youth Services</u>   ✔✔✔✔
keywords: **writing, children's literature, books**

Figure 13.4 Search results are presented like this, with a few lines about each guide along with its overall Argus Clearinghouse rating.

Children's Literature Web Guide

Guide Information

`http://www.ucalgary.ca/~dkbrown/index.html`

Keywords
<u>children's literature</u>

Compiled by
D. K. Brown (dkbrown@acs.ucalgary.ca)
University of Calgary

Rating
Overall: ✔✔✔✔✔
Resource Description: 5
Resource Evaluation: 5
Guide Design: 5
Organization Schemes: 5
Guide Meta-information: 5
(<u>Rated</u> 03/97)

Last Checked by Argus Clearinghouse
March 31, 1997

Figure 13.5 This is the information page for the award-winning Children's Literature Web Guide created by D.K. Brown at the University of Calgary.

Table 13.1

Argus Clearinghouse Quick Reference		
FOR THIS TYPE OF SEARCH:	DO THIS:	EXAMPLES:
Phrase Search	Type the phrase as a sequence of words enclosed in **double quotes**.	"news media"
Wildcard Search	Use an **asterisk** (*) to search for wildcard characters at the end of a word. The example would find *biology* as well as *biological* and *biologist*.	biolog*
AND Search (multiple words and phrases, each of which *must* be present)	Use **AND** to connect two or more words or phrases. The example would find guides whose titles or keywords include both words.	Asia AND business
OR Search (multiple words and phrases, any one of which may be present)	Use **OR** to connect two or more words or phrases, either one of which might appear in the guide's title or keywords.	justice OR judicial
Nested Search	Use **parentheses** to group search expressions into more complex queries. The example would find references to *art museum*, *art gallery*, and *art galleries*.	art AND (museum OR galler*)

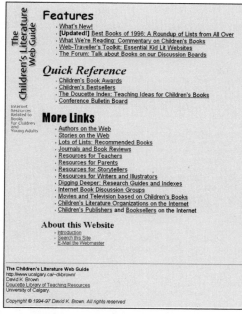

Figure 13.6 And here's the home page for the Children's Literature Web Guide itself, well-organized and full of useful information—just what you'd expect from a top-rated Clearinghouse guide.

SEARCHING FOR PEOPLE WITH FOUR11

www.four11.com

What you can search

- E-mail directory of over 10 million addresses for people all over the world

- Telephone directory of some 100 million U.S. residential listings

- Special directories for government officials and celebrities

Contact information

Four11 Corporation
Menlo Park, CA
415/617-2000
www.four11.com

Sending and receiving e-mail is without a doubt the most popular of all online and Internet features. Newsgroups, mailing lists, and chat rooms all have their devoted fans, and most online users venture at least occasionally onto the World Wide Web. But virtually *everyone* who's online sends and receives e-mail on a regular basis and counts it among their top two or three reasons for being online in the first place.

That being the case, it's no wonder that Web sites specializing in e-mail directories and other *people-finding* tools rank consistently among the Internet's 100 most frequently visited sites. We'll take a look here at one of the premier directory sites, the Four11 Internet White Pages Directory. It's the site we check first whenever we need to locate an e-mail address, and we suggest that you do the same.

If Four11 doesn't have what you're looking for (and that's bound to happen from time to time), try one of these e-mail directory sites, which are also quite good:

- **BigFoot**   www.bigfoot.com
- **Switchboard**   www.switchboard.com
- **WhoWhere?**   www.whowhere.com

FOUR11

There's simply no single, comprehensive source for all of the world's e-mail addresses, nor will there be any time soon. Four11 and these other e-mail directory sites provide a great service, but they currently list only a fraction of the millions of e-mail addresses that are out there.

✔ Tips

- The name Four11 (pronounced "four-one-one") refers, of course, to the long-established practice of dialing 411 for local directory assistance.

- The reason Four11 and similar people-finding sites are often referred to as *white pages* directories is that their databases typically include residential telephone numbers and street addresses—just like you'd find in your local telephone company white pages. The difference is that you can search for anyone, anywhere in the United States.

- When we say "anyone, anywhere," we mean it quite literally. You can use Four11 and other such sites to find parents, grandparents, neighbors, and friends who have never so much as touched a computer keyboard, let alone gone online.

- Because they allow you to cast such a wide net, white pages directories are terrific for locating former classmates, tracking down long-lost military buddies, and doing genealogical research. Four11 is attempting to make the process even easier by encouraging people to add descriptive keywords to their listings. It's a free service you can take advantage of when you add or update your Four11 listing.

- Learn to use at least a couple of white pages directories. But keep in mind that sometimes the best way to find out a person's e-mail address is to do it the "old-fashioned" way: Pick up the telephone and call!

FOUR11

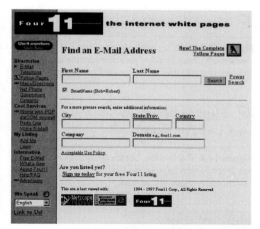

Figure 14.1 Four11's home page includes the E-mail Address search form and a menu of options for other Four11 directories, services, and company information.

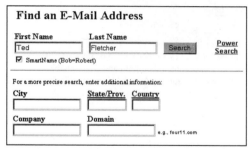

Figure 14.2 To look for an e-mail address, start by completing just the First and Last Name fields. You can always go back and enter more information to narrow your search.

Figure 14.3 To modify a search, click on this button on the Search Results page.

Figure 14.3 To modify a search, click on this button on the Search Results page.

Finding e-mail addresses with Four11

There are just a few things you need to know to take full advantage of Four11's people-finding features. Point your Web browser at **www.four11.com** to get to the Four11 home page (**Figure 14.1**). That's where you'll find the search form for looking up e-mail addresses. Other features (telephone number searches, special directories for government officials and celebrities, Four11 company information, and so forth) are accessible from the menu on the left side of the page.

To search for e-mail addresses:

1. Use the E-mail Address search form (**Figure 14.2**) on the Four11 home page. Start with a broad search, completing just the First and Last Name fields. For common names like Smith or Jones, go ahead and complete the State or Country field as well. Leave out the person's middle initial, even if you know what it is. (Four11 isn't currently set up to handle middle initials.)

2. Click on the Search button to submit your query. If you find the person you're looking for, great. If you come up empty (or with too many hits), click on Modify Search (**Figure 14.3**) on the search results page and try again.

3. To search Group Connections—the descriptions people have added to their Four11 listings (education, military service, business background, hobbies, special interests, etc.)—click on Power Search (**Figure 14.4**) and use Four11's Advanced Search page.

4. If you can't find the e-mail address you're looking for with Four11, try another directory site: BigFoot (**www.bigfoot.com**), Switchboard (**www.switchboard.com**), or WhoWhere? (**www.whowhere.com**).

✔ Tips

■ It's usually best to start with a name-only search. If you get too many hits, complete additional fields one at a time, in this order: Country, State/Province, City, Company or Domain, Group Connections.

■ Another good way to reduce the number of hits is to turn off the SmartName feature (**Figure 14.5**). With SmartName on, Four11 searches automatically for variations on popular first names. (A search for John will also find Jack and Jonathan.) To turn SmartName off, remove the check mark by clicking on it.

■ If you're not sure of the spelling of a last name, use an asterisk (*) to do a wildcard search. A search for **Anders*** in the Last Name field, for example, would find listings for Andersen, Anderson, and Andersson. (Wildcards can be used in the First Name, City, and Group Connections fields as well.)

■ The Flexible Search feature (**Figure 14.6**) on the Advanced Search page tells Four11 to look for wildcard matches automatically. Searching for **Mary** (no asterisk) would also find Marylou. Turn this feature off if your search returns too many hits.

■ You'll find a summary of Four11 search features in the Four11 Quick Reference on page 169. For answers to other questions, click on Help/FAQ in the Information menu (**Figure 14.7**) on the Four11 home page.

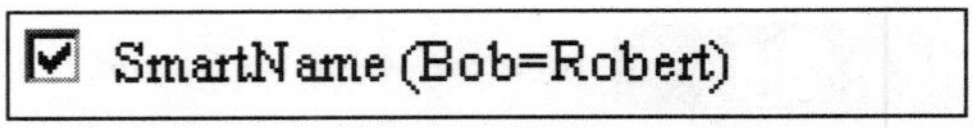

☑ SmartName (Bob=Robert)

Figure 14.5 With SmartName on (indicated by the check mark), Four11 searches automatically for nicknames associated with popular first names.

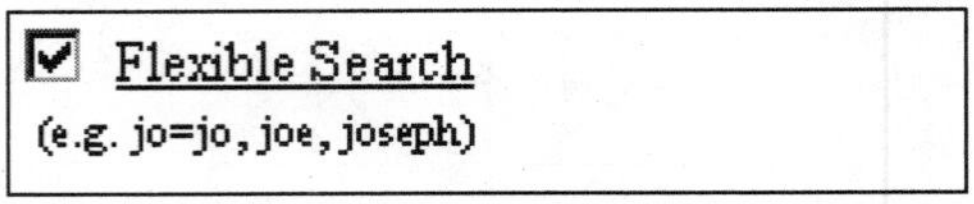

☑ Flexible Search
(e.g. jo=jo, joe, joseph)

Figure 14.6 The Flexible Search feature on Four11's Advanced Search page works just like a wildcard search, but without the asterisk.

Figure 14.7 Click on Help/FAQ to take advantage of Four11's excellent online help and a searchable database of Frequently Asked Questions (FAQ).

Figure 14.8 To search for home addresses and telephone numbers, you first have to access the Telephone Directory from this menu.

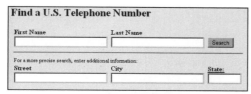

Figure 14.9 Four11's U.S. Telephone Number search form.

Finding home addresses and telephone numbers with Four11

The search form on the Four11 home page allows you to look for e-mail addresses worldwide. But what if the person you're trying to find doesn't have an e-mail address? (Most people don't.) And you can't call Directory Assistance because you're not even sure in which city or state the person lives.

The solution: use Four11's Telephone Directory feature. If the person lives in the United States, chances are you can find both an address (including 9-digit ZIP code) and telephone number with Four11.

To search for home addresses and telephone numbers:

1. From the Four11 home page (www.four11.com), click on Telephone in the Directories menu (**Figure 14.8**). That will take you to the U.S. Telephone Number search form (**Figure 14.9**).

2. Here, too, it's a good idea to start with a broad search, completing just the First and Last Name fields—unless the name is quite common, in which case you might want to complete the State field as well.

3. Click on Search and review the results. If you get too many hits, go back and narrow the search. (Try adding State, then City, then Street.) If you get too few or none at all, check your spelling. Or try a wildcard search in the First Name, Last Name, or City fields.

✔ Tips

- Four11 gets home addresses and telephone numbers from the Regional Bell Operating Companies (RBOCs) and updates its database about four times a year. If the person you're looking for has moved recently, it may take three months or so for the new information to make its way into the Four11 Telephone Directory.

- Keep in mind that many people list themselves in the phone book with a first initial instead of a full name. If your search for, say, Janet Parker is unsuccessful, try a wildcard search for J* Parker.

- Four11 offers two special directories, Government and Celebrity, both accessible from the Directories menu on any page (**Figure 14.10**). Click on Government to locate a member of Congress. Click on Celebrity to search for famous people (actors, authors, journalists, sports stars, etc.).

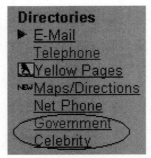

Figure 14.10 Click on Government or Celebrity in the Four11 Directories menu to search these special databases.

Table 14.1

Four11 Quick Reference		
FOR THIS TYPE OF SEARCH:	**DO THIS:**	**EXAMPLES:**
E-mail Address Search (worldwide)	Start by completing just the First and Last Name fields. To narrow your search, complete additional fields one at a time, in this order: • Country • State/Province • City • Company or Domain • Group Connections (Available on Advanced Search page only. Click on Power Search to get there.) Note: You can also narrow a search by turning off Four11's SmartName feature. On the Advanced Search page, turn off both SmartName *and* Flexible Search. Use an **asterisk** (*) to do a wildcard search. The example would find listings for *Jane Anderson, Andersen*, and *Andersson.* Note: You can use wildcards in the First Name, Last Name, and City fields.	First Name: Ted Last Name: Fletcher [Search] ☑ SmartName (Bob=Robert) First Name: Jane Last Name: Anders* [Search] ☑ SmartName (Bob=Robert)
Home Address and Phone Number Search (U.S. only)	Click on Telephone in the Directories menu on the Four11 home page to access the U.S. Telephone Number search form. Start by completing the First and Last Name fields. To narrow your search, complete more fields one at a time, in this order: • State • City • Street Use an **asterisk** (*) to do a wildcard search in the First Name, Last Name, or City fields. The example would find listings in the cities of *Greensboro* and *Greenville.*	First Name: Alan Last Name: Fowler [Search] Street: City: Green* State: NC
Government Search (White House and Congress)	Click on Government in the Directories menu on the Four11 home page. Then follow the links to find the e-mail addresses and home pages for the White House and members of Congress.	Directories E-Mail ▶ Telephone Yellow Pages Maps/Directions Net Phone Government Celebrity
Celebrity Search	Click on Celebrity in the Directories menu on the Four11 home page. From the Celebrity search page, you can by category (Actors, Authors, Sports Stars, etc.). But your best bet is to click on Full Celebrity Listings and search the entire database alphabetically.	Directories E-Mail ▶ Telephone Yellow Pages Maps/Directions Net Phone Government Celebrity Cool Services

Searching for Businesses with Zip2 Yellow Pages

www.zip2.com

What you can search

- Directory of U.S. businesses, searchable by name or category

- Database of driving directions and maps

Contact information

Zip2 Yellow Pages
Zip2 Corporation
Mountain View, CA
415/429-4400
415/429-4500 (fax)
info@zip2.com
www.zip2.com

You can use virtually any Web search engine to find information on businesses like Barnes and Noble, Disney, Federal Express, and Microsoft. Product announcements, catalogs, press releases, stock quotes, earnings reports—all these (and more) are available on the World Wide Web.

But what about the vast numbers of businesses, large and small, that have yet to establish a presence on the Web? The fact is, most companies, like most people, are not online.

And what if the information you're looking for is pretty straightforward? For example, you want a street address or phone number so that you can visit the company or call to ask a specific question. Surprisingly, many business Web sites don't even include this information, or they bury it so deep that it's almost impossible to find.

The answer to both of these questions is to use a *yellow pages directory*. The one we'll focus on here is the Zip2 Yellow Pages, a relative newcomer in a crowded field. It's well designed, easy to use, and extremely fast. Other directories like BigBook, BigYellow, and GTE SuperPages get more attention, but having tried them all, we like the Zip2 Yellow Pages the best.

With Zip2, you can search for businesses by name or type—a standard feature of all the major yellow pages directories. Zip2 far outshines the competition, however, when it comes to displaying the results of a search. It's also especially good at handling *near* matches of business names and types. For example, a Zip2 search for *dry cleaners* will return matches for companies listed under the category *cleaners*, instead of reporting "no results found" as some of its competitors do.

Another Zip2 feature you'll appreciate is the ability to set up a *search profile*. Fill out a simple form with your home and work addresses and tell Zip2 to store the information. From then on, whenever you do a search, you can automatically look for businesses that are "Near My Home" or "Near My Work." No need to worry about specifying multiple cities, ZIP codes or area codes. Zip2 will present the results in order by *distance*, with the closest ones listed first.

As good as Zip2 is, you may from time to time have to check another yellow pages directory—either because the site is down or overloaded, or because you need to do a type of search that Zip2 doesn't offer.

For general searching, BigBook comes closest to Zip2 in ease of use. BigYellow (which can be excruciatingly slow) and GTE SuperPages offer features like ZIP code and area code searches—neither of which are available with Zip2. BigYellow also provides links to business directories for countries outside the United States. And AT&T's Toll-Free Directory is, of course, the place to look for 800 and 888 numbers.

Here's where to find these sites when you need them:

- **AT&T Toll-Free Directory**   www.tollfree.att.net
- **BigBook Yellow Pages**   www.bigbook.com
- **BigYellow**   www.bigyellow.com
- **GTE SuperPages**   yp.gte.net

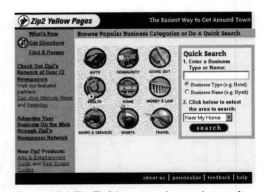

Figure 15.1 The Zip2 home page lets you browse for businesses by category or search for a specific company with the Quick Search form.

Figure 15.2 Use Zip2's Personalize feature to record home and work locations so you can search for nearby businesses automatically.

Figure 15.3 The Zip2 Quick Search form makes it easy to locate businesses in a particular area.

Figure 15.4 To search for businesses near your office or some other location, use the Quick Search form's drop-down menu.

Click on the icons next to a business to :	Get Directions	Visit Web Site	

Bed & Breakfast Accommodations closest to your address (1 - 15) listed

Distance		Name / Address	Phone
2.0 miles		Inn To The Woods B & B 150 Glenwood Dr. Washington Crsng, PA.	(215) 493-1974
5.0 miles		Temperance House 5 S State St. Newtown, PA.	(215) 860-0474
5.2 miles		Pineapple Hill Bed & Breakfast 1324 River Rd. New Hope, PA.	(215) 862-1790
8.0 miles		Hollileif Bed & Breakfast 677 Durham Rd. Newtown, PA.	(215) 598-3100
8.6 miles		Chimney Hill Farm 207 Goat Hill Rd. Lambertville, NJ.	(609) 397-1516
9.3 miles		Inn Of The Hawke 74 S Union St. Lambertville, NJ.	(609) 397-9555
9.4 miles		Mansion Inn 9 S Main St. New Hope, PA.	(215) 862-1231
9.5 miles		Bridgestreet House 75 Bridge St. Lambertville, NJ.	(609) 397-2503
9.6 miles		44 Coryell Bed & Breakfast 44 Coryell St. Lambertville, NJ.	(609) 397-8292

Figure 15.5 Zip2 search results are presented like this, with the closest ones listed first.

Finding businesses with Zip2

To look for businesses with Zip2 Yellow Pages, point your Web browser at **www.zip2.com**. That will take you to the Zip2 home page (**Figure 15.1**), where you can browse by category (Auto, Community, Going Out, etc.) or use the Quick Search form to search by business name or type.

If this is your first visit to Zip2, click on Personalize in the menu bar at the bottom of the screen (**Figure 15.2**) and complete the information about your home and work addresses. Once you've filled out and recorded the form, you'll be able to search automatically for businesses that are near your home or office.

To search for businesses:

1. Enter the type of business or a specific business name in the space provided on the Quick Search form (**Figure 15.3**). (Case doesn't matter.) Be sure to activate the appropriate radio button (Business Type or Business Name) depending on the kind of search you are doing.

2. Use the drop-down menu (**Figure 15.4**) to choose the area you want to search. The default is Near My Home, but other options include Near My Work; Near Address; Other City, State; and Search in Map. (You'll be prompted to supply address information for locations other than home and work.)

3. Click on the Search button to display your results (**Figure 15.5**), 15 listings to a page. They'll be presented in order by distance from the location you specified on the Quick Search form. Icons next to each one take you to driving directions and (on rare occasions) the business's Web site.

4. If your search produces more than 15 listings, a menu bar at the bottom of the page (**Figure 15.6**) lets you sort and search them alphabetically, or view the next page of results with the Next button.

5. Click on any item on the results page for more information. In the example shown here for Pineapple Hill Bed & Breakfast (**Figure 15.7**), you could search automatically for other bed & breakfast accommodations, just in case this one is booked up. Or use the Nearby Businesses option to produce a list of restaurants close to the inn.

6. To get back to the Zip2 home page, click on the Go button (**Figure 15.8**) on any page. (The arrow next to the Go button leads to a drop-down menu for other options.)

✔ Tips

■ If you want to look for a particular type of business but aren't sure what search terms to use, do a Business Name search instead. Use a specific company you'd expect to find on the list. Once you know how that business is classified, you can click on the link labeled "Search related types of businesses" (**Figure 15.7**) to find others like it.

■ In order to show up in a yellow pages directory, companies must have a "business listing" with the telephone company. Many home-based businesses choose not to pay the higher rates for such listings, so you won't find them in Zip2 or any of the other online yellow pages. Instead, try a white pages directory like Four11 (www.four11.com) and search on the business owner's name.

A B C D E F G H I J K L M N O P

Figure 15.6 A menu bar at the bottom of the search results page lets you sort and view the list alphabetically or move on to the next page.

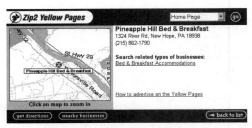

Figure 15.7 Here's a sample Zip2 listing, with a map and links to additional information.

Figure 15.8 Use the Go button and drop-down menu at the top of any Zip2 page to get back to the home page or access other features.

Table 15.1

Zip2 Yellow Pages Quick Reference		
FOR THIS TYPE OF SEARCH:	**DO THIS:**	**EXAMPLES:**
Business Name Search	To search for a specific business, enter its name (or one or two unique words) in the Quick Search form and activate the Business Name radio button. By default, Zip2 searches for businesses near your home. To select another area, use the drop-down menu.	Quick Search 1. Enter a Business Type or Name: Yellowhouse Gallery ○ Business Type (e.g. Hotel) ● Business Name (e.g. Hyatt) 2. Click below to select the area to search: Other City, State Near My Home Near My Work Near Address Other City, State Search in Map
Business Category Search	To search for all the businesses in a particular category, type one or two unique words in the Quick Search form and activate the Business Type radio button. Be sure to specify the area you want to search using the drop-down menu.	Quick Search 1. Enter a Business Type or Name: shoe repair ● Business Type (e.g. Hotel) ○ Business Name (e.g. Hyatt) 2. Click below to select the area to search: Near My Home Near My Home Near My Work Near Address Other City, State Search in Map
Point-to-Point Driving Directions and Maps	Click on the Get Directions icon next to any listing in your Zip2 search results. For point-to-point directions without searching, click on Get Directions on the Zip2 home page.	Yellowhouse Galleries (919) 441-6928 2902 S Virginia Dare Trl. Nags Head, NC. Get Directions

SEARCHING FOR EVERYTHING FROM AUTHORS TO ZIP CODES

You've seen what a breeze it can be to use highly specialized search engines like the Four11 Internet White Pages (**www.four11.com**) and the Zip2 Yellow Pages (**www.zip2.com**). Because they're designed for a single, relatively narrow task—looking for people and businesses in telephone-like directories—the search forms are simple and there's very little complexity to master. Just fill in the blanks and away you go.

For the most part, that's what you'll find with the 25 special-purpose search engines profiled in this chapter. Each is designed to handle searching for a particular type of information really well—whether it's the latest book by a favorite author or Microsoft's Technical Support phone numbers or your Aunt Harriet's ZIP code. Many offer Help pages and search tips, but for most of them, you won't need to learn any special search rules and commands. In our experience, about the only thing that's difficult about special-purpose search engines is remembering to use them.

That being the case, what we'll focus on here is where to find these 25 special-purpose sites and the subject matter or type of information you can search with each one. We encourage you to read through the descriptions and visit some or all of the sites. Add the ones you think you might use on a regular basis to your Web browser's Bookmarks or Favorites list (or commit them to memory). That way you can zip to them easily whenever you need them.

Amazon.com Books

Amazon.com's mission is to sell books, and they do a superb job of that from their Web site, billed as "Earth's Biggest Bookstore." But the Web site is worth learning about even if you have no intention of ever placing a book order. Imagine being able to search a database of some 2.5 million books by author, title, subject, or keyword. You can produce a master list of all the books by a favorite author, for example, or search for every book with the word *chocolate* in the title. You'll also find current bestseller lists, author interviews, and book reviews from *The New York Times*, NPR, Oprah, and elsewhere.

If there's a book you're looking for that's not in the Amazon.com database (either because it's out of print or not yet published), let them know and they'll try to find it. If and when they do, you'll be contacted by e-mail.

CDNow

Like Amazon.com, CDNow is in the business of selling things—in this case, CDs and videos. To do so, they offer a searchable database of some 165,000 CDs and 35,000 movies. You can search the CD database by title or artist. The site also includes Top 20 lists, buyer's guides, sound clips, biographies, and entertainment news.

www.shareware.com

C|Net's Shareware.com

C|Net's Shareware.com is a "virtual software library" that lets you search a catalog of some 190,000 shareware programs of all types—games, utilities, screensavers, word-processor add-ons, fonts, etc. (Shareware is "software on the honor system." Try the program for a designated period—usually 30 days—and then register and pay for it if you decide to keep it on your system.) The programs themselves are located in shareware archives and corporate sites throughout the Internet, but they can be downloaded directly from Shareware.com.

A related C|Net search service called Download.com is available from the Shareware.com home page. The names are confusing at first, since, as we've said, you can both search for and download shareware from Shareware.com. So what's Download.com? It's a searchable catalog of demos, drivers, and patches offered by the creators of *commercial* (rather than shareware) programs.

Consumer World

Consumer World is a master search site for consumer-related information. The site's creator has identified over 1,500 consumer resources available on the Internet, categorized them for easy browsing, and added a search capability. Consumer agencies, product reviews and buyer's guides, travel bargains, the best credit card deals, health insurance options—you'll find information on these and more with a Consumer World search.

www.consumerworld.org

DineNet Menus Online

How's this for a neat idea: collect reviews, menus, and prices for hundreds of the best restaurants all over the United States and make them available (and searchable) on the Web? That's what DineNet Menus Online offers for these major metropolitan areas:

www.menusonline.com

Atlanta	Miami
Boston	New Orleans
Chicago	New York
Dallas	Philadelphia
Houston	San Diego
Kansas City	San Francisco
Long Island	Seattle
Los Angeles	Washington/Baltimore

Additional cities are sure to be added as this idea catches on. You can search for restaurants in a given area by location, type of cuisine, or "amenities" (things like wheelchair access, parking, special menus, smoking rules, entertainment, outdoor dining, and so forth).

Edmund's Automobile Buyer's Guides

Edmund's Buyer's Guides are required reading for anyone in the market for a new or used car. This Web site lets you look for the information online, when you need it: reviews by make and model, road test reports, dealer prices, used car and truck prices, loan and lease quotes, and more. It's actually a directory rather than a search engine, but the site is so well designed and organized that you really won't mind.

Automobile Buyer's Guides
www.edmunds.com

Electric Library

www.elibrary.com

Electric Library is an incredible research tool. It gives you access to a searchable database of more than 150 full-text newspapers, 800 magazines, 2,000 classic books, two international news wires, and countless maps, photographs, and TV and radio transcripts. You can pose a question in plain English and launch a search of the entire Electric Library database, or focus on one or more types of sources. This is a subscription service, but at $10 a month or $60 a year, it's a real bargain. You can sign up for a 30-day free trial at the Electric Library Web site.

Epicurious Food

www.epicurious.com

Created by Condé Nast, the publisher of *Gourmet* and *Bon Appétit* magazines, this Web site is a cook's and food-lover's delight. You'll find complete menus, practical cooking tips and techniques, and cookbook reviews and recommendations. But the best part about the site is its Recipe File, a searchable database of more than 6,000 recipes that have appeared in *Gourmet* and *Bon Appétit*. If you're a subscriber to one or both magazines, you'll appreciate not having to root through the recycle pile to find a recipe you forgot to clip out. Just search the database, using one or two keywords to identify the type of recipe and a unique ingredient: **eggplant and appetizer**, for example. Chances are, you'll find it.

FedEx Package Tracking

If you use overnight courier services on a regular basis, the FedEx Web site is one you should definitely get to know. It can be a real time-saver when the FedEx phone lines are busy, or any time you want to find out quickly whether your FedEx shipment has arrived at its destination or the location of your nearest FedEx dropbox.

www.fedex.com

With FedEx Package Tracking, you can search the company's shipping database by airbill number to find out exactly when your shipment was delivered and who signed for it. The Drop-off Locator, another searchable database, will help you identify the nearest self-service and staffed FedEx locations and the cutoff times for dropping off your package.

FindLaw Internet Legal Resources

FindLaw is one of the premier sites for doing legal research on the Web. You can browse the site's legal resources directory, which is organized by topic. Or use one of several FindLaw search services:

Internet Legal Resources
www.findlaw.com

- **LawCrawler Search** to find cases, codes, and regulations at legal sites throughout the Internet.

- **Supreme Court Decisions Search**, for cases dating back to 1937.

- **Law Reviews Search**, for the full text of law review articles on the Internet.

For best results, be sure to visit the FindLaw Help & Information page and read the "Primer Geared Toward Legal Research" offered there. You might also want to print a copy of the Search Help page, which is more complicated and extensive than you'll find at most special-purpose search engine sites. (To find Search Help, click on Options next to the FindLaw search form.)

www.healthatoz.com

www.imdb.com

HealthAtoZ

There's enough medical and health-related information on the Internet to make your heart race and your head spin, so it's no wonder that HealthAtoZ has become such a popular search tool. Designed for both health-care professionals and consumers, HealthAtoZ is a searchable database of resources on the Net—mostly Web sites, but newsgroups and mailing lists as well.

Nothing gets into the database without being reviewed first by a team of medical professionals who also tag the sites with appropriate keywords so that they can be found easily. You can search the entire HealthAtoZ database, or limit your search to a specific topic in the site's multi-level directory.

Internet Movie Database

"Where have I seen that character before?" If you've ever left a movie theater puzzling over that question, you need the Internet Movie Database (IMDb). With information on over 80,000 movies and hundreds of thousands of actors, actresses, and crew members, IMDb is the single best film resource we've encountered on the Web. You can search for a specific actor or actress (or crew member) for a brief biography and a complete list of other movie credits. Or you can search by movie title to find out when a particular film was made and who was involved in the production—director, cast, and crew.

MapQuest

MapQuest specializes in worldwide maps and driving directions between any two places in the United States. The maps won't replace your trusted road atlas or the large, fold-out variety you keep in the glove compartment of your car. But the point-to-point directions, which include estimated mileage, are a neat feature. Based on our experience, you'll still want to consult your favorite map or road atlas to verify the suggested route, but in general, MapQuest is pretty reliable. Give it a try before your next road trip.

www.mapquest.com

Microsoft Technical Support

If you've ever tried calling a major software company for technical support, you know how frustrating it can be to get even the simplest question answered. You either get a busy signal right from the start, or you work your way intently through the company's voice-mail menu system, only to be put on hold. Microsoft does a better job than most at handling technical support calls, but they also supplement their phone operation with this outstanding technical support Web site.

www.microsoft.com/support/

You'll want to be sure to learn how to use the Microsoft Knowledge Base. It's the place to look for answers to questions about any Microsoft product. (Click on Search Hints for advice and sample searches.) Other searchable databases offered at the site include Troubleshooting Wizards, Frequently Asked Questions, Help Files & Service Packs, and Microsoft Newsgroups.

If all else fails and you simply have to talk to a real person, click on Telephone Numbers for a directory of Microsoft Technical Support numbers and service options, organized by product.

"WHERE TO FIND WHAT TO READ"

www.nytimes.com/books/

The New York Times Book Reviews

One of several "New York Times on the Web" features, this site gives you access to all the book reviews, book news, and author interviews that have appeared in *The New York Times* since 1980, searchable by title, author, or keyword. You can also browse the current issue of *The New York Times Book Review*, which is supplemented by Web-only features like author interviews, complete first chapters of selected books, and expanded versions of the hardcover and paperback bestseller lists (30 titles instead of 15).

There's one important search tip to keep in mind for this site. To look for a book title or an author's name (or any phrase), enclose the words in single (rather than double) quotes: 'The Perfect Storm' or 'Sebastian Junger'.

Online Career Center

The Online Career Center (OCC) is one of the Internet's most popular job-hunting sites. You can search the OCC jobs database by keyword, company, industry, or location. The site also provides links to other job-related Internet resources like the online version of the *Occupational Outlook Handbook*, salary surveys, career fairs, and relocation services.

Online Career Center
The Internet's first and foremost career center

www.occ.com

SEARCHING FOR EVERYTHING

Parent Soup

Whether you're awaiting the birth of your first child or packing the last one off to college, you're sure to have questions and concerns, and Parent Soup's searchable Parenting Library may just have the answers. The database includes more than 4,000 articles on all aspects of parenting, from very specific concerns (like how to deal with the Beanie Baby craze) to more general issues like baby-proofing your house and financing your child's college education. Other popular search features at the site include the Baby Name Finder and the Directory of Parenting Organizations, both of which are searchable alphabetically—not by name or keyword, unfortunately.

www.parentsoup.com

Peterson's Education & Career Center

Brought to you by the publishers of *Peterson's Guide to Four-Year Colleges* and dozens of other well-known education and career guides, this site makes much of that same information available online in searchable form. There are separate databases for kindergarten and elementary schools, colleges and universities, graduate programs, studying abroad, camps and summer programs, special schools, and (for those who question whether learning can be fun) learning adventures and holidays.

www.petersons.com

www.promo.net/pg/

Project Gutenberg

Project Gutenberg was started more than 25 years ago by Michael Hart at the University of Illinois. His objective was to make all of the world's great works of literature available online so that students and researchers could study them at no cost. Volunteers from all over the world do the typing, and the project survives solely on donations.

Today, the Project Gutenberg archive includes more than 1,000 works, all of which are in the public domain, so no laws are being broken. You can search the archive for the complete text of *Aesop's Fables*, *Alice in Wonderland*, the *Bill of Rights*, *The Book of Mormon*, and the *King James Bible*, to name just a few examples. The project is also slowly expanding to include musical scores and important images (like the original Tenniel illustrations for *Alice in Wonderland* and an MPEG file of the moon landing).

Of course only the most dedicated and under-funded scholars would choose to read *Moby Dick* on their computer screens. The real advantage to having great works of literature available online is that they can be down-loaded to your computer and then searched using any word processor.

Tax Information: 1040.com

Have you ever sat down to work on your taxes, only to find that you're missing one vital form? It's probably an obscure one, too—one that's not likely to be available at the post office or library, even if they're still open when you make your discovery.

www.1040.com

Thanks to 1040.com, a service of Drake Software, you never need face this problem again. You can download Federal and State tax forms, along with all the relevant instructions and publications, at any time of the day or night. (The IRS Web site at **www.irs.ustreas.gov** offers tax forms, too, but 1040.com is faster and the address is easier to remember.) You'll need the Adobe Acrobat reader to view and print the forms, but that, too, is available for downloading at 1040.com.

Thomas Legislative Information

Hosted by the Library of Congress, this site was named in honor of Thomas Jefferson, who founded that institution by donating his substantial collection of books to it. Thomas is the place to look for the full text of legislation under consideration by Congress, the *Congressional Record*, Committee Reports, and historical documents like the *Declaration of Independence* and the *Constitution*.

thomas.loc.gov

You can search for legislation by keyword or sponsor, and you can limit your search in a number of ways: House bills only, Senate bills only, bills that were the subject of floor action, bills that have been signed into law, etc. A detailed explanation of the whole legislative process ("How Our Laws Are Made") is also offered at the site. Last but not least, you'll find a master list of links for all the official U.S. Government Web sites—every agency in the Executive, Legislative, and Judicial branches.

www.ups.com

www.wsj.com

www.zdnet.com/findit/

UPS Package Tracking

Not to be outdone by FedEx, rival UPS also offers Package Tracking and Drop-off Locator features at its Web site. For Package Tracking, you simply key in the UPS tracking number to check on the status of your shipment. The Drop-off Locator helps you find the nearest place (often your neighborhood grocery or office-supply store) that will accept packages for shipping by UPS.

The Wall Street Journal Interactive Edition

Don't cancel your subscription to the traditional paper version of *The Wall Street Journal* that's delivered in time to enjoy with your morning coffee. But if you'd like to be able to search online for articles that have appeared in the *Journal* during the past two weeks, spring for an extra $29 per year ($49 for non-subscribers) for access to *The Wall Street Journal* Interactive Edition at this Web site.

Subscribers to the Interactive Edition can also search the Dow Jones News/Retrieval Publications Library—more than 3,600 newspapers, news wires, magazines, trade and business journals, transcripts, and newsletters. Searching this database is provided as part of your Interactive Edition subscription, but any articles you choose to view and print or save to disk are billed at $2.95 each (or $9.95 per month for up to 15 articles).

ZDNet Software Library and Reviews

ZDNet is the online home for *PC Magazine* and more than a dozen other Ziff-Davis computer publications. It's one of the best technology sites on the Internet and a great place to search for hardware and software reviews, public domain and shareware software, and profiles of high-tech companies. The site's Find It feature lets you search four major ZDNet databases:

- Articles, reviews, and buyer's guides from Ziff-Davis computer magazines and newspapers.

- ZDNet's Software Library of public domain and shareware software for DOS and Windows PCs.

- MacUser's Software Central collection of public domain and shareware software for the Macintosh.

- Company profiles and contact information (sales, technical support, etc.) from ZDNet's Company Finder.

The next time you're considering a hardware or software purchase or face a computing problem of some sort, check here first. You won't be disappointed.

ZIP Code Lookups

The U.S. Postal Service is the target of lots of criticism and jokes, but here's an example of something they're really doing right: a convenient, easy-to-use ZIP code locator. Just key in a street address, city, and state, and the system will tell you almost instantly what the nine-digit ZIP+4 code is for that location.

When you think about the time and effort required to travel to the Post Office and thumb through that big fat ZIP code directory they keep there, this is a wonderful innovation. And a great example to leave you with as we end this chapter (and this part of the book) on special-purpose search engines.

www.usps.gov

APPENDIX A: SEARCH ENGINE QUICK REFERENCE

For each search engine covered in this book, we've assembled the most important commands and other essential information into one or more Quick Reference guides. How do you do an AND search with AltaVista or Excite? Are Infoseek queries case sensitive? What Boolean operators are allowed with Lycos? This is the information we have always wanted to have at hand for our own online searches but could never find all in one place.

The Quick Reference guides appear throughout the book in the individual search engine chapters. But we've collected all of them into this appendix, arranged in alphabetical order by search engine name, to make them easier to find. If you're like us, you'll be turning to these pages often as you explore the Web with your favorite search engines.

AltaVista

AltaVista Simple Search Quick Reference		
FOR THIS TYPE OF SEARCH:	DO THIS:	EXAMPLES:
Phrase	Type the phrase as a sequence of words surrounded by **double quotes**.	"Battle of Trafalgar"
Wildcard	Use an **asterisk** at the end of or within a word with at least three letters of the search term.	Brit* col*r
AND Search (multiple words and phrases, each of which *must* be present)	Use a **plus sign** in front of each word or phrase that must appear in the results.	+London +"art museum"
OR Search (multiple words and phrases, any one of which may be present)	Type words or phrases separated by spaces, without any special notation.	Stratford Shakespeare
NOT Search (to exclude a word or phrase)	Use a **minus sign** in front of word or phrase you want to exclude from results.	+python —monty
Proximity Search	Not available with Simple Search. Use Advanced Search.	
Nested Search	Not available with Simple Search. Use Advanced Search.	
Case-Sensitive Search	Use lowercase to find *any combination* of upper- and lower-case. Use capital letters to force an *exact match* of your search term. Example would match *Bath* but not *bath* or *BATH*.	Bath
Date Search	Not available with Simple Search. Use Advanced Search.	
Field Search	Type field-search keyword in lowercase, followed by a colon and your search word or phrase. (See page 193 for Web page field-search keywords.)	title:"Victoria and Albert Museum" host:cambridge.edu domain:com
Weighted Keyword Search	Not available with Simple Search. Use Advanced Search.	

AltaVista

AltaVista Web Page Field Search Quick Reference

FIELD	DESCRIPTION	EXAMPLES
title:	Limits search to the part of the Web page that the author labeled as the title.	title:"John Lennon"
host:	Searches just the *host name* portion of Web addresses.	host:beatlefest.com host:oxford.edu host:BBC
domain:	Searches Web addresses for a specific domain (com, edu, gov, net, org, etc.) or two-letter Internet country code. (See Appendix B for complete list.)	domain:edu domain:uk
applet:	Searches for names or addresses of Java applets (small programs embedded in a Web page). If you don't know the name of the applet, try combining an applet wildcard search with some other search term.	applet:beatles applet:*
image:	Searches Web pages for the filenames of images matching your search term.	image:ringo.gif image:*.gif
link:	Searches for hypertext links (URL) embedded in a Web page.	link:beatles.com
object:	Searches Web for ActiveX objects.	object:crescendo object:*
text:	Searches for text in the body of the Web page.	text:"Strawberry Fields"
url:	Searches for text in complete Web addresses (URLs).	url:beatles.html

AltaVista Usenet Newsgroup Field Search Quick Reference

FIELD	DESCRIPTION	EXAMPLES
newsgroups:	Allows you to limit your search to specific newsgroups or newsgroup categories (alt, comp, rec, news, etc.)	newsgroups:rec.music.beatles newsgroups:rec.*
from:	Searches the newsgroup message *from* field containing the sender's e-mail address and possibly also the sender's real name, nickname, and/or company name.	from:"Prince Charles" from:royalfamily.com
subject:	Searches the subject field of newsgroup messages for the text you specify.	subject:"Beatles Poster" subject:"for sale"
summary:	Searches the summary field. Of limited value, because most people don't bother to provide summary information for their postings.	summary:"Paul McCartney"
keywords:	Searches for keywords (if any) provided by the person who posted the message.	keywords:musician

APPENDIX A

AltaVista

AltaVista Advanced Search Quick Reference

FOR THIS TYPE OF SEARCH:	DO THIS:	EXAMPLES:
Phrase	Type the phrase as a sequence of words surrounded by **double quotes**.	"Tower of London"
Wildcard	Use an **asterisk** at the end of or within a word with at least three letters of the search term.	bicycl*
AND Search (multiple words and phrases, each of which *must* be present)	Use **AND** between words or phrases to specify that both must be present in the results.	Oxford AND Cambridge
OR Search (multiple words and phrases, any one of which may be present)	Use **OR** between words or phrases to specify that you want to find references to either or both items.	Oxford OR Cambridge
NOT Search (to exclude a word or phrase)	Use **AND NOT** in front of the word or phrase you want to exclude from the query.	Oxford AND NOT Cambridge
Proximity Search	Use **NEAR** to find words or phrases that appear within 10 words of each other. The example would find *bed and breakfast* as well as *bed & breakfast* and *breakfast in bed.*	bed NEAR breakfast
Nested Search	Use **parentheses** to group search expressions into more complex queries. The example would find *Prince of Wales* as well as *Prince and Princess of Wales.*	(Prince OR Princess) NEAR "of Wales"
Case-sensitive Search	Use lowercase to find *any combination* of upper- and lower-case. Use capital letters to force an *exact match* of your search term, as shown in the example.	"Round Table"
Date Search	Type the date or range of dates you want to search in the Start Date and End Date boxes. Use the form DD/MMM/YY.	01/Jul/97
Field Search	Type field-search keyword in lowercase, immediately followed by a colon and your search word or phrase. (See page 193 for Web page field-search keywords.)	title:"Castle Howard" host:royalfamily.com domain:edu
Keyword Weighting	In the Results Ranking Criteria box, type the word or phrase that should be given the greatest weight. Web pages or newsgroup postings meeting your criteria will appear at the head of the list.	See page 47 for a sample search.

Argus Clearinghouse

Argus Clearinghouse Quick Reference		
FOR THIS TYPE OF SEARCH:	DO THIS:	EXAMPLES:
Phrase Search	Type the phrase as a sequence of words enclosed in **double quotes**.	"news media"
Wildcard Search	Use an **asterisk** (*) to search for wildcard characters at the end of a word. The example would find *biology* as well as *biological* and *biologist*.	biolog*
AND Search (multiple words and phrases, each of which *must* be present)	Use **AND** to connect two or more words or phrases. The example would find guides whose titles or keywords include both words.	Asia AND business
OR Search (multiple words and phrases, any one of which may be present)	Use **OR** to connect two or more words or phrases, either one of which might appear in the guide's title or keywords.	justice OR judicial
Nested Search	Use **parentheses** to group search expressions into more complex queries. The example would find references to *art museum*, *art gallery*, and *art galleries*.	art AND (museum OR galler*)

Deja News

Deja News Stopwords Quick Reference

Stopwords are words that search engines ignore because they are too common and therefore don't really help to narrow a search. Here's the current list of Deja News stopwords.

1994	as	gmt	lines	organization	that
1995	be	have	may	path	the
1996	but	i	message-id	re	there
a	can	if	newsgroups	references	this
an	date	in	nntp-posting-host	s	to
and	do	is	of	sender	uuneo
any	for	it	on	subject	with
are	from	jan	or	t	you

Deja News

Deja News Quick Search and Power Search Quick Reference

FOR THIS TYPE OF SEARCH:	DO THIS:	EXAMPLES:
Phrase Search	Type the phrase as a sequence of words surrounded by **double quotes**. (Note: Deja News searches are *not* case sensitive.)	"forensic medicine"
	Restrictions: Wildcards cannot be used within phrases. Also, phrases must contain at least two words that are not Deja News *stopwords*. For a list of stopwords, see page 195.	
Wildcard Search	Use an **asterisk** (*) to search for wildcard characters. The example would find *therapeutic, therapist,* and *therapy.*	therap*
	You can also use **braces** to search for a range of words. The example would find all words that fall alphabetically between *therapeutic* and *therapy.*	{therapeutic therapy}
AND Search (multiple words and phrases, each of which *must* be present)	Use **AND** or **&** to connect two or more words or phrases. Or simply type the words or phrases separated by a space. All three of the examples would produce the same results.	cholesterol AND exercise cholesterol & exercise cholesterol exercise
OR Search (multiple words and phrases, any one of which may be present)	Use **OR** or **|** to connect two or more words or phrases. Both examples would find newsgroup postings that mention either fitness or nutrition.	fitness OR nutrition fitness | nutrition
NOT Search (to exclude a word or phrase)	Use **NOT** or **&!** in front of a word or phrase you want to exclude from your results. To look for postings about vitamins but not multi-level marketing deals, for example, you might want to exclude *mlm.*	vitamins NOT mlm vitamins &! mlm
Proximity Search	Use **^** to find words that appear in close proximity to each other. The default distance is 5 *characters,* but you can change that by including a number following the **^** symbol. The second example would look for the two words within 30 characters of each other.	infertility ^ treatment infertility ^30 treatment
	Restrictions: Phrases aren't allowed with Deja News proximity searches. Also, neither search term can be on the Deja News stopwords list. (See page 195 for stopwords.)	
Nested Search	Use **parentheses** to group search expressions into more complex queries. The example would find postings that mention a *clinical study* or *clinical trial.*	clinical & (study | trial)
Field Search	Use one of the **field-search operators** shown below in front of your search term to zero in on a specific field in newsgroup postings: Author: **~a** Subject: **~s** Group name: **~g** Date Created: **~dc**	~a bjones ~s lyme disease ~g sci.med.diseases.* ~dc 1997/04/01
	For even easier (fill-in-the-blank) field searching, use the Deja News Search Filter.	

Excite

Excite Quick Reference		
FOR THIS TYPE OF SEARCH:	DO THIS:	EXAMPLES:
Phrase	Type the phrase as a sequence of words surrounded by **double quotes**. Excite will search for that phrase *and* related concepts.	"Kentucky Derby"
Concept or idea	Simply type a phrase or question that expresses the idea or concept. Use as many words as necessary.	thoroughbred racing Kentucky Where can I find information about thoroughbred racing in Kentucky?
AND Search (multiple words and phrases, each of which *must* be present)	Use a **plus sign** in front of each word or phrase that *must* appear in the results. Alternatively, you can use **AND** (all caps) between the words or phrases. Using AND tells Excite to turn off its concept-based searching.	+racing + "Churchill Downs" racing AND "Churchill Downs"
OR Search (multiple words and phrases, any one of which may be present)	Type words or phrases separated by a space, without any special notation. Excite will search for either term *and* for related concepts. Alternatively, you can use **OR** (all caps) between each word or phrase. (If you use OR, Excite will turn off concept-based searching and return just those sites containing references to at least one of the search terms.)	Derby Preakness Derby OR Preakness
NOT Search (to exclude a word or phrase)	Use a **minus sign** in front of a word or phrase you want to exclude from results. Or use AND NOT (all caps) in front of the word or phrase you want to exclude. (Concept-based searching will be turned off.)	"horse race" —Derby "horse race" AND NOT Derby
Nested Search	Use **parentheses** to group search expressions into more complex queries.	racing AND (horse OR thoroughbred)
Query by Example	Click on "More Like This" next to any item on the search results page.	

Four11

Four11 Quick Reference		

FOR THIS TYPE OF SEARCH:	DO THIS:	EXAMPLES:
E-mail Address Search (worldwide)	Start by completing just the First and Last Name fields.	First Name: Ted, Last Name: Fletcher, Search, ☑ SmartName (Bob=Robert)
	To narrow your search, complete additional fields one at a time, in this order: • Country • State/Province • City • Company or Domain • Group Connections (Available on Advanced Search page only. Click on Power Search to get there.) Note: You can also narrow a search by turning off Four11's SmartName feature. On the Advanced Search page, turn off both SmartName *and* Flexible Search.	
	Use an **asterisk** (*) to do a wildcard search. The example would find listings for *Jane Anderson*, *Andersen*, and *Andersson*. Note: You can use wildcards in the First Name, Last Name, and City fields.	First Name: Jane, Last Name: Anders*, Search, ☑ SmartName (Bob=Robert)
Home Address and Phone Number Search (U.S. only)	Click on Telephone in the Directories menu on the Four11 home page to access the U.S. Telephone Number search form. Start by completing the First and Last Name fields.	First Name: Alan, Last Name: Fowler, Search
	To narrow your search, complete more fields one at a time, in this order: • State • City • Street	
	Use an **asterisk** (*) to do a wildcard search in the First Name, Last Name, or City fields. The example would find listings in the cities of *Greensboro* and *Greenville*.	Street: , City: Green*, State: NC
Government Search (White House and Congress)	Click on Government in the Directories menu on the Four11 home page. Then follow the links to find the e-mail addresses and home pages for the White House and members of Congress.	Directories menu: E-Mail, ▶ Telephone, Yellow Pages, Maps/Directions, Net Phone, Government, Celebrity
Celebrity Search	Click on Celebrity in the Directories menu on the Four11 home page.	Directories menu: E-Mail, ▶ Telephone, Yellow Pages, Maps/Directions, Net Phone, Government, Celebrity, Cool Services
	From the Celebrity search page, you can by category (Actors, Authors, Sports Stars, etc.). But your best bet is to click on Full Celebrity Listings and search the entire database alphabetically.	

HotBot

HotBot Quick Reference	

FOR THIS TYPE OF SEARCH:	DO THIS:
Phrase Search	Type the phrase without any special punctuation and select "**the exact phrase**" on the drop-down menu.
	Alternatively, you can type phrases as a sequence of words surrounded by **double quotes** (" ") and select "**all the words**" or "**any of the words**" from the drop-down menu.
AND Search (multiple words and phrases, each of which *must* be present)	Type words or phrases and select "**all the words**" from the drop-down menu.
	You can also combine words and phrases with **AND** and select "**the Boolean expression**" from the menu.
OR Search (multiple words and phrases, any one of which may be present)	Type words or phrases separated by spaces and select "**any of the words**" from the menu.
	Alternatively, combine words and phrases with **OR** and choose "**the Boolean expression**" from the menu.
NOT Search (to exclude a word or phrase)	Use a **minus sign** (−) in front of a word or phrase you want to exclude from the results.
	Or use **NOT** in front the word or phrase and specify "**the Boolean expression**."
Nested Search	Combine search terms with **parentheses** and select "**the Boolean expression**" from the menu.
Case-Sensitive Search	Use lowercase to find *any combination* of upper- and lowercase. Use the correct combination of upper- and lowercase letters (for example, HotWired or NeXT) to force an *exact match* of your search term.
Date Search	Open the **Date tool** and select a time frame (days, months, or years) or a specific "before" or "after" date.
Location Search (Web site, domain, country, or geography)	Open the **Location tool** and choose CyberPlace to search for a specific Web site, Internet domain (.com, .edu, .gov, etc.), or country. Choose GeoPlace to search by geography.
Field Search (Media Type)	Open the **Media Type tool** and choose the file types and/or file extensions you want to find.
Field Search (Other)	See HotBot **Meta Words** on page 200.
Weighted Keyword Search	Put a **plus sign** (+) in front of a word or phrase that should be ranked higher in the results and select "all the words" or "any of the words" from the menu.

APPENDIX A

HotBot

HotBot Meta Words*	
META WORD FORMAT	**WHAT IT DOES**
domain:*name*	Restricts search to the domain name selected. Domains can be specified up to three levels: **domain:com domain:ford.com domain:www.ford.com**
depth:*number*	Limits how deep within a Web site your search goes. To go three pages deep, use **depth:3**.
linkdomain:*name*	Restricts search to pages containing links to the domain you specify. For example, **linkdomain:edmunds.com** finds pages that point to the Edmund's Car Guides Web site.
linkext:*extension*	Restricts search to pages containing embedded files with a particular extension. For example, **linkext:ra** finds pages containing RealAudio files.
scriptlanguage:JavaScript	Allows you to search for pages containing JavaScript.
scriptlanguage:VBScript	Allows you to search for pages containing VBScript.
newsgroup:*newsgroup name*	Restricts Usenet newsgroup searches to articles that have been posted to the specified newsgroup.
feature:*name*	Limits your query to pages containing the specified feature.
feature:embed	Detects plug-ins
feature:script	Detects embedded scripts
feature:applet	Detects embedded Java applets
feature:activex	Detects ActiveX controls or layouts
feature:audio	Detects audio formats
feature:video	Detects video formats
feature:acrobat	Detects Acrobat files
feature:frame	Detects frames in HTML documents
feature:table	Detects tables in HTML documents
feature:form	Detects forms in HTML documents
feature:vrml	Detects VRML files
feature:image	Detects image files (GIF, JPEG, etc.)
after:*day/month/year*	Restricts search to documents created or modified after a specific date: **Explorer AND after:30/09/97**.
before:*day/month/year*	Restricts search to documents created or modified before a specific date: **"buyer's guide" AND before:01/01/97**.
within:*number/unit*	Restricts search to documents created or modified within a specific time period. *Unit* can be *days*, *months*, or *years*. **Jeep AND within:3/months**.

*Note: The words shown in italics are variables. You'll find examples of the terms you can use for each of these variables in the column labeled "What It Does."

Infoseek

Infoseek Quick Reference		
FOR THIS TYPE OF SEARCH:	**DO THIS:**	**EXAMPLES:**
Plain-English Question	Simply type a phrase or question that expresses the idea or concept. Use as many words as necessary.	Where can I find information about "study abroad" programs in France?
Phrase Search	Type the phrase as a sequence of words surrounded by **double quotes**. Or put **hyphens** between the words that must appear together.	"youth hostel" study-abroad-program
AND Search (multiple words and phrases, each of which *must* be present)	Use a **plus sign** in front of each word or phrase that must appear in the results.	+Princeton +"financial aid"
OR Search (multiple words and phrases, any one of which may be present)	Type words or phrases separated by spaces, without any special punctuation.	grants scholarships loans
NOT Search (to exclude a word or phrase)	Use a **minus sign** in front of word or phrase you want to exclude from results.	"Shirley Temple" —cocktail
Case-Sensitive Search	Use lowercase to find *any combination* of upper- and lowercase. Use upper- and lowercase to force an exact match. The example would find *Java* but not *java* or *JAVA*.	Java
	Use initial caps to search for a person's name. To search for several names (or two versions of the same name), separate them with commas.	Steven Spielberg Hitchcock, Alfred Hitchcock
Field Search (title, URL, Web link, Web site)	Type field-search keyword in lowercase, followed by a colon and your search word or phrase.	title:"Jurassic Park" url:www.travelocity.com link:mrshowbiz site:disney.com
	To search a specific Web site for a word or phrase, you must put a plus (+) sign in front of each search term.	+site:disney.com +Dalmatian
Image Search	Click on Ultraseek, then Imageseek, and type your search term in the Search text box.	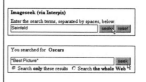
Set Search	Using the main (Ultrasmart) search form, do your first search. Scroll down to the bottom of the page, add one or more new search terms, and use the "Search Only These Results" feature to perform a new search.	
	Using the Ultraseek search form, add a **pipe symbol** (|) and another search term or phrase to your original query. Then click on Seek to look for the new term within your previous set of search results.	Oscars | "Best Picture"

Lizst

Liszt Quick Reference		
FOR THIS TYPE OF SEARCH:	DO THIS:	EXAMPLES:
Word or Phrase Search	Enclose the word or phrase in **double quotes**. (Without the quotes, Liszt performs a *string search* and thus might find references to the Marshall family reunion as well as the planet Mars.)	"mars" "handwriting analysis"
Wildcard Search	Use an **asterisk** (∗) to search for wildcard characters, or simply type a sequence of letters and Liszt will perform a string search. The first two examples would find both *dance* and *dancing*. The third would find *baseball* and *basketball*.	danc∗ danc b∗ball
AND Search (multiple words and phrases, each of which *must* be present)	Use **and** (lowercase) to connect two or more words or phrases. Or simply type the words or phrases separated by a space, since AND searching is the default.	ballroom and swing ballroom swing
OR Search (multiple words and phrases, any one of which may be present)	Use **or** (lowercase) to connect two or more words or phrases.	bird or birding
NOT Search (to exclude a word or phrase)	Use **not** (lowercase) in front of a word or phrase you want to exclude from your results.	music not jazz
Nested Search	Use **parentheses** to group search expressions into more complex queries.	games and (board or card)
Case-Sensitive Search	Click on Advanced Search Options on the Liszt home page and activate the Case Sensitive radio button.	⦿ Case sensitive ○ Case insensitive

APPENDIX A

Lycos

Lycos Basic Search Quick Reference		
FOR THIS TYPE OF SEARCH:	DO THIS:	EXAMPLES:
Phrase Search	Type the phrase as a sequence of words surrounded by **double quotes**.	"oyster mushroom"
AND Search (multiple words and phrases, each of which *must* be present)	Use a **plus sign** in front of each word or phrase that must appear in the results.	"oyster mushroom" +recipe
OR Search (multiple words and phrases, any one of which may be present)	Type words and phrases separated by a space without any special punctuation. Lycos will search for documents containing either term.	mushrooms mycology
NOT Search (to exclude a word or phrase)	Use a **minus sign** in front of a word or phrase you want to exclude from the results.	magazine —computer
Plain-English Search	Not available on basic search form. Use Lycos Pro with Java Power Panel and choose The Natural Language Query option (see page 205).	
Boolean Search (including Proximity Search)	Not available on basic search form. Use Lycos Pro with Java Power Panel and choose The Boolean Expression option (see page 205).	
Multimedia Files	Choose Sounds or Pictures in the search form's drop-down menu. Or click on the Pictures & Sounds button at the top of the Lycos home page.	
Web Site Reviews	To search for reviews, choose Top 5% in the search form's drop-down menu. To browse the directory of reviews, click on the Top 5% button at the top of every Lycos page.	

Lycos

Lycos Pro Custom Search Quick Reference

FOR THIS TYPE OF SEARCH:	DO THIS:	EXAMPLES:
Phrase Search	Type the phrase as sequence of words surrounded by **double quotes**.	"French table wines"
AND Search (multiple words and phrases, each of which *must* be present)	Type the words (or phrases in quotes) in the search form text box and choose All the Words from the drop-down menu.	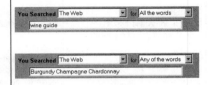
OR Search (multiple words and phrases, any one of which may be present)	Type the words (or phrases in quotes) in the search form text box and choose Any of the Words from the drop-down menu.	
NOT Search (to exclude a word or phrase)	Use a **minus sign** in front of a word or phrase you want to exclude from the results.	Chardonnay —California
Plain-English Search	Not available with Lycos Pro Custom Search. Use Lycos Pro with Java Power Panel and choose The Natural Language Query option (see page 205).	
Boolean Search (including Proximity Search)	Not available with Lycos Pro Custom Search. Use Lycos Pro with Java Power Panel and choose The Boolean Expression option (see page 205).	
Multimedia Files	Choose Sounds or Pictures in the search form's drop-down menu and type your query using any of the commands described in this Quick Reference.	
Web Site Reviews	Choose Top 5% in the search form's drop-down menu and type your query using any of the commands described in this Quick Reference.	

Lycos

Lycos Pro with Java Power Panel Quick Reference

FOR THIS TYPE OF SEARCH:	DO THIS:	EXAMPLES:
Phrase	Type the phrase in the search form text box and choose The Exact Phrase from the drop-down menu. Note that you don't need quotation marks if you specify The Exact Phrase.	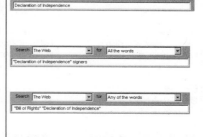
AND Search (multiple words and phrases, each of which *must* be present)	Type the words (or phrases in quotes) in the search form text box and choose All the Words from the drop-down menu.	
OR Search (multiple words and phrases, any one of which may be present)	Type the words (or phrases in quotes) in the search form text box and choose Any of the Words from the drop-down menu.	
Plain-English Search	Type your question in the search form text box and choose The Natural Language Query from the drop-down menu.	
Boolean Search	Type your query in the search form text box using Boolean operators and choose The Boolean Expression from the drop-down menu.	
	You can use any of the following Boolean operators. (We've used uppercase, but lowercase works as well.)	
	• *Combine* terms with AND, OR, NOT.	Leonardo AND Michelangelo Chico OR Zeppo Marx NOT Brothers
	• *Require* or *exclude* terms with plus (+) or minus (−) signs. Produces much the same results as AND and NOT.	Leonardo +Michelangelo Marx −Brothers
	• For *phrases*, use quotation marks.	"Panama hat"
	• For more *complex queries*, group search terms with parentheses, or with [ ], < >, or {}. This is often referred to as a *nested search*.	"clip art" AND (animals OR tiger)
	• For *proximity searches*, use ADJ (words adjacent to each other in any order) or NEAR (within 25 words). Also available (but less useful) are FAR (at least 25 words apart), and BEFORE.	car ADJ race "Jimmy Stewart" NEAR career
	• For more precise proximity searches, add a forward slash (/) and any word count you choose: **NEAR/5**, for example, to look for search terms within five words of each other.	"Men in Black" NEAR/5 review
Multimedia Files	Choose Sounds or Pictures in the search form's drop-down menu and type your query using any of the commands described in this Quick Reference.	
Web Site Reviews	Choose Top 5% in the search form's drop-down menu and type your query using any of the commands described in this Quick Reference.	

APPENDIX A

Yahoo!

Yahoo! Quick Reference

FOR THIS TYPE OF SEARCH:	DO THIS:	EXAMPLES:
Phrase Search	Type the phrase as a sequence of words surrounded by **double quotes**.	"Russian lacquer boxes"
AND Search (multiple words and phrases, each of which *must* be present)	Use a **plus sign** in front of a word or phrase that *must* appear in the results. The plus sign in front of the first word is not required, but we've found you get more precise results if you include it.	+antiques +18th-century
OR Search (multiple words and phrases, any one of which may be present)	Type words or phrases separated by a space, without any special notation.	"Carl Faberge" "Faberge egg"
NOT Search (to exclude a word or phrase)	Use a **minus sign** in front of a word or phrase you want to exclude from your results. To find software Easter eggs, for example, you might want to exclude the word *Fabergé*.	"Easter eggs" —Faberge
Wildcard Search *lacquerware.*	Use an **asterisk** (*) with at least the first three letters of your search term. The example would find references to *lacquer* as well as *lacquered* and	lacq*
Field Search	Use **t:** directly in front of a word or phrase to limit your search to *titles* of Web page documents. Use **u:** to search for the word or phrase in document URLs.	t:"oriental rugs" u:"oriental rugs"
Date Search	Click on Options to get to the Search Options page and use the drop-down menu to select a timeframe (1 day to 3 years).	Find only new listings added during the past

APPENDIX A

Zip2 Yellow Pages

Zip2 Yellow Pages Quick Reference

FOR THIS TYPE OF SEARCH:	DO THIS:	EXAMPLES:
Business Name Search	To search for a specific business, enter its name (or one or two unique words) in the Quick Search form and activate the Business Name radio button. By default, Zip2 searches for businesses near your home. To select another area, use the drop-down menu.	
Business Category Search	To search for all the businesses in a particular category, type one or two unique words in the Quick Search form and activate the Business Type radio button. Be sure to specify the area you want to search using the drop-down menu.	
Point-to-Point Driving Directions and Maps	Click on the Get Directions icon next to any listing in your Zip2 search results. For point-to-point directions without searching, click on Get Directions on the Zip2 home page.	

APPENDIX B:
INTERNET DOMAINS
AND COUNTRY CODES

Many search engines let you look for Web sites based on Internet *domains* and *country codes*. Searching by domain allows you to focus your search on a particular *type* of organization: commercial, education, government, etc. Searching by country code makes it possible to zero in on (or avoid) sites that originate in a specific country.

To help you take full advantage of domain and country code search options, this appendix includes three lists:

- Common Internet Domains

- Country Codes (Alphabetical by Country)

- Country Codes (Alphabetical by Code)

Even if you never have occasion to do a domain or country code search, this information may come in handy from time to time, simply for deciphering an e-mail or Web site address. Internet domains are pretty obvious, but you'll find that country codes aren't always easy to guess: AU, for example, is Australia (not Austria, which is AT).

Common Internet Domains

DOMAIN	TYPE
COM	Commercial
EDU	Education
GOV	Government
INT	International
MIL	Military (U.S.)
NET	Network
ORG	Non-Profit Organization

Country Codes (Alphabetical by Country)

COUNTRY	CODE	COUNTRY	CODE	COUNTRY	CODE
Afghanistan	AF	Chad	TD	Greece	GR
Albania	AL	Chile	CL	Greenland	GL
Algeria	DZ	China	CN	Grenada	GD
American Samoa	AS	Christmas Island	CX	Guadeloupe (French)	GP
Andorra	AD	Cocos (Keeling) Islands	CC	Guam (U.S.)	GU
Angola	AO	Colombia	CO	Guatemala	GT
Anguilla	AI	Comoros	KM	Guernsey (Channel Islands)	GG
Antarctica	AQ	Congo	CG	Guiana (French)	GF
Antigua and Barbuda	AG	Congo (formerly Zaire)	ZR	Guinea	GN
Argentina	AR	Cook Islands	CK	Guinea Bissau	GW
Armenia	AM	Costa Rica	CR	Guyana	GY
Aruba	AW	Croatia	HR	Haiti	HT
Australia	AU	Cuba	CU	Heard and McDonald Islands	HM
Austria	AT	Cyprus	CY	Honduras	HN
Azerbaijan	AZ	Czech Republic	CZ	Hong Kong	HK
Bahamas	BS	Denmark	DK	Hungary	HU
Bahrain	BH	Djibouti	DJ	Iceland	IS
Bangladesh	BD	Dominica	DM	India	IN
Barbados	BB	Dominican Republic	DO	Indonesia	ID
Belarus	BY	East Timor	TP	Iran	IR
Belgium	BE	Ecuador	EC	Iraq	IQ
Belize	BZ	Egypt	EG	Ireland	IE
Benin	BJ	El Salvador	SV	Isle of Man	IM
Bermuda	BM	Equatorial Guinea	GQ	Israel	IL
Bhutan	BT	Eritrea	ER	Italy	IT
Bolivia	BO	Estonia	EE	Ivory Coast	CI
Bosnia-Herzegovina	BA	Ethiopia	ET	Jamaica	JM
Botswana	BW	Falkland Islands (Malvinas)	FK	Japan	JP
Bouvet Island	BV	Faroe Islands	FO	Jersey (Channel Islands)	JE
Brazil	BR	Fiji	FJ	Jordan	JO
British Indian Ocean Territory	IO	Finland	FI	Kazakhstan	KZ
Brunei Darussalam	BN	France	FR	Kenya	KE
Bulgaria	BG	France (European Territory)	FX	Kiribati	KI
Burkina Faso	BF	French Southern Territories	TF	Korea (North)	KP
Burundi	BI	Gabon	GA	Korea (South)	KR
Cambodia	KH	Gambia	GM	Kuwait	KW
Cameroon	CM	Georgia	GE	Kyrgyz Republic	KG
Canada	CA	Germany	DE	Laos	LA
Cape Verde	CV	Ghana	GH	Latvia	LV
Cayman Islands	KY	Gibraltar	GI	Lebanon	LB
Central African Republic	CF	Great Britain	GB	Lesotho	LS

Country Codes (Alphabetical by Country)

COUNTRY	CODE	COUNTRY	CODE	COUNTRY	CODE
Liberia	LR	Oman	OM	Suriname	SR
Libya	LY	Pakistan	PK	Svalbard and Jan Mayen Islands	SJ
Liechtenstein	LI	Palau	PW	Swaziland	SZ
Lithuania	LT	Panama	PA	Sweden	SE
Luxembourg	LU	Papua New Guinea	PG	Switzerland	CH
Macau	MO	Paraguay	PY	Syria	SY
Macedonia	MK	Peru	PE	Tadjikistan	TJ
Madagascar	MG	Philippines	PH	Taiwan	TW
Malawi	MW	Pitcairn	PN	Tanzania	TZ
Malaysia	MY	Poland	PL	Thailand	TH
Maldives	MV	Polynesia (French)	PF	Togo	TG
Mali	ML	Portugal	PT	Tokelau	TK
Malta	MT	Puerto Rico (U.S.)	PR	Tonga	TO
Marshall Islands	MH	Qatar	QA	Trinidad and Tobago	TT
Martinique (French)	MQ	Reunion (French)	RE	Tunisia	TN
Mauritania	MR	Romania	RO	Turkey	TR
Mauritius	MU	Russian Federation	RU	Turkmenistan	TM
Mayotte	YT	Rwanda	RW	Turks and Caicos Islands	TC
Mexico	MX	Saint Lucia	LC	Tuvalu	TV
Micronesia	FM	San Marino	SM	Uganda	UG
Moldova	MD	Saudi Arabia	SA	Ukraine	UA
Monaco	MC	Senegal	SN	United Arab Emirates	AE
Mongolia	MN	Seychelles	SC	United Kingdom	UK
Montserrat	MS	Sierra Leone	SL	United States	US
Morocco	MA	Singapore	SG	United States Minor Outlying Islands	UM
Mozambique	MZ	Slovakia (Slovak Republic)	SK	Uruguay	UY
Myanmar	MM	Slovenia	SI	Uzbekistan	UZ
Namibia	NA	Solomon Islands	SB	Vanuatu	VU
Nauru	NR	Somalia	SO	Vatican City State	VA
Nepal	NP	South Africa	ZA	Venezuela	VE
Netherland Antilles	AN	South Georgia and South Sandwich Islands	GS	Vietnam	VN
Netherlands	NL	Soviet Union	SU	Virgin Islands (British)	VG
New Caledonia (French)	NC	Spain	ES	Virgin Islands (U.S.)	VI
New Zealand	NZ	Sri Lanka	LK	Wallis and Futuna Islands	WF
Nicaragua	NI	St. Helena	SH	Western Sahara	EH
Niger	NE	St. Pierre and Miquelon	PM	Western Samoa	WS
Nigeria	NG	St. Tome and Principe	ST	Yemen	YE
Niue	NU	St. Vincent and Grenadines	VC	Yugoslavia	YU
Norfolk Island	NF	St.Kitts Nevis Anguilla	KN	Zambia	ZM
Northern Mariana Islands	MP	Sudan	SD	Zimbabwe	ZW
Norway	NO				

APPENDIX B

Country Codes (Alphabetical by Code)

CODE	COUNTRY	CODE	COUNTRY	CODE	COUNTRY
AD	Andorra	CK	Cook Islands	GN	Guinea
AE	United Arab Emirates	CL	Chile	GP	Guadeloupe (French)
AF	Afghanistan	CM	Cameroon	GQ	Equatorial Guinea
AG	Antigua and Barbuda	CN	China	GR	Greece
AI	Anguilla	CO	Colombia	GS	South Georgia and South Sandwich Islands
AL	Albania	CR	Costa Rica		
AM	Armenia	CU	Cuba	GT	Guatemala
AN	Netherland Antilles	CV	Cape Verde	GU	Guam (U.S.)
AO	Angola	CX	Christmas Island	GW	Guinea Bissau
AQ	Antarctica	CY	Cyprus	GY	Guyana
AR	Argentina	CZ	Czech Republic	HK	Hong Kong
AS	American Samoa	DE	Germany	HM	Heard and McDonald Islands
AT	Austria	DJ	Djibouti	HN	Honduras
AU	Australia	DK	Denmark	HR	Croatia
AW	Aruba	DM	Dominica	HT	Haiti
AZ	Azerbaijan	DO	Dominican Republic	HU	Hungary
BA	Bosnia-Herzegovina	DZ	Algeria	ID	Indonesia
BB	Barbados	EC	Ecuador	IE	Ireland
BD	Bangladesh	EE	Estonia	IL	Israel
BE	Belgium	EG	Egypt	IM	Isle of Man
BF	Burkina Faso	EH	Western Sahara	IN	India
BG	Bulgaria	ER	Eritrea	IO	British Indian Ocean Territory
BH	Bahrain	ES	Spain	IQ	Iraq
BI	Burundi	ET	Ethiopia	IR	Iran
BJ	Benin	FI	Finland	IS	Iceland
BM	Bermuda	FJ	Fiji	IT	Italy
BN	Brunei Darussalam	FK	Falkland Islands (Malvinas)	JE	Jersey (Channel Islands)
BO	Bolivia	FM	Micronesia	JM	Jamaica
BR	Brazil	FO	Faroe Islands	JO	Jordan
BS	Bahamas	FR	France	JP	Japan
BT	Bhutan	FX	France (European Territory)	KE	Kenya
BV	Bouvet Island	GA	Gabon	KG	Kyrgyz Republic
BW	Botswana	GB	Great Britain	KH	Cambodia
BY	Belarus	GD	Grenada	KI	Kiribati
BZ	Belize	GE	Georgia	KM	Comoros
CA	Canada	GF	Guyana (French)	KN	St.Kitts Nevis Anguilla
CC	Cocos (Keeling) Islands	GG	Guernsey (Channel Islands)	KP	Korea (North)
CF	Central African Republic	GH	Ghana	KR	Korea (South)
CG	Congo	GI	Gibraltar	KW	Kuwait
CH	Switzerland	GL	Greenland	KY	Cayman Islands
CI	Ivory Coast	GM	Gambia	KZ	Kazakhstan

Country Codes (Alphabetical by Code)

CODE	COUNTRY	CODE	COUNTRY	CODE	COUNTRY
LA	Laos	NR	Nauru	SZ	Swaziland
LB	Lebanon	NU	Niue	TC	Turks and Caicos Islands
LC	Saint Lucia	NZ	New Zealand	TD	Chad
LI	Liechtenstein	OM	Oman	TF	French Southern Territories
LK	Sri Lanka	PA	Panama	TG	Togo
LR	Liberia	PE	Peru	TH	Thailand
LS	Lesotho	PF	Polynesia (French)	TJ	Tadjikistan
LT	Lithuania	PG	Papua New Guinea	TK	Tokelau
LU	Luxembourg	PH	Philippines	TM	Turkmenistan
LV	Latvia	PK	Pakistan	TN	Tunisia
LY	Libya	PL	Poland	TO	Tonga
MA	Morocco	PM	St. Pierre and Miquelon	TP	East Timor
MC	Monaco	PN	Pitcairn	TR	Turkey
MD	Moldova	PR	Puerto Rico (U.S.)	TT	Trinidad and Tobago
MG	Madagascar	PT	Portugal	TV	Tuvalu
MH	Marshall Islands	PW	Palau	TW	Taiwan
MK	Macedonia	PY	Paraguay	TZ	Tanzania
ML	Mali	QA	Qatar	UA	Ukraine
MM	Myanmar	RE	Reunion (French)	UG	Uganda
MN	Mongolia	RO	Romania	UK	United Kingdom
MO	Macau	RU	Russian Federation	UM	United States Minor Outlying Islands
MP	Northern Mariana Islands	RW	Rwanda		
MQ	Martinique (French)	SA	Saudi Arabia	US	United States
MR	Mauritania	SB	Solomon Islands	UY	Uruguay
MS	Montserrat	SC	Seychelles	UZ	Uzbekistan
MT	Malta	SD	Sudan	VA	Vatican City State
MU	Mauritius	SE	Sweden	VC	St. Vincent and Grenadines
MV	Maldives	SG	Singapore	VE	Venezuela
MW	Malawi	SH	St. Helena	VG	Virgin Islands (British)
MX	Mexico	SI	Slovenia	VI	Virgin Islands (U.S.)
MY	Malaysia	SJ	Svalbard and Jan Mayen Islands	VN	Vietnam
MZ	Mozambique	SK	Slovakia (Slovak Republic)	VU	Vanuatu
NA	Namibia	SL	Sierra Leone	WF	Wallis and Futuna Islands
NC	New Caledonia (French)	SM	San Marino	WS	Western Samoa
NE	Niger	SN	Senegal	YE	Yemen
NF	Norfolk Island	SO	Somalia	YT	Mayotte
NG	Nigeria	SR	Suriname	YU	Yugoslavia
NI	Nicaragua	ST	St. Tome and Principe	ZA	South Africa
NL	Netherlands	SU	Soviet Union	ZM	Zambia
NO	Norway	SV	El Salvador	ZR	Congo (formerly Zaire)
NP	Nepal	SY	Syria	ZW	Zimbabwe

APPENDIX B

APPENDIX C: USENET NEWSGROUP HIERARCHIES

Deja News and other search engines greatly simplify the process of finding information in Usenet newsgroups. It's no longer necessary to know exactly which newsgroups deal with a particular topic. Just tell your favorite search engine that you want to search newsgroups instead of the Web and let it take care of the details.

Eventually, though, you may want to employ the power-searching technique of limiting your newsgroup queries to specific newsgroups. Or you may simply want to know what those "alt-dot-something" names mean and how they get assigned. The key concept is newsgroup *hierarchies*.

The first part of a newsgroup name is the major topic or *top-level* hierarchy—**alt** for the wildly popular "alternative" newsgroups, **biz** for business-related groups, **comp** for computer hardware and software, **sci** for science, and so forth. Each of these major topics is then broken down into subtopics, and those are broken down again and again as newsgroups are created for discussions of greater and greater specificity.

For example, in the **alt** hierarchy, a group called **alt.music** might be formed to discuss music in general. Over time, some participants decide they want to focus on a specific type of music like jazz, while others prefer to discuss bluegrass. So two new groups are formed: **alt.music.jazz** and **alt.music.bluegrass**. Things can get even more specific as

people decide to focus on a favorite jazz or bluegrass musician. The newsgroup name gets longer and longer as the topic of discussion becomes more and more specific.

Of the hundreds of top-level newsgroup hierarchies, here are the ones you're most likely to encounter, along with a brief description.

Usenet Newsgroup Hierarchies	
TOPIC	DESCRIPTION
alt	Alternative newsgroups—everything from sexually oriented topics to the truly offbeat. They're called "alternative" because they don't fit neatly anywhere else. Many Usenet servers don't carry these groups.
bionet	Biology network.
bit	Articles from Bitnet LISTSERV mailing lists, used mainly by the academic community.
biz	Business-related newsgroups. This is the place for advertisements, marketing, and other commercial postings (product announcements, product reviews, demo software, etc.).
clari	ClariNet News, a commercial service providing UPI wire news, newspaper columns like Dave Barry, and lots more to sites that subscribe.
comp	Computer-related newsgroups. Topics of interest to computer professionals and hobbyists, including computer science, software source code, and information on hardware and software systems.
gnu	The GNU project and the Free Software Foundation.
hepnet	Higher Energy Physics network.
humanities	Discussions of humanities and the arts.
ieee	Institute of Electrical and Electronic Engineers.
k12	Topics of interest to teachers of kindergarten through grade 12 (curriculum, language exchanges with native speakers, and classroom-to-classroom projects designed by teachers).
microsoft	Microsoft products and services.
misc	A catch-all category for groups that address topics not easily classified anywhere else. Two of the most popular are **misc.jobs** and **misc.forsale**.
news	Groups concerned with the Usenet network (*not* current affairs, as you might think). The newsgroups **news.announce.newusers**, **news.newusers.questions**, and **news.answers** are the places to check for information aimed at first-time Internet and newsgroup users.
rec	Groups focusing on recreational activities and hobbies of all sorts.
schl	Resources for elementary and secondary school teachers (similar to **k12**).
sci	Discussions of scientific research and applied sciences.
soc	Groups devoted to social issues, often related to a particular culture.
talk	Debates and long-winded discussions without resolution and with very little useful information.

THE WEB
SEARCHER'S TOOLKIT

The Web Searcher's Toolkit at a Glance

- Compression and Conversion Tools (2 disks)
- Encryption Tools
- Graphic Workshop
- Paint Shop Pro (2 disks)
- Software Tools: Cache Master & CCLink
- Sound Tools: GoldWave
- Text Treater Tools

Forget the learned essays on the significance of cyberspace. What the Internet really means is "anything you want, whenever you want it." You need a program that will display GIF and JPEG graphics files? Or one that will help you compress and uncompress ZIP files? Or a set of file encryption tools? No problem! Just check the Net.

But there are, in fact, two problems. First, Internet sites come and go, and the names of specific files change over time. So it's pointless for us to say "Go to site XYZ and download the file called ABC.ZIP." As you read this, the site may no longer exist, and if it does, the filename may have changed to something like ABC-01P.ZIP.

Second, there's no way to know what you're going to need until you actually need it. For example, a Web page may alert you to a file that contains a marvelous image of a rare butterfly. You opt to download it, only to discover that you can't display the image because it's in PCX (PC Paintbrush) format. Now you've got to go search for and download a viewer program that can handle PCX files. What a nuisance!

Essential Tools for Windows Users

This appendix is designed to eliminate—or at least reduce—such hassles for our fellow Windows users. Certainly we can't anticipate absolutely every need. But with more than 20 years of online experience, we have a pretty good idea of what most people are likely to require as they wade into cyberspace.

There isn't a file on any of the disks offered here that you can't get online from the Internet, America Online, CompuServe, Prodigy, or some other online system. We know, because that's where we got most of them ourselves.

We've located, tested, and selected the best programs and files for our own use. But it occurred to us that readers might appreciate the opportunity to benefit from our experience, not to mention the convenience of being able to get most of the tools they need from one place. So we've collected the programs we use to support our online searching activities and put them on 3.5-inch high-density disks, each of which is described in this appendix.

Compression and Conversion Tools

Our goal with this two-disk set was to create the ultimate collection of compression and conversion programs. The real standout is the award-winning WinZip, which can handle ZIP files and most other compression formats you're likely to encounter on the Internet.

Another excellent program, WinCode, makes it exceptionally easy to deal with files like images, sound clips, and programs that have been converted from their original binary form to plain ASCII text. Years ago, the only way to send binary files via e-mail was to

A Word About Shareware

Most of the programs in the Web Searcher's Toolkit are *shareware*, which means that if you decide to use them on a regular basis, you're honor-bound to send the creators a modest registration fee—usually no more than about $25. Once you see how good and useful these programs are, you'll be glad to support the programmers' efforts.

convert them first to plain ASCII, and some people still follow that practice. You'll also encounter such files in Usenet newsgroup postings. When you do, WinCode is the tool to use to convert them back to their original binary format.

Encryption Tools

It isn't likely to happen, but if someone really wants to read your e-mail, they can probably find a way to do so. Should you ever want to encrypt a text or binary file so that no one can read it without the decoding "key," then this is the disk for you. You'll find several encryption programs here, but the famous one is Phil Zimmermann's Pretty Good Privacy (PGP) program.

Graphic WorkShop

Graphic WorkShop (GWS) is the ultimate viewer and converter for graphic image files. Written by Steven Rimmer, GWS is designed to display, scale, alter, and convert files in all major graphics formats (GIF, TIF, JPEG, PCX, MAC, IMG, EPS, and many others). The Windows versions allow you to display thumbnail images showing quick renditions of each graphic file on your disk. Since there are no standard graphics formats, if you do much downloading from the Internet or other online systems, you will almost certainly need a tool like GWS. It's available in DOS, Windows 3.x, and Windows 95 versions.

Paint Shop Pro

Offered as a two-disk set, Paint Shop Pro (PSP) is designed to let you display, edit, and alter images you find online and elsewhere. PSP can accept and save files to almost two dozen of the most common file formats.

Software Tools: Cache Master and CCLink

Web browser programs store all of the HTML text and the graphics files they reference in their disk caches. So any Web page you've seen recently can be made to appear on your screen very quickly indeed. (After all, the text and graphics are coming from your hard drive and not from the Internet.)

Storing pages on disk is a neat concept. But unfortunately, Web browsers store page components using obscure filenames like M0P36UCG.GIF and M0P22N0.HTM. That's where Cache Master comes in. It will process your cache (Netscape Navigator only as of this writing) and build a database of Web pages that you can view with your browser—without having to go back online. Cache Master even remembers the links you followed when you visited the sites.

The program has many other features, including the power to search for text in your previous online sessions, display the images in your cache, and delete items much as you would with a file manager.

CCLink, the other program on this disk, is for people who use an internal modem. Written by Gary Shaboo, the package includes a terminal program. But what we

like is the little window designed to give you the equivalent of an external modem's LED lights. With CCLink loaded, you can tell whether or not your commands are getting out the door by watching the SD (send data) light. And you can confirm that your system is receiving files by looking at the flickering RD (receive data) light. This is a neat feature to have on those days when the Internet is especially slow. You can't speed it up, but you can at least see what's happening.

Sound Tools: GoldWave

GoldWave is a sound editor, player, recorder, and converter for Windows 95/NT. It supports all multimedia PC (MPC) sound cards (Sound Blaster and others) and features built-in support for WAV, VOC, AU, and other sound-file formats. The program includes all the tools you need for editing, altering, enhancing, mixing, or merely clipping out sounds.

Text Treater Tools

This disk includes 45 programs specifically selected to manipulate, filter, and prepare a text file in any way you can imagine. These tools are particularly convenient when dealing with text you get from e-mail correspondents and Internet sites.

A program called Text, for example, lets you remove all leading white space on each line of a file, remove all trailing blanks, or convert all white space into the number of spaces you specify. Chop will cut a large file into any number of smaller pieces. CRLF makes sure that every line in a text file ends with a carriage return and line feed so that it can be displayed and edited properly. There's also a package by Peter Norton to create an index for a report, document, book, or whatever.

Order Form

You can use the order form on the next page (or a photocopy) to order the disks described here, as well as a selection of our books. Or you may simply write your request on a piece of paper and send it to us.

We accept American Express, MasterCard, Visa, and checks or money orders made payable to **Glossbrenner's Choice** (U.S. funds drawn on a U.S. bank, or international money orders). For additional information, write or call:

Glossbrenner's Choice
699 River Road
Yardley, PA 19067-1965
215-736-1213 (voice)
215-736-1031 (fax)

books@mailback.com (information about Glossbrenner books)

gloss@gloss.com (all other correspondence)

Glossbrenner's Choice Order Form

for Readers of *Search Engines for the World Wide Web: Visual QuickStart Guide*

Name _____

Address _____

City _____ State _____ ZIP _____

Province/Country _____ Phone _____

Payment ☐ Check or Money Order payable to **Glossbrenner's Choice**

        ☐ Amex/MC/Visa _____ Exp ___/___

Signature _____

Mail, fax, phone, or e-mail your order to:

Glossbrenner's Choice   215-736-1213 (voice)
699 River Road   215-736-1031 (fax)
Yardley, PA 19067-1965   gloss@gloss.com

The Web Searcher's Toolkit

_____ Compression and Conversion Tools (2 disks) **$10**   _____

_____ Encryption Tools **$5**   _____

_____ Graphic Workshop (___ DOS ___ Win3.x ___ Win95) **$5**   _____

_____ Paint Shop Pro (2 disks) **$10**   _____

_____ Software Tools: Cache Master and CCLink **$5**   _____

_____ Sound Tools: GoldWave **$5**   _____

_____ Text Treater Tools **$5**   _____

_____ Complete Toolkit (all 9 disks) **$35**   _____

TOTAL for Disks _____

Shipping for disk orders: **$3** to U.S. addresses; **$5** outside the U.S. _____

Glossbrenner Books (Prices include $3 for Book Rate shipping.)

_____ *Search Engines for the World Wide Web/**Peachpit Press** ($20)*   _____

_____ *The Little Web Book/**Peachpit Press** ($20)*   _____

_____ *Computer Sourcebook/**Random House** ($38)*   _____

_____ *The Information Broker's Handbook/**McGraw-Hill** ($38)*   _____

_____ *Online Resources for Business/**John Wiley & Sons** ($28)*   _____

_____ *Making More Money on the Internet/**McGraw-Hill** ($23)*   _____

_____ *Internet 101: A College Student's Guide/**McGraw-Hill** ($23)*   _____

TOTAL _____

Pennsylvania residents, please add 6% Sales Tax. _____

GRAND TOTAL ENCLOSED _____

INDEX

1040.com   188

A

actors and actresses, searching for   183
AIIP (Association of Independent Information
      Professionals)   27
AltaVista   35–36
   banner ads   38
   contact information   35
   databases   35
   help   38, 48
   Quick Reference guides
      Advanced Search   49, 194
      Simple Search   39, 192
      Usenet Newsgroup Field Search   45, 193
      Web Page Field Search   43, 193
   refining searches with LiveTopics   50–55
   results, display options   38, 48
   search forms
      Advanced Search   46
      Simple Search   36–37
   searching
      Usenet newsgroups   44–45, 48
      World Wide Web   37, 42–43, 47
   search tools and techniques
      AND, OR, and NOT searches   39, 40, 47, 49
      case-sensitive searches   39, 41, 49
      date searches   39, 46, 47, 49
      field searches   39, 42–43, 44–45, 49
      keyword weighting   39, 46, 47, 49
      nested searches   39, 46
      phrase searches   39, 40, 49
      proximity searches   39, 46, 49
      wildcard searches   39, 40, 49
   spider   6, 7, 35
   strengths   24, 36
Amazon.com Books   178
America Online   58
AND searches   17. See also individual search engines
Answers.com   27
archives, Usenet newsgroup   146, 147
Argus Clearinghouse   157–158
   contact information   157
   Digital Librarian's Award   158
   Quick Reference guide   161, 195
   rating system   158, 160
   searching by keyword   159–160

Association of Independent Information
      Professionals (AIIP)   27
AT&T Toll-Free Directory   172
audio files. See multimedia, searching for
authors, searching for   178
automobile guides, searching for   180

B

background color, customizing Web page   78
banner ads   38, 114
best Web sites. See reviews, Web site
BigBook Yellow Pages   171, 172
BigFoot   163, 165
BigYellow   94, 95, 171, 172
Bon Appétit magazine   181
Bookmarks, adding search engines to   29
book reviews, New York Times   185
books, searching for   178
Boolean searching   16
business information, searching for   88, 127,
      173–174, 189

C

Cache Master   219
card catalog, library   9–10
career information, searching for   185, 186
car guides, searching for   180
Carnegie Mellon University   113
case-sensitive searches   13
      with AltaVista   41
      with HotBot   84
      with Infoseek   99
CCLink   219
CDNow   178
celebrities, searching for   165, 168, 169
Channels, Excite   57, 60, 68
City.Net Travel, Excite   57–58, 74–75
classifieds, searching   127, 132
Clearinghouse. See Argus Clearinghouse
clip art. See multimedia, searching for
C|Net's Search.com   25
C|Net's Shareware.com   179
colleges and universities, searching for   186
color, customizing Web page background   78
Communicator, Netscape. See Netscape Navigator

companies, searching for
    with AltaVista   42
    with HotBot   82
    with Infoseek   108
    with Lycos   127–128
    with Yahoo!   132
    with Zip2 Yellow Pages   171–175
complex queries   21. *See also* nested searches
com portion of Web addresses   5
Compression and Conversion Tools disk   218
concept-based searching, Excite   21, 57, 61, 63
Congressional Record   188
Consumer World   179
country codes, Internet   xii
    lists of   209–213
    searching
        with AltaVista   43
        with HotBot   83
        with Infoseek   101
crawlers, Web   6, 7
Cuckoo's Egg, The   3
current events. *See* newspapers and magazines, searching
customizing Web browsers   28–29
CyberPlace option, HotBot   82–83

D

da Silva, Stephanie   152
date searches
    AltaVista   46
    HotBot   79, 82, 85
    Yahoo!   136, 137
Deja News   145–146
    accessing from other search engines
        Excite   70–71
        Infoseek   103–104
        Yahoo!   136
    contact information   145
    help   148
    Quick Reference guides
        Deja News Stopwords   146, 195
        Quick Search and Power Search   149, 196
    search forms   147–148
    search tools and techniques
        AND, OR, and NOT searches   146, 149
        case-sensitive searches   147
        field searches   148, 149
        Interest Finder   148
        nested searches   147, 149
        phrase searches   149
        proximity searches   146, 149
        recent postings *vs.* archives   146, 147–148
        Search Filter   148
        stopwords   22, 146
        wildcard searches   148
Digital Equipment Corporation   35
DineNet Menus Online   180
directories
    mailing list   151–152
    subject-specific Internet guides   157–158
    Web site   4, 7
        Excite   4, 60, 68–69
        HotBot   88–89
        Infoseek   93, 94
        Lycos   119–120, 125, 126
        Yahoo!   129–131, 138–141
    white pages   163–164
    yellow pages   171–172

domains, Internet   xii
    list of common   209
    searching
        with AltaVista   42–43
        with HotBot   82–83
        with Infoseek   101
Dow Jones News/Retrieval Publications Library   189
driving directions. *See* maps and driving directions
Dun and Bradstreet company database   127

E

Edmund's Automobile Buyer's Guides   180
Education & Career Center, Peterson's   186
Electric Library   181
e-mail directories   163–164
Encryption Tools disk   218
Epicurious Food   181
Excite   57–58
    Channels   57, 60, 68
    contact information   57
    customizing Web browser for   58
    databases   57
    foreign language editions   75
    Guided Web Tours   69
    help   65
    Quick Reference guide   63, 197
    results, display options   62, 73
    search forms
        main search page   59–60
        Power Search   66–67, 73, 75
    searching
        current news   72–73
        News Channel   57, 72–73
        selected Web sites   66–67
        Travel Channel   57–58, 74–75
        Usenet newsgroups   70–71
        Web sites by topic   68–69
        World Wide Web   61–62
    search tools and techniques
        AND, OR, and NOT searches   63, 64, 65, 67
        concept-based searching   21, 57, 61, 63
        idea and concept searches   64
        "More Like This" option   57, 61, 63
        nested searches   63, 65
        phrase searches   64
        Reference Tools   60
    strengths   24, 57–58
    Web site reviews   57, 67, 68
ExciteSeeing Tours   69
excluding words and phrases   19

F

Favorites list, adding search engines to   29
FedEx package tracking   182
field searches   9–10
    with AltaVista   42, 44–45
    with Deja News   148, 149
    with HotBot   85, 87
    with Infoseek   100–101, 102, 111
    with Yahoo!   134, 137
Filo, David   129
FindLaw Internet Legal Resources   182
foreign-language sites. *See* country codes, Internet
Four11   163–164
    contact information   153
    databases   163

help   166
   Quick Reference guide   169, 198
   searching
      for celebrities and government
         officials   165, 168, 169
      for e-mail addresses   165–166
      for home addresses and telephone
         numbers   167–168
      for members of a group   165
full-text searching   9–10

G

general-purpose search engines   4, 144
geography, searching by. *See* country codes, Internet
GeoPlace option, HotBot   83
Global Excite   75
Glossbrenner, Alfred and Emily
   e-mail address   iii
   other books   iv, 221
Glossbrenner's Choice   220–221
GoldWave sound tools   219
Gourmet magazine   181
government information, searching for   188
government officials, searching for   165, 168, 169
graphics. *See* multimedia, searching for
Graphic Workshop   218
GTE SuperPages   127, 171, 172

H

habits, search   24–27
Hanover Hacker   3
hardware and software reviews, searching for   189–190
HealthAtoZ   183
hierarchies, Usenet newsgroup   xii, 44, 215–216
hits   4
Home location, Web browser   28–29
HotBot   77–78
   contact information   77
   databases   77
   help   85
   Quick Reference guides   86–87, 199–200
   refining searches   79, 82–83, 84–85
   results, display options   80
   saving search settings   79, 81, 83
   search form   79–81
   searching
      Usenet newsgroups   80–81
      Web sites by topic   88–89
      World Wide Web   80–81
   search tools and techniques
      AND, OR, and NOT searches   81, 84, 86
      case-sensitive searches   84, 86
      Date tool   79, 82, 85, 86
      field searches   85, 86, 87
      keyword weighting   84, 86
      Location tool   79, 82–83, 86
      Media Type tool   79, 83
      Meta Words   85, 87
      Modify tool   79, 82
      nested searches   81, 86
      people searches   81
      phrase searches   80, 81, 86
      URL links searches   81
   spider   7, 78
   strengths   24, 77–78
   Wired Source directory   77, 88–89

HotWired, Inc.   77
http:// portion of Web addresses   5

I

images. *See* multimedia, searching for
index, search engine   6
Information Broker's Handbook, The   27, 221
Infoseek   91–92
   contact information   91
   databases   91
   foreign-language versions   95
   help   99
   Quick Reference guide   102, 201
   results, display options   97
   search forms
      Ultraseek   92, 93, 101, 110–111
      Ultrasmart   93–95
   searching
      company profiles   108
      current news articles   105–106
      e-mail addresses   107
      newsgroup FAQs   109
      for related topics   97, 98
      Usenet newsgroups   103–104
      Web directory   93, 94
      World Wide Web   96–97
   search tools and techniques
      AND, OR, and NOT searches   98–99, 102
      BigYellow   94, 95
      case-sensitive searches   99, 102
      field searches   100–101, 102, 111
      image searches   102, 111
      News Center   94
      phrase searches   98, 102
      plain-English searches   96, 98, 102
      reference tools   94
      set searches   12, 92, 98, 102, 111
      Smart Info   94
      Special Searches page   101
      Ultrashop   95
   strengths   24, 91–92
Inktomi Corp.   77
Internal Revenue Service   188
Internet
   country codes (*See* country codes, Internet)
   domains (*See* domains, Internet)
   guides to search tools   5
   mailing lists   151–152
   perils of searching   3
Internet Explorer. *See* Microsoft's Internet Explorer
Internet Movie Database   183

J

Java   51
jobs, searching for   185
jokes, searching for   25

K

keyboard shortcuts   30
keywords   2
   choosing unique   11–13, 25
   importance of   9
   searching for multiple   16–22

keywords (continued)
  weighting
    AltaVista   46
    HotBot   84

L

legal resources, searching for   182
Legislative Information, Thomas   188
librarians   27
library card catalog   9–10
Linnaeus   129
List of Lists, Vivian Neou's   152
Liszt Mailing List Directory   151–155
  color code   154
  contact information   151
  Info Files   154
  Quick Reference guide   155, 202
  search form   153
  search tools and techniques
    AND, OR, and NOT searches   155
    case-sensitive searches   155
    Junk Filter   153
    string searches   153, 155
    wildcard searches   155
literary works, searching for   25, 187
Little Web Book, The   x, 221
LiveTopics, AltaVista
  Java Interface   52–53
  JavaScript and Text Interfaces   54–55
  refining searches with   50–51
Location tool, HotBot   79, 82–83
Lycos   113–114
  banner ads   114
  contact information   113
  customizing Web browser for   114
  databases   113, 127–128
  Quick Reference guides
    Basic Search   118, 203
    Lycos Pro Custom Search   125, 204
    Lycos Pro with Java Power Panel   126, 205
  results, display options   120
  search forms
    Basic Search   115–117
    Lycos Pro Custom Search   123, 124, 125
    Lycos Pro with Java Power Panel   123, 126
  searching
    images and sounds database   121–122
    Top 5% Directory and reviews   119–120,
      125, 126
    Web sites by topic   117
    World Wide Web   115–116
  search tools and techniques
    AND, OR, and NOT searches   118, 123, 125, 126
    multimedia searches   118, 121–122, 125, 126
    phrase searches   118, 123, 125, 126
    plain-English searches   123, 125, 126
    proximity searches   126
  strengths   24, 113–114
  WebGuides   115, 117
  Web site reviews   114, 117, 118, 119–120

M

magazines. See newspapers and magazines, searching
mailing lists, Internet   151–152

MapQuest   128, 184
maps and driving directions   128, 132, 173–174, 184
Mauldin, Michael "Fuzzy,"   113
Media Type tool, HotBot   79, 83
medical information, searching for   183
menus, searching for restaurant   180
message threads, Usenet newsgroup   148
meta-search engines   25
Meta Words, HotBot   85, 87
Microsoft's Internet Explorer
  Favorites list   29
  keyboard shortcuts   30
  Search button   29
  Start Page   28
  Web address shortcuts   5
  Web page background colors   78
Microsoft Technical Support   184
Modify tool, HotBot   79, 82
"More Like This" option, Excite   61
Movie Database, Internet   183
multimedia, searching for
  with HotBot   79, 83, 87
  with Lycos   113, 114, 121–122
multiple words and phrases, searching for   16–22
music, searching for   178

N

natural-language searching. See plain-English searching
Navigator, Netscape. See Netscape Navigator
NEAR searches   20
  with AltaVista   39, 46, 49
  with Deja News   146, 149
  with Lycos   126
Neou, Vivian   152
nested searches   21
  with AltaVista   39, 46
  with Deja News   147, 149
  with Excite   63, 65
  with HotBot   81, 86
  with Liszt   155
NetFind, America Online's   58
Netscape Navigator
  customizing   28–29, 78
  guide to search engines and tools   5
  keyboard shortcuts and time-savers   30–31
News Channel, Excite   57, 72–73
newsgroups. See Usenet newsgroups
newspapers and magazines, searching
  with Electric Library   181
  with Excite   72–73
  with HotBot   88
  with Infoseek   94, 105–106
  with Yahoo!   132, 134, 139, 141
NewsTracker, Excite   57, 72–73
New York Times Book Reviews   185
NOT searches   19. See also individual search engines

O

Occupational Outlook Handbook   185
Online Career Center   185
operators, Boolean   16
order form, Glossbrenner's Choice   220–221
OR searches   18. See also individual search engines

P

package tracking   128, 182, 189
Paint Shop Pro   219
PAML (Publicly Accessible Mailing Lists)   152
Parent Soup   186
PC Quote   128
Peachpit Press
    Visual QuickStart series   ix
    Web site   58
people-finding tools   163–164
Perl programming language   154
Peterson's Education & Career Center   186
plain-English searching   16
    with Excite   61
    with Infoseek   96, 98, 102
    with Lycos   123, 125, 126
poetry, searching for   25
Pretty Good Privacy (PGP)   218
professional searchers   27
Project Gutenberg   187
proximity searches   20
    with AltaVista   39, 46, 49
    with Deja News   146, 149
    with Lycos   126
publications. *See* newspapers and magazines, searching
public domain software   xii, 179, 217–221
Publicly Accessible Mailing Lists (PAML)   152

Q

query by example, Excite   63
Quick Reference guides   xi, 13, 191
    AltaVista Advanced Search   49, 194
    AltaVista Simple Search   39, 192
    AltaVista Usenet Newsgroup Field Search   45, 193
    AltaVista Web Page Field Search   43, 193
    Argus Clearinghouse   161, 195
    Deja News Quick Search and Power Search   149, 196
    Deja News Stopwords   146, 195
    Excite   63, 197
    Four11   169, 198
    HotBot   86, 199
    HotBot Meta Words   87, 200
    Infoseek   102, 201
    Liszt   155, 202
    Lycos Basic Search   118, 203
    Lycos Pro Custom Search   125, 204
    Lycos Pro with Java Power Panel   126, 205
    Yahoo!   137, 206
    Zip2 Yellow Pages   175, 207
quotations, searching for   25

R

recipes, searching for   181
reference librarians   27
reference tools
    Dow Jones News/Retrieval Publications Library   189
    Electric Library   181
    Excite   60
    HotBot   88
    Infoseek   94
    Yahoo!   132
relevancy, methods for calculating   6
research and reference tools. *See* reference tools
research services   27
restaurant menus, searching for   180

reviews, Web site
    Excite   57, 67, 68
    Lycos   114, 117
    Yahoo!   141
robot programs   6, 7

S

Scooter   6, 35
search basics   xi, 2
Search.com, C|Net's   25
search engines. *See also* specific search engines
    all-purpose contrasted with special-purpose   144
    basic search tools   15–22
    choosing unique keywords   11–13, 25
    directories and guides   5, 24–25
    field searching with   10
    how they work   6–7
    leading   xi
        features of   4
        strengths of   24
        Web addresses for   29
    Quick Reference guides   xi, 13, 191
    spiders and crawlers   6–7
    topic directories   4, 7
    using multiple   26
Search Engines for the World Wide Web
    assumptions about readers   x
    organization of   xi–xii
    purpose of   ix
searching
    challenges of full-text   9–10
    habits for effective   24–27
    set searching   12, 92, 98, 111, 133
"Seven Habits of Highly Effective Web Searchers,"   24–27
shareware   218
    C|Net's Shareware.com   179
    Web Searcher's Toolkit   xii, 217–221
    ZDNet Software Library and Reviews   189–190
Shareware.com, C|Net's   179
shopping Web sites, searching for   95
shortcuts
    entering Web addresses   5, 31
    keyboard   30
Silicon Snake Oil   3
single-subject search tools   144
Slurp   78
software
    searching for   179, 189–190
    shareware and public domain   xii, 179, 217–221
sound files. *See* multimedia, searching for
Sound Tools disk   219
Southwick, Scott   151, 152
spamdexing   6
special-purpose search engines   144, 177. *See also*
        specific search engines
spelling errors   13
spiders   6, 7, 35, 78
Stanford University   129
Startup location, Web browser   28–29
stock quotes   128
Stoll, Clifford   3, 4
stopwords   22, 146
string search   153
subject guides, Internet. *See* Argus Clearinghouse
Supreme Court Decisions   182
Switchboard   163, 165

T

tax forms and information, searching for   188
Technical Support, Microsoft   184
telephone directories   163–164
Text Treaters Tools disk   219
Thomas Legislative Information   188
threads, Usenet newsgroup message   148
titles, searching Web page   12
   with AltaVista   42
   with Infoseek   100
   with Yahoo!   134, 137
toll-free directory, AT&T   172
Toolkit, Web Searcher's   xii, 217–221
Top 5% Directory, Lycos   119–120
topic directories, search engine   4, 7
   Excite   4, 60, 68–69
   HotBot   88–89
   Infoseek   93, 94
   Lycos   119–120, 125, 126
   Yahoo!   129–131, 138–141
top-rated Web sites. See reviews, Web site
Trade-Direct   127
travel information
   Excite   57–58, 74–75
   Lycos   128

U

University of Michigan   157
UPS package tracking   128, 189
URL (Uniform Resource Locator)
   searching for
      with AltaVista   43
      with HotBot   81
      with Infoseek   100, 102
   shortcuts for entering   5
Usenet newsgroups
   archives   146, 147
   author profiles   71, 104, 146
   date searches   148
   hierarchies   xii, 44, 215–216
   importance of checking   26, 71
   popular categories   44
   searching
      with AltaVista   38, 44–45, 48
      with Deja News   145–149
      with Excite   70–71
      with HotBot   80–81
      with Infoseek   103–104
      with Yahoo!   136

V

videos, searching for   178
Visual QuickStart series   ix
Vonnegut, Kurt   9–10

W

Wall Street Journal Interactive Edition   189
Web
   accuracy of information on   26
   addresses   5
   browsing vs. searching   4
   perils of searching   3
   top-rated sites (See reviews, Web site)

Web addresses
   for leading search engines   29
   shortcuts   5, 31
Web browsers
   customizing for searching   28–29
   keyboard shortcuts   30
   opening multiple   31
   Web address shortcuts   5
Web pages, searching with Edit, Find   31
Web Searcher's Toolkit   xii, 217–221
white pages directories   163–164
WhoWhere?   163, 165
wildcard searches   21
   with AltaVista   39, 40, 49
   with Deja News   148
   with Liszt   155
   with Yahoo!   134, 137
Wired magazine   77, 78, 88
Wired Source, HotBot   77, 88–89
World Wide Web. See Web
www portion of Web addresses   5

Y

Yahoo!   129–131
   contact information   129
   databases   129
   help   134
   menu bar   132
   Quick Reference guide   137, 206
   reference tools   132
   results, display options   136
   reviews, Web site   141
   search forms
      main   131
      Search Options page   135–136
   searching
      e-mail addresses   136
      newspapers and magazines   132, 134, 139, 141
      Usenet newsgroups   136
      Web directory   133, 135–136, 138–141
   search tools and techniques
      AND, OR, and NOT searches   133–134, 135, 137
      case-sensitive searches   134
      date searches   136, 137
      field searches   134, 137
      name searches   135
      phrase searches   134, 135, 137
      set searches with "Search only in" feature   133
      wildcard searches   134, 137
   strengths   24
   Web directory   129–131, 133, 135–136, 138–141
Yahoo! Internet Life   141
Yang, Jerry   129
yellow pages directories   94, 95, 171–175

Z

ZDNet Software Library and Reviews   189–190
Ziff-Davis   141, 189–190
ZIP code locator   190
Zip2 Yellow Pages   171–175
   contact information   171
   creating search profile   172, 173
   databases   171
   maps and driving directions   173–174, 175
   Quick Reference guide   175, 207
   searching for businesses   173–174

INDEX